RED ALERT

China's Global Power and How it Threatens U.S. National Security

Military – Economic - Diplomatic

Antonio Graceffo, PhD, China-MBA

First published December 25, 2023 by Mary Labita Press

For permissions contact: Webantonio67@gmail.com

ISBN: 979-8-9897950-0-0

Table of Contents

Introduction

"Under the rule of the Chinese Communist Party (CCP), the People's Republic of China (PRC) is seeking to expand its influence culturally, economically, politically, and militarily," Melanie W. Sisson of the Talbott Center for Security, Strategy, and Technology, told the House Armed Services Committee on February 7, 2023.[1] By 2027, China hopes to develop the People's Liberation Army (PLA) into a world class force, capable of rivaling the United States. By 2049, Xi Jinping has set the goal of China becoming the dominant global power, exceeding the U.S. in terms of military power, economic power, and diplomatic power.[2]

The 2022 Department of Defense Report on Military and Security Developments Involving the People's Republic of China characterized the CCP as the "the most consequential and systemic challenge to U.S. national security and the free and open international system."[3] The DOD's assessment indicated that the PLA had successfully achieved its modernization objectives for 2020. Throughout 2021, the CCP increasingly relied on the PLA to execute its foreign missions. With the initial phase of modernization now accomplished, the PLA has shifted its focus to its next objective: "to accelerate the integrated development of mechanization, informatization, and intelligentization of the armed forces" by 2027.[4] This encompasses enhancements in the PLA's

---

[1] https://www.brookings.edu/articles/the-pressing-threat-of-the-chinese-communist-party-to-us-national-defense/
[2] https://www.bloomberg.com/news/articles/2022-10-26/xi-s-vow-of-world-dominance-by-2049-sends-chill-through-markets
[3] DOD Military and Security Developments Involving the People's Republic of China 2023 Report to Congress
[4] Ibid.

nuclear, space, counterspace, electronic warfare, and cyberspace operations.

As it grows in power, the CCP regime is progressively challenging the United States in realms such as trade, investment, and diplomacy. The U.S.-China cold war has indeed arrived, although it differs from the Cold War with the USSR. Nevertheless, akin to all cold wars, it will conclude either when one contender loses its capacity to compete, or when it transforms into a hot conflict. This book will focus on the latter scenario: a hot war involving the U.S. and China. It will begin with an examination of the new cold war and the China threat, followed by a comprehensive analysis of China's overall global power, assessed across multiple dimensions encompassing military, technological, economic, and diplomatic spheres.

1

Assessing the Current Threat Landscape

Over the past ten years, as relations between the United States and the People's Republic of China have steadily deteriorated, analysts, policymakers, and academics have debated whether the U.S. and China are embroiled in a cold war. However, this debate is unnecessary, as Washington-Beijing enmity matches the textbook definition of a cold war being played out in Taiwan, Ukraine, and the Middle East. When people ask whether the U.S. and China are in a cold war, what they truly mean to ask is whether the U.S. and China are locked in a cold war similar to the Cold War between the U.S. and the USSR. The answer to that question is no, and the reasons are complex.

A cold war can be defined as a war "being fought not in the traditional manner of clashing armies, but by all other means short of actual combat."[5] A cold war is a condition of political and ideological tension, rivalry, and non-violent conflict between major powers or blocs. It is typified by the absence of direct military engagement or declared hostilities. Instead, opposing nations or alliances compete through tactics such as espionage, propaganda, and proxy conflicts. The cold war period is marked by the maintenance of a delicate balance of power and a climate of suspicion that may potentially escalate into open warfare.

Cold wars are relatively common. Examples from the 20th and 21st centuries include India versus Pakistan, Saudi Arabia

---

[5] https://news.osu.edu/whats-a-cold-war-a-historian-explains-how-rivals-us-and-soviet-union-competed/

versus Iran, North Korea versus South Korea, and possibly India versus China. Cold wars are not new: The 19th-century Great Game, played out between the British and Russian empires in Central Asia, never escalated to open warfare. The same was true of the Scramble for Africa, where European powers competed against each other, with open combat being fought by proxies.

The Cold War between the United States and the USSR was a prolonged geopolitical and ideological rivalry[6] that lasted from the end of World War II in 1945 to the collapse of the USSR in 1991. During this period, Washington and Moscow, along with their respective allies, engaged in a state of political and military tension without their armies ever exchanging shots. The Cold War was characterized by ideological differences, a battle of capitalism/democracy against communism/autocracy,[7] the nuclear arms race, and proxy conflicts in places such as Korea, Vietnam, and Central America. The two countries also spied on one another, and both nations remained on constant alert, anticipating a nuclear exchange.

This Cold War is Different

The ongoing cold war between the U.S. and China is playing out on multiple fronts, with both nations seeking support, influence, and political advantages in Taiwan, Ukraine, and the Middle East. China's interest in Taiwan (the Republic of China, ROC) is straightforward, as it aims to annex the island nation, while the U.S. supports Taiwan without seeking annexation. In Ukraine, both countries are working through proxies: China supports Moscow, while the United States and NATO support Kyiv. In the Middle

---

[6] https://www.history.com/topics/cold-war/cold-war-history
[7] https://www.jfklibrary.org/learn/about-jfk/jfk-in-history/the-cold-war

East, Washington provides direct support to Israel, while Beijing indirectly supports Hamas and Hezbollah through its support for Tehran. These proxy conflicts resemble events during the Cold War with the Soviet Union, but there are significant differences between the current Cold War with the PRC and the previous one with Moscow.

One of these is economic competition. The U.S. and China are major economic rivals, whereas the difference in wealth between the U.S. and USSR was so immense that no competition was possible or necessary. China wants the yuan (RMB, renminbi) to replace the U.S. dollar as the global exchange currency. The ruble, by contrast, was never even considered for global trade.

The USSR built a bloc of Warsaw Pact and Soviet-allied states. China similarly builds blocs through the Belt and Road Initiative, BRICS, and the Shanghai Cooperation Organization. However, the Soviet blocs were all or nothing. Members were bound by trade, economic, diplomatic, and defense agreements which excluded them from following independent foreign policies. However, the China-led groupings have no such agreements, nor exclusivity, neither is there a contractual loss of sovereignty for members.

Beyond Soviet-aligned nations, the USSR had no real diplomatic power. It did not dictate the behavior of nations outside of the bloc. China, by contrast, convinced almost the entire world to adopt Beijing's strategy for virus containment during the Covid-19 pandemic. Additionally, China is a "plus" member, dialogue partner, or observer in numerous regional partnerships, such as ASEAN Regional Forum, the Organization of American States (OAS), the China-Arab States Summit and Gulf Cooperation Council (GCC), the China-Africa Cooperation Forum and the African Union (AU), and the Pacific Islands Forum.

Ideology: Both the USSR and the PRC were/are driven by ideology. However, the USSR's goal was to export communism, to convince other countries to adopt the same governmental system, and then to bring them into the fold as an official member. China, by contrast, has no interest in exporting socialism or changing the systems followed by other nations. Instead, Beijing just wants other nations to behave in a way that benefits Beijing.

Proxy Wars: One could argue that the Korean War was a proxy war, fought between the U.S. and China. But it would be more accurate to say that it was a proxy war between the U.S. and the USSR, and that China was the proxy army. Apart from that conflict, the U.S. and China have not really fought a proxy war. China backs Iran and Iran backs Hamas and Hezbollah, but so far, the U.S. has only fought Iran's allies through proxies in Yemen and Syria. While China would have been happy to benefit from those conflicts, China was not very involved. This contrasts with the communist uprisings in Latin America in the 1980s, where Washington backed one side and Moscow backed the other.

Military Buildup: The U.S. and USSR were in a massive arms race, as well as a race to space. The U.S. and China are also engaged in an arms race, but it does not have the feverish pace of the U.S.-Soviet arms race. One reason for this is that the U.S. has had very clear arms superiority during the entire time of competition and will remain on top as long as Congress keeps approving large defense budgets. The space race is similar. The U.S. was there first. The best China can do is tie. The U.S. is much closer to achieving a manned mission to Mars than China. Even if China wins the race to Mars, it will not have a fraction of the impact of the first American on the moon.

Espionage and Intelligence: The USSR and the U.S. spied on each other, but it generally consisted of intelligence-gathering related to the military, counterintelligence operations, and military technology. China engages in economic/industrial espionage on a massive scale, to obtain U.S. civilian and military technology, to earn money, as well as to bolster its military capabilities. Additionally, China's opportunities for espionage are far greater than those afforded the USSR. Chinese comprise the largest percentage of foreign students in the U.S.,[8] and the U.S. is home to about 2.4 million immigrants from China.[9] Some 75,000 to 130,000 Americans live in China.[10] Both countries welcome tourists. The U.S. also funds joint research projects[11] and labs in China, something that never happened during the Cold War with the USSR.

Maintaining peace during a cold war requires the United States to maintain strength, relying on its defense capabilities as a deterrent. Xi Jinping, in his role as the leader of the PRC, aspires to establish a global order where China dominates and shapes international rules to serve its own interests. Engaging in a conflict and losing to the U.S. would jeopardize the realization of this vision. The multifaceted threat posed by China is persistent, with China continually probing for vulnerabilities across various domains, both domestically and abroad, within the United States' defenses. Therefore, it is imperative for the U.S. to evaluate and define the various dimensions of the China threat, enabling the reinforcement of defenses in areas where vulnerabilities exist.

---

[8] https://www.axios.com/2023/05/08/chinese-students-us-education
[9] https://www.migrationpolicy.org/article/chinese-immigrants-united-states
[10] https://www.hiredchina.com/how-many-americans-live-and-work-in-china
[11] https://www.gao.gov/products/gao-22-105313

Assessing the China Threat

The 2023 Annual Threat Assessment of the U.S. Intelligence Community anticipates the joint challenges of China and Russia to be the most pervasive threat to the current rules-based global order,[12] which Beijing and Moscow want to reshape to serve their interests. Russia's invasion of Ukraine demonstrates Russia's capacity to challenge the international order through land-based warfare. China, on the other hand, has the capacity to challenge the current international paradigm in multiple regions and across a broad array of domains.

The 2010 U.S. Nuclear Posture Review anticipated that the PRC will remain the country's most significant competitor for decades to come.[13] This conclusion was based on increasingly frequent attempts by the PRC to remake the Indo-Pacific region, as well as the international system, according to Beijing's authoritarian preferences. Even more, the PRC has a stated goal of quickly modernizing and expanding the PLA. In recent years, Beijing is increasingly combining growing military power[14] with its economic, technological, and diplomatic influence, to ensure the continued rule of the CCP in China, safeguard what it considers its sovereign territories, exert regional supremacy, and advance its global impact.

To realize its policy objectives, the PRC relies on its influential positions within critical global supply chains and deploys a coordinated, whole-of-government approach to showcase its power, compelling neighboring nations to conform to its preferences. These preferences encompass territorial claims on

---

[12] Annual Threat Assessment of the U.S. Intelligence Community February 6, 2023
[13] DOD Nuclear Posture Review Report April 2010
[14] Annual Threat Assessment of the U.S. Intelligence Community February 6, 2023

land, sea, and air within the region, as well as its assertions of sovereignty over Taiwan.

Nonetheless, China confronts a plethora of international and domestic challenges that could impede the aspirations of CCP leaders. These challenges encompass an aging population, a decelerating economy, high levels of debt, economic disparities, and mounting resistance to the PRC's repeated threats toward Taiwan and other nations. China also grapples with growing skepticism from foreign countries and businesses, accelerating the process of de-risking and gradual decoupling from China. This has resulted in a decline in foreign direct investment and the redirection of trade toward nations including India, Vietnam, and Indonesia, all of which has been driven by China losing its appeal as a manufacturing hub. In 2023, Mexico overtook China as the United States' top trading partner.[15]

Despite encountering more resistance now than during the early years of Xi's leadership, Beijing persists in its efforts to expand its influence on the global stage through a range of initiatives, such as the Belt and Road Initiative, the Shanghai Cooperation Organization, BRICS, the Global Security Initiative, the China-Arab States Cooperation Forum (CASCF), and the Regional Comprehensive Economic Partnership (RCEP), as well as through its roles as an advisor and dialogue partner in other regional trade agreements and groupings, such as the Association of Southeast Asian Nations (ASEAN).

Beijing has sought to leverage these programs and initiatives to promote a China-led alternative to the international development and security forums typically dominated by the U.S.

---

[15] https://www.businessinsider.com/us-mexico-china-trade-world-economy-changing-2023

and Western powers, to alter international norms so they align with China's interests.

Beijing remains committed to enhancing its domestic defense production capabilities for weapons of mass destruction and advanced conventional armaments. Its objective is to establish a military force by 2027 with the primary purpose of deterring potential U.S. intervention in a future cross-Strait crisis. Notably, the PLA Navy and PLA Air Force stand as the largest forces in the region, consistently incorporating cutting-edge platforms to strengthen China's capacity for achieving air superiority and projecting power beyond the initial island chain. Additionally, it is likely that the PLA Rocket Force already possesses short-, medium-, and intermediate-range conventional systems capable of posing a threat to U.S. forces and regional bases.

The PLA is working to establish overseas military installations and secure access agreements, with the goal of projecting power and safeguarding China's interests abroad. To achieve these objectives, the PLA employs tailor-made strategies designed to suit each individual country it seeks to engage with. Customized strategies, involving trade, investment, grants, and loans, are aimed at addressing local concerns while fostering improved relations and advancing China's overseas basing objectives. Currently, Beijing possesses military and dual-use facilities in Argentina, Cambodia, Cuba, Djibouti, and Myanmar. In addition, it has outfitted ports capable of hosting PLA Navy vessels in Sri Lanka and elsewhere.

China is additionally challenging the U.S. through technology, cyber activities, malign influence operations, espionage, accelerated development of AI, and the utilization of extensive big data analytics capabilities. Furthermore, China's scope of influence extends beyond Earth, as it enhances its space warfare capabilities by engaging in space exploration, launching satellites — including what could be "killer satellites" — and developing space-based weapons. The PRC also has ambitions related to colonization on celestial bodies such as the moon and Mars.

A Possible Hot War: Taiwan

One key potential trigger for a conflict between the United States and China is the Taiwan question. Officially named the Republic of China (ROC), Taiwan lies 130 km (81 miles) from China's southeastern coast, bordering the East China Sea, the Philippine Sea, the South China Sea, and the Taiwan Strait. More than 97 percent of the island's 23.8 million inhabitants are ethnic Chinese; most of the remainder are indigenous Austronesian peoples.[16]

The country was a Japanese colony until 1945. After the Kuomintang (KMT) forces led by Chiang Kai-shek faced military defeat in the Chinese Civil War, they relocated to Taiwan. The UN and the U.S. shifted recognition from the ROC to the PRC in 1971 and 1979, respectively. Chiang Kai-shek quit the UN, a move that set the stage for the next half century of ambiguity and impending peril for Taiwan. Taiwan is now recognized as an independent country by just 13 countries, including the Holy See.[17]

In 1996, when Taiwan held the first direct presidential elections, the PRC carried out missile tests in the Taiwan Strait, trying to intimidate voters into voting for the pro-unification party. Invoking the Taiwan Relations Act, the U.S. dispatched two aircraft carrier battle groups to the region, ending the missile tests.

---

[16] https://www.britannica.com/place/Taiwan/Climate
[17] https://worldpopulationreview.com/country-rankings/countries-that-recognize-taiwan

In 2000, KMT rule finally came to an end, with the election of Chen Shui-bian of the Democratic Progressive Party (DPP).

Today, Taiwan is a multiparty democracy with an average income of $25,000 per year,[18] putting them in the top 15 percent of countries in terms of per capita income. The current president of Taiwan, Tsai Ing-wen of the DPP,[19] is in her second term, having won a resounding victory in 2020. Her statements that Taiwan will not unify with the PRC[20] have angered Beijing, but match public sentiment among Taiwanese voters.[21]

Beijing claims sovereignty over both Taiwan and its territorial waters. In 2005, the CCP passed a law giving Beijing the authority to use military action to annex Taiwan.[22] In 2019, Xi said: "We make no promise to renounce the use of force and reserve the option of taking all necessary means."[23] He reaffirmed this stance in 2022, and in August 2023, the PRC government released a new map of China which showed Taiwan as part of China, sparking outrage in Taiwan.[24] Almost immediately afterwards, the U.S. State Department's Foreign Military Financing program, normally reserved for sovereign nations, was extended to include equipment transfers to Taiwan.[25]

Washington's approach to Taiwan is known as "strategic ambiguity." The United States adheres to a "One China" policy,

---

[18] https://www.ceicdata.com/en/indicator/taiwan/forecast-nominal-gdp-per-capita
[19] https://english.president.gov.tw/NEWS/6523
[20] https://www.aljazeera.com/news/2020/5/20/taiwans-tsai-ing-wen-says-no-to-one-country-two-systems
[21] https://www.brookings.edu/articles/why-is-unification-so-unpopular-in-taiwan-its-the-prc-political-system-not-just-culture/
[22] https://www.asianews.it/news-en/Beijing-anti-secession-law-and-Taiwan-anti-annexation-bill-2642.html
[23] https://www.xinhuanet.com/english/2019-01/02/c_137715300.htm
[24] https://www.newsweek.com/china-border-map-neighbors-reaction-territorial-claims-1823648
[25] https://edition.cnn.com/2023/08/30/politics/us-taiwan-foreign-military-financing-program/index.html

refraining from taking a position on whether Taiwan is a part of China. Nevertheless, the TRA stipulates that the U.S. advocates for a peaceful resolution of Taiwan's status. Furthermore, in accordance with the TRA, the U.S. commits to equipping Taiwan for its self-defense against China. President Biden has publicly expressed the U.S. commitment to fight for Taiwan on several occasions, although the White House subsequently walked the statement back, CNN reported on March 27, 2022. Notably, under both the Trump and Biden administrations, the U.S. has consistently increased arms sales to Taiwan. President Trump sent the first U.S. troops to Taiwan since 1979. And Biden said that he was planning to quadruple the number.[26] The roughly 200 soldiers sent to Taiwan as trainers and advisers would make no significant difference in the event of an invasion, yet the act of deploying them sent an important signal to the CCP that the U.S. will conduct its foreign policy as it sees fit, irrespective of trade relations.

As tensions between Washington and Beijing escalate, some U.S. lawmakers have called for an end to strategic ambiguity.[27] This was echoed in April 2022 by Japan's former prime minister, the late Shinzo Abe.[28] As Japan views its own defense becoming more closely entwined with that of Taiwan,[29] Tokyo wants to know if they can count on the U.S. if conflict were to break out. Abe said that doubts about the U.S. willingness to fight may make the situation more dangerous, as it would embolden China.

Another perspective on strategic ambiguity suggests that it could serve as a more effective deterrent compared to a public

---

[26] https://www.wsj.com/articles/u-s-to-expand-troop-presence-in-taiwan-for-training-against-china-threat-62198a83

[27] https://thehill.com/policy/defense/575842-lawmakers-call-for-end-to-strategic-ambiguity-on-taiwan/

[28] https://www.project-syndicate.org/commentary/us-taiwan-strategic-ambiguity-must-end-by-abe-shinzo-2022-04

[29] https://www.ft.com/content/f4140801-a688-4703-825d-236fab4818e1

commitment to engage in war over Taiwan. A clear and official commitment could potentially trigger a conflict. Moreover, China might be inclined to attack U.S. forces in Japan[30] if they were certain the U.S. would respond with military action. In contrast, if they perceived uncertainty regarding the U.S. stance, they might immediately invade Taiwan while taking precautions to avoid inadvertently dragging Japan or the U.S. into the conflict. Consequently, strategic ambiguity may be the preferred strategy because it keeps Beijing uncertain about its course of action. China would not risk a preemptive strike on the U.S. because this would almost certainly lead to war with Japan, the U.S., and Taiwan. The UK, Australia, New Zealand, India, as AUKUS and Quad partners would likely enter the conflict against China as well.

As Beijing attempts to isolate Taiwan, sometimes even the U.S. has to compromise. Washington rejected Taiwan's bid to join the new Indo-Pacific Economic Framework (IPEF) in spite of the fact that Taiwan has the seventh largest economy in Asia[31] and plays a crucial role in global supply chains, particularly for microchips. The reason Taiwan was excluded was a fear of scaring off Southeast Asian nations who depend heavily on China. Shortly after, U.S. Trade Representative Katherine Tai met with her Taiwanese counterpart to discuss deepening trade relations between the two countries.

Each time the U.S. sends representatives to Taiwan, or when U.S. and Taiwanese officials meet to find a way that Taiwan can meaningfully participate in the UN, the WHO, or the global community, the PRC issues strong statements of condemnation and sends ships and jets to challenge the sea and airspace around

---

[30] https://www.nytimes.com/2022/05/27/opinion/biden-taiwan-defense-china.html
[31] https://edition.cnn.com/2022/05/27/business/taiwan-us-new-economic-talks-intl-hnk/index.html

Taiwan. Beijing does the same on China's National Day[32] and Taiwan's National Day.

Whether or not the United States intends to defend Taiwan remains to be seen. However, it is clear that the U.S. is intensifying its economic engagement with the island nation in addition to its commitment to provide Taiwan with the weapons and strategies to defend itself from the CCP regime. Apart from the Taiwan Relations Act, thwarting China's annexation of Taiwan holds immense significance in advancing U.S. policy objectives.

Support for Taiwan is driven not only by an ideological dedication to democracy, but also by the strategic significance of Taiwan. If China were to take control of Taiwan, they would effectively command both shores of the Taiwan Strait, allowing Beijing to assert sovereignty over the vital international shipping lanes in between. This has already happened in the disputed Spratly Islands,[33] where Beijing issued new maritime rules[34] that certain types of foreign vessels had to notify Chinese authorities before sailing through. Annexing Taiwan would embolden the PRC to claim the South China Sea and parts of the Indo-Pacific region. This would give Beijing control over 60 percent of the world's maritime shipping.[35]

Taiwan is also a significant component in Washington's Asia policy.[36] Maintaining freedom and stability in the region is predicated on Taiwan remaining independent of China. Currently, the U.S. maintains troops in Thailand, the Philippines, and Guam, with larger troop strengths in Japan and South Korea. Additionally,

---

[32] https://www.nytimes.com/2021/10/09/world/asia/united-states-china-taiwan.html
[33] https://www.maritime-executive.com/article/u-s-navy-increases-activity-in-the-south-china-sea
[34] https://www.hstoday.us/subject-matter-areas/maritime-security/china-stokes-anxiety-with-new-maritime-law/
[35] https://chinapower.csis.org/much-trade-transits-south-china-sea/
[36] https://www.state.gov/u-s-relations-with-taiwan/

the U.S. Navy conducts "Freedom of Navigation Operations" in the South China Sea.[37]

Countries which have maritime disputes with the PRC in the South China Sea include Brunei, Taiwan, Indonesia, Malaysia, the Philippines, and Vietnam. None of them is strong enough to stand up to the PLA Navy. In addition to issues of territorial sovereignty, trillions of dollars' worth of cargo passes through the region,[38] including 40 percent of the world's liquefied natural gas. If the U.S. loses Taiwan, or loses an Indo-Pacific showdown, maritime disputes would be decided by China, and the free use of shipping lanes would end.

Japan also has a territorial dispute with China, while New Zealand and Australia have a strong interest in maintaining freedom of navigation in the South China Sea and the Indo-Pacific. The Five Eyes intelligence-sharing alliance, AUKUS, and the Quad defense grouping are dedicated to containing China, a task made much easier by maintaining a free Taiwan, with freedom of movement in Taiwanese waters and airspace.

China, of course opposes all three alliances,[39] saying "Five Eyes could be poked blind if China's sovereignty and security are harmed."[40] By sovereignty, they mean their claim over Taiwan. Not only does the PRC resent the U.S. arms sales to Taiwan, but even registered "strong indignation" when President Trump accepted a call from Taiwan President Tsai Ing-wen, congratulating him on his victory in the U.S. presidential election.[41] The CCP views any positive engagement with Taiwan

---

[37] https://www.maritime-executive.com/article/u-s-navy-increases-activity-in-the-south-china-sea
[38] https://www.cfr.org/global-conflict-tracker/conflict/territorial-disputes-south-china-sea
[39] https://www.bloomberg.com/news/articles/2021-09-23/why-the-aukus-quad-and-five-eyes-pacts-anger-china-quicktake
[40] https://www.globaltimes.cn/content/1207378.shtml
[41] http://www.xinhuanet.com/english/2020-05/20/c_139072717.htm

as an infringement on China's sovereignty. North Korea, China's only official ally, echoed the CCP line, issuing a statement, saying that the U.S. should stop supporting Taiwan.[42]

Under China's Anti-Secession Law, Beijing claims legal authority to take Taiwan by force.[43] Liu Weidong, a U.S. affairs specialist at the Chinese Academy of Social Sciences, said "China cannot accept any country to develop official relations with Taiwan." He went on to say that there was a general trend of countries increasing their engagement with Taiwan, and issued a vague threat to those who dared support the island nation, *South China Morning Post* reported on October 24, 2021.

A Chinese Blockade of Taiwan is Likely

A PLA blockade on Taiwan would thwart U.S. policy objectives in the Indo-Pacific as much as China annexing the island nation. And the likelihood of a blockade is high. The only question is whether Xi Jinping will use the blockade itself as a weapon to defeat Taiwan, or if he will employ a blockade in conjunction with a military invasion.

During the October 5, 2023 China's Power Conference at the CSIS, U.S. Assistant Secretary of Defense for Indo-Pacific Security Affairs Ely Ratner explained that Xi Jinping has set a timeline for the modernization of the PLA, which many people believe coincides with the timeline for invading Taiwan. To counter a Chinese invasion, the U.S. military has increased its presence in the Indo-Pacific, including the South China Sea and the Taiwan Strait. Taiwan's military has also developed significant capabilities focused on repelling an invasion, such as launching missiles and artillery shells from land bases.

---

[42] https://www.taiwannews.com.tw/en/news/4323453
[43] https://www.newsweek.com/china-military-force-taiwan-diplomacy-1507263

Beijing is aware that a full-scale invasion of Taiwan could provoke a response from not only the United States, but also potentially draw in Japan, AUKUS, the Quad partners, and even NATO allies, with the potential to escalate into a global conflict. Another option in Beijing's arsenal would be a blockade. China could cut off access to Taiwan, preventing the island nation from receiving supplies of fuel, ammunition, and even food.

According to Lonnie Henley, a senior fellow at the Foreign Policy Research Institute also at the CSIS event, a blockade is also expected to elicit a response from the U.S. and its allies, although it would carry a lower likelihood of igniting a world war. However, if the U.S. and its allies opt for a military response to the blockade, neither the U.S. nor the Taiwanese armed forces are adequately prepared. Both military establishments have dedicated decades to preparing for an invasion scenario rather than a blockade.

Another conference attendee, Phil Saunders, director of the National Defense University's Center for the Chinese Military Affairs, concurred that a blockade would be less taxing on the PLA, resulting in fewer casualties. It would also be easier to sell diplomatically to the world community. The UN and EU would quickly condemn an invasion, apply harsh sanctions, and then vote on whether or not to send troops. The response to a blockade might just be a strongly-worded letter, urging both sides to find a peaceful resolution.

Saunders also pointed out that a blockade on Taiwan would become a de facto blockade on China, a nation which depends on imports of both food and energy. The CCP regime has never liked chaos, and the civilian population of China would react badly if they found themselves on reduced food and fuel rations. Saunders conjectured that Beijing might seek to shift blame onto Taipei for the blockade, redirecting public anger toward Taiwan. The CCP could simultaneously leverage this contrived blame as a diplomatic instrument when explaining the blockade to the international community. Beijing's rationale for an invasion could then be magnified through social media channels[44] and the CCP's extensive network of wumao trolls, bots, and compromised journalists, to undermine foreign support for any military intervention.

Despite the numerous advantages of a blockade, Saunders expressed the view that the drawbacks would significantly exceed the benefits. A blockade on Taiwan would be costly to the global economy, and could trigger an aggressive reaction by countries suffering as a result of losing access to Taiwan-made chips. The allies would immediately blockade China. Shipping through and fishing in the Taiwan Strait and the South China Sea would grind to a halt, causing hunger in Southeast Asia, as well as a global financial crisis. This would bring most of the world into the conflict, on Taiwan's side.

Another drawback with a blockade, observed Saunders, is that it would last for an indeterminate time, as there would be no way of knowing when Taiwan would surrender. And each day that passes would deepen Beijing's economic woes. At the same time, the world would attempt to resupply Taiwan. The PLA could sink resupply ships and shootdown planes doing food drops, but this would escalate the blockade into a world war, which is exactly what Beijing would be trying to avoid in a blockade scenario.

A further point Saunders made was that a blockade would involve bombing ports, container facilities, airports, and other infrastructure to prevent Taiwan from using them. To observers

---

[44] https://www.hrw.org/news/2023/08/14/chinas-social-media-interference-shows-urgent-need-rules

around the world, this would look very much like an invasion, and they would react accordingly.

Ultimately, he believed that a military invasion was Xi Jinping's best option. If the invasion could be executed swiftly, it would limit the opportunity for the U.S. and its allies to respond. Moreover, if the CCP established a presence on Taiwanese soil, the allies may become less inclined to attempt their removal. The invasion might offer the advantages of greater speed, cost-effectiveness, and decisiveness compared to a blockade. Additionally, from the perspective of the CCP's global power projection, it would not only damage the reputation of the United States, but also sow doubt among U.S. allies about the extent of American security guarantees.

Henley felt that in the event of Beijing taking action against Taiwan, the imposition of a blockade, either preceding or following an invasion, was nearly certain. Given this, a blockade was the most probable scenario. Moreover, if the CCP were to gain control on the ground in Taiwan, the international community might be inclined to engage in negotiations with China to reopen global shipping as soon as possible.

Direct Threats to the U.S. Homeland

In addition to threatening U.S. interests in the Indo-Pacific, China also poses a threat to U.S. citizens at home. CCP entities are engaged in various activities within the United States, including cyberattacks, espionage, supporting drug trafficking from Mexico, the collection of American DNA data, as well as the operation of bio labs and cryptocurrency mining facilities, all of which are perceived as potential national security concerns.

Cyberattacks on the Department of Defense

According to the DOD's Military and Security Developments Involving the People's Republic of China 2023 Report to Congress, PRC-based cyber intrusions target computer systems worldwide including those owned by the U.S. Government. These intrusions exploit known vulnerabilities to actively breach government networks, aiming to pilfer intellectual property and establish access to sensitive networks. The PRC employs its cyberspace capabilities not only for intelligence gathering against various U.S. sectors, but also for extracting sensitive data from vital defense infrastructure and research institutions. This activity is undertaken to gain economic and military advantages and potentially prepare for cyberattacks.

The stolen information can benefit China's high-tech defense industries, aid in military modernization, provide insights into U.S. plans and intentions, and support diplomatic negotiations. Furthermore, it allows Beijing's cyberspace forces to construct an operational view of U.S. defense networks, military positioning, logistics, and related capabilities, which could be exploited during a crisis. The access and skills required for these intrusions closely resemble those necessary for conducting cyberspace operations aimed at deterring, delaying, disrupting, and degrading DOD operations ahead of or during a conflict. Collectively, these cyber-enabled campaigns have a direct or indirect impact on Washington's ability to project or defend against military actions.

Espionage

The PRC poses a sophisticated and ongoing threat to military and critical infrastructure systems using cyber-enabled means to obtain advanced technologies and information.[45] There have been several U.S. criminal indictments since 2015, targeting PRC nationals,

---

[45] Ibid.

U.S. citizens, and individuals with ties to the PRC who have engaged in illegal efforts to acquire information and technology to modernize the PLA. The PRC has dedicated significant resources to support its defense modernization, utilizing the Military-Civil Fusion (MCF) strategy and espionage to access sensitive, dual-use, and military-grade equipment. Furthermore, the PRC has implemented substantial reforms within its defense industry, with a focus on enhancing R&D, acquisition, testing, evaluation, and production of weapon systems.

Espionage cases involving individuals with ties to the PRC encompass various charges, including the procurement and export of controlled items to China and acts of economic espionage. The U.S. Department of Justice regards these cases as significant in U.S. export enforcement. Beijing's efforts have covered a wide range of technologies, including aviation, radiation-hardened components, integrated circuits, microwave technology, sensors, naval and marine systems, signals decoding, trade secrets related to syntactic foam, space communications, military communications jamming equipment, and dynamic random access memory.

The Chinese regime poses a sophisticated and enduring cyber-enabled threat to military and vital infrastructure systems[46] as part of its initiatives to develop, acquire, and gain access to advanced technologies and information. Their detected cyberspace operations have encompassed telecommunications companies, managed service providers, and software developers. Prominent targets involve proprietary technologies in commercial and military domains, as well as research institutions affiliated with defense, energy, and various other sectors. The PRC's objectives include creating disruptive and destructive effects, ranging from denial-of-service attacks to physically disrupting critical infrastructure, with the aim of influencing decision-making and

---

[46] Ibid.

disrupting military operations in both the initial and ongoing stages of a conflict. Compared to a decade ago, China's recent actions in cyberspace represent a distinct, intricate, and pressing challenge to U.S. national security.

CCP Spies and Coercion

The FBI and the Department of Homeland Security are ramping up efforts to counter CCP intelligence operations in the United States. In May 2023, the FBI arrested an alleged Chinese spy in Boston, accusing him of spying on Chinese dissidents based in the U.S. and critics of the CCP regime.[47] This latest arrest comes as part of an ongoing campaign by the CCP to silence critics abroad.[48] To dissuade pro-democracy activists and others who speak out against the CCP, Beijing uses physical threats, online harassment, and clandestine operations in foreign countries.

Chinese security forces have implemented campaigns, such as Operation Fox Hunt, to coerce people wanted by the regime to return and stand trial.[49] This is often achieved through intimidation, threatening the person's family back in China, or outright abduction. In April 2023, the FBI raided a secret Chinese police station in New York City, which prosecutors identified as part of the CCP's "transnational repression" campaign.[50]

The regime is carrying out an increasing number of intelligence and covert operations in Western democracies, where human rights and personal freedoms are often exploited to avoid detection. Allegations of and investigations into secret police

---

[47] https://www.foxbusiness.com/politics/feds-arrest-alleged-chinese-spy-boston
[48] https://www.reuters.com/world/china/china-keeps-up-campaign-pressure-critics-abroad-despite-western-backlash-2023-05-10/
[49] https://edition.cnn.com/2022/10/20/china/us-justice-department-charged-china-fugitive-family-intl-hnk/index.html
[50] https://www.voanews.com/a/us-brings-charges-over-secret-chinese-police-outpost/7054291.html

stations have cropped up in Canada and in Europe.[51] So far, 14 countries are investigating secret Chinese police stations on their territory.[52] And Canada has expelled a Chinese diplomat for attempting to intimidate a Canadian lawmaker who challenged the CCP on human rights grounds.

Beijing's covert networks are extensive, not only in the number of countries they cover, but also in the number of agents employed. At the same time that the Chinese police station was raided in New York City, 34 officials of China's Ministry of Public Security were charged by U.S. prosecutors with creating thousands of fake online accounts which they used to harass and menace opponents of the regime.[53]

The CCP regime is targeting not only Chinese nationals or ethnic Chinese, but also Americans who could be of use to the regime either by providing political influence or by stealing U.S. secrets. These efforts are directed at businesses, academic institutions, researchers, lawmakers, and the general public. The FBI has identified countering the severe threat of the CCP's counterintelligence and economic espionage campaign as a top priority.[54] CCP tactics are meant to influence lawmakers and public opinion to support government policies that are more favorable to Beijing. To achieve Xi Jinping's goal of China displacing the United States, the CCP employs a number of tools, including predatory lending and business practices, theft of intellectual property, forced intellectual property transfer,[55]

---

[51] https://www.theguardian.com/world/2023/apr/20/explainer-chinas-covert-overseas-police-stations

[52] https://www.voanews.com/a/chinese-refugees-in-italy-wary-of-beijing-outposts/6848100.html

[53] https://www.justice.gov/usao-edny/pr/34-officers-peoples-republic-china-national-police-charged-perpetrating-transnational

[54] https://www.fbi.gov/investigate/counterintelligence/the-china-threat

[55] FBI Office of Private Sector, Counterintelligence Division and Training Division. *Made in Beijing: The Plan for Global Market Domination* (film).

industrial espionage, acquisition of foreign companies, and cyber hacking. This economic espionage[56] converges with overseas influence operations on campuses, in R&D departments, and in research labs in the U.S. where Chinese researchers are often co-opted or coerced, or have their families threatened if they refuse to steal secrets[57] for Beijing.

In April 2021, the FBI announced that they were opening a new China-related espionage investigation roughly once every ten hours.[58] In early 2023, the DHS announced an initiative to combat malicious artificial intelligence controlled by China.[59] This included attempts to influence public opinion and legislation by spreading misinformation, or outright attacks on U.S. critical infrastructure, such as power grids. Apart from silencing critics, the DHS reported that Beijing was exploiting immigration and travel systems to spy on the U.S. government as well as private companies and individuals.

The Foreign Agents Registration Act (FARA) and Section 951 of the Espionage Act[60] make it clear that anyone inside the United States and acting on behalf of China can be classified as a foreign agent. If they fail to register as such, they can be subject to arrest and prosecution. In 2022, the Justice Department invoked FARA to arrest and charge 25 people. While this is a step in the right direction, the real number of people meeting the definition of foreign agent is surely much higher, and it includes people paid by the CCP to lobby, spy, or engage in "influence operations." As of

---

[56] https://www.bbc.com/news/world-asia-china-64206950
[57] https://edition.cnn.com/2023/01/25/politics/chinese-engineer-sentence-spying-intl-hnk/index.html
[58] https://edition.cnn.com/2021/04/14/politics/fbi-director-china-investigations-intl-hnk/index.html
[59] https://www.voanews.com/a/us-targeting-china-artificial-intelligence-threats-/7061020.html
[60] https://www.justice.gov/nsd-fara/fara-related-statutes

early 2022, the FBI had more than 2,000 open investigations into Chinese spying activity in the U.S.[61]

In addition, Beijing is also guilty of killing Americans with illegal drugs, by allowing shipments of precursor chemicals for fentanyl being shipped from China to Mexico.[62] Some U.S. lawmakers want the drug cartels officially designated as international terrorist organizations.[63] If that happens, China could be held accountable for supplying materials to the cartels and for helping them launder money. By similar logic, could drug dealers in the U.S. be considered foreign agents, working on the behalf of Beijing? At a time when China is expanding its own Counter-Espionage Law,[64] making business consulting and some other common business services effectively illegal, it seems that a U.S. accountant in China could be charged with spying for auditing the books of his clients, while CCP agents can operate out of secret police stations in the U.S., influencing opinion, shutting down dissenters, or forcing graduate students to steal secrets.

TikTok Matches Definition of Foreign Agent

FARA "requires the registration of, and disclosures by, an 'agent of a foreign principal' who, either directly or through another person, acts on behalf of a foreign government within the United States," and it seems that short-form video hosting serviceTikTok matches the definition of a foreign agent. Some U.S. lawmakers — among them former House Speaker Kevin McCarthy — favor banning it, to protect American data from being shared with Beijing.

---

[61] https://www.nbcnews.com/politics/politics-news/fbi-director-wray-says-scale-chinese-spying-us-blew-away-rcna14369

[62] https://www.brookings.edu/articles/chinas-role-in-the-fentanyl-crisis/

[63] https://www.cbsnews.com/news/mexican-drug-cartels-terrorist-organization-what-would-that-mean/

[64] https://www.dw.com/en/china-anti-espionage-law-heightens-risks-for-foreign-firms/a-65528537

In March 2023 — when a bipartisan House committee questioned TikTok CEO Shou Zi Chew about data security issues and the degree of control which the CCP has over the company[65] — Beijing complained that singling out a Chinese company was racially motivated. Chew said that TikTok had never been asked to hand over user data to the CCP. This may or may not be true, yet, if TikTok were asked, the company would be required to comply. TikTok says they plan to store American user data on U.S. soil. But under the terms of PRC law, it does not matter where the data is stored.[66] Chinese companies must turn over data when Beijing requests it.

The connection between TikTok and the CCP is quite clear. The CCP has invested heavily in ByteDance, TikTok's parent company, and the party holds a seat on the board of directors. ByteDance also has an internal CCP cell, and it solidified its control over the app when its former CFO began serving as CEO of TikTok in April 2021.[67] Beijing's strong opposition when it was suggested that ByteDance, an allegedly private company, should sell the app,[68] proves the CCP has a stake in both ByteDance and TikTok. Moreover, Beijing accusing Washington of singling out the Chinese app seems hypocritical, given China's blocking of Google and Western media outlets.

Even though TikTok is prohibited in China, Beijing said any potential TikTok ban would represent an overreach of U.S. authority. In the United States, TikTok is already banned on Federal Government and military devices. TikTok is also banned

---

[65] https://www.cbsnews.com/news/tiktok-hearing-ceo-shou-zi-chew-house-committee-testimony/

[66] https://www.lawfaremedia.org/article/beijings-new-national-intelligence-law-defense-offense

[67] https://www.nationalreview.com/2023/03/tiktok-digs-deeper-hole/

[68] https://www.cnbc.com/2023/03/24/tiktok-wants-to-distance-from-china-but-the-governments-getting-involved.html

or restricted in the UK, India, and several other countries.[69] The Netherlands' national intelligence agency warned that using apps from China, Russia, North Korea and Iran increase the risk of espionage,[70] especially in light of China's aggressive program of cyberattacks and data theft.

Along with attacks and data theft, there are issues with the CCP controlling the flow of information on TikTok, disseminating its own views, and censoring opposing opinions. For example, in Russia, TikTok restricts uploads that criticize the government or the military.[71] The app is also used to track journalists, a fact which sparked an investigation by the DOJ.[72]

A report submitted to the Australian Parliament's Select Committee on Foreign Interference through Social Media found that describing ByteDance as a private enterprise was no longer accurate. The Australian Strategic Policy Institute has concluded that ByteDance collaborates with Chinese public security bureaus, including the one in Xinjiang.[73] And in its March 24, 2023 Daily Brief, Human Rights Watch said TikTok is "beholden to China's authoritarian government… ultimately, the ruling Chinese Communist Party (CCP) has total control over it."

Deng Yuwen, a former editor of the CCP Central Party School's *Journal Study Times*, was quoted in a March 21, 2023 Asia Nikkei report as saying that a recent government restructuring is "mobilizing nationwide resources to achieve breakthroughs." This makes CCP control of ByteDance even more conspicuous. It

---

[69] https://mashable.com/article/tiktok-ban-countries

[70] https://www.euronews.com/next/2023/04/04/which-countries-have-banned-tiktok-cybersecurity-data-privacy-espionage-fears

[71] https://www.washingtonpost.com/technology/2022/04/13/tiktok-russia-censorship-propaganda-tracking-exposed/

[72] https://abcnews.go.com/Politics/doj-investigating-tiktok-owners-surveillance-us-journalists-sources/story?id=97945747

[73] https://www.washingtonexaminer.com/news/justice/new-details-tiktok-ties-ccp-revealed

confirms that ByteDance, TikTok, and other Chinese companies operating in the United States pose a national security threat.

CCP Hacking, Spying, and Co-opting

"There is no country that presents a broader, more severe threat to our innovation, our ideas and our economic security than China does," said FBI Director Christopher Wray. told NBC News on February 2, 2022. The following week, the Justice Department announced criminal charges against Hytera,[74] a Chinese company previously the subject of a national security blacklisting proposal.[75] The charges allege that Hytera conspired with employees of Motorola Solutions Inc to steal digital mobile radio technology.

In early 2022, News Corp. — owners of *The Wall Street Journal* and *New York Post* — reported being the target of a cyberattack linked to China.[76] Previously, CCP-linked hackers penetrated both the *New York Times* and *The Wall Street Journal*. In 2014 and 2015, the Federal Government's Office of Personnel Management was breached, with China-linked hackers stealing information on 20 million current and former federal employees. Beijing's proven history of cyberattacks on businesses, government agencies, and universities, prompted the Trump administration to launch an initiative to counter such intrusions.

Within China, the CCP regime uses spycraft to monitor and control its own people, with security officials creating a system to track journalists and scholars, Reuters reported on November 30, 2021. The Chinese region of Xinjiang has become synonymous with advanced AI, facial recognition, and surveillance

---

[74] https://www.reuters.com/business/media-telecom/us-charges-chinese-company-with-conspiring-with-ex-motorola-staff-steal-2022-02-07/

[75] https://broadbandbreakfast.com/2021/09/hytera-and-huawei-respond-to-fcc-blocking-chinese-equipment-as-u-s-players-react/

[76] https://www.washingtonpost.com/politics/2022/02/07/news-corp-breach-illustrates-how-badly-china-wants-hack-us/

technology.[77] It is suspected that all attendees at the Beijing Olympics were monitored, surveilled, and tracked with the latest spy gear, including health apps, phone taps, and state-approved VPNs. Even more worrying is that the DNA of foreign athletes, officials, and diplomats may have been collected and categorized, as a result of a strict schedule of daily Covid-19 testing.[78]

Beijing exports this type of repression to stifle dissenters in immigrant communities in the U.S., and hacks media outlets to discover the names and locations of informants who oppose the CCP. Once these people are found, they may be subject to intimidation, and their families back in China threatened. In the most extreme cases, they could become targets of extrajudicial harassment[79] aimed at overseas Tibetans, Uyghurs, Falun Gong practitioners, and pro-democracy advocates. In the most extreme cases, these people may be kidnapped from the streets of foreign countries, and returned to China to be jailed or otherwise controlled.

More subtle types of infiltration occur when Chinese embassies and consulates send out messages to U.S. businesses, advising that if they wish to continue doing business in China, they should promote pro-China legislation in Congress.[80] Similarly, China threatened to cut lucrative contracts with the NBA's Houston Rockets when coach Daryl Morey "liked" a post by Hong Kong pro-democracy protesters. Using economic pressure, the CCP seeks to control U.S., Chinese, and foreign citizens and companies, regardless of which country they are in.

---

[77] https://warontherocks.com/2021/11/turning-ghosts-into-humans-surveillance-as-an-instrument-of-social-engineering-in-xinjiang/

[78] https://thehill.com/homenews/administration/558648-cotton-warns-of-china-collecting-athletes-dna-at-2022-olympics/

[79] https://www.fbi.gov/news/speeches/countering-threats-posed-by-the-chinese-government-inside-the-us-wray-013122

[80] Ibid.

Industrial and Economic Espionage

Beyond spying, as a form of social and political control, the regime also engages in industrial and economic espionage, in order to further the country's development. Beijing's Made in China 2025 policy encompasses broad goals, such as increasing China's dominance in robotics, green energy, electric vehicles, aerospace, and biopharma.[81] Beijing is so determined to achieve these goals that it throws massive quantities of money and resources at them, as well as resorting to unfair competition, technology theft, and spying.

FBI chief Wray has estimated that China's IP theft costs the United States government and industries between $300 and $600 billion per year.[82] As of November 2023, a survey of Chinese espionage in the U.S. maintained by the CSIS listed "224 reported instances of Chinese espionage directed at the United States since 2000. It does not include espionage against other countries, against U.S. firms or persons located in China, nor the many cases involving attempts to smuggle controlled items from the U.S. to China" — or the 1,200-plus IP-theft lawsuits brought by U.S. companies against Chinese entities in either the U.S. or China. According to the same survey, 42 percent of the alleged perpetrators worked for China's government or the PLA; 32 percent were private Chinese citizens; and 26 percent were non-Chinese, usually Americans, persuaded to act on Beijing's behalf. Moreover, the prevalence of economic spying has increased over the past decade.

Despite Liu Pengyu, a spokesperson for the PRC Embassy in Washington, saying that "China is a staunch defender of

---

[81] Ibid.
[82] https://www.theguardian.com/world/2020/feb/06/china-technology-theft-fbi-biggest-threat

cybersecurity,"[83] the CCP regime maintains a state hacking apparatus larger than that of any other nation. In a single incident, hackers linked to China's Ministry of State Security (MSS) stole terabytes of data from a network, representing 10,000 American companies.[84] The FBI has identified Chinese attempts to steal the designs for everything from vaccines and computer chips to nuclear power plants and smartphones.

Apart from hacking, some of the spying is done through workers, students, or researchers physically planted in the target organization. These co-opted agents may provide cover, identify assets and targets, facilitate communication, or otherwise aid in intelligence gathering. On November 16, 2022, NPR reported the conviction of Chinese MSS officer Xu Yanjun. He was sentenced to 20 years' imprisonment for trying to steal high-tech aviation trade secrets from GE.

Chinese entities often make strategic investments in American companies, in order to gain access to proprietary information. Sometimes, the true ownership of a state-owned or state-controlled company may be obscured. An example is China's HNA Group, which showed an interest in buying *Forbes* magazine.[85] Major shareholders in HNA — which already owned American technology distributor Ingram Micro — include state-owned enterprises.

FBI and Justice Department Respond

Some Asian-American groups have accused the FBI and the Justice Department of overreach or Asian hate, by profiling

---

[83] https://www.npr.org/2022/02/04/1078259252/news-corp-china-hacking-cyberattack
[84] https://www.fbi.gov/news/speeches/countering-threats-posed-by-the-chinese-government-inside-the-us-wray-013122
[85] https://www.cnbc.com/2017/05/11/10-iconic-american-companies-owned-by-chinese-investors.html

Chinese nationals in spying investigations.[86] Additionally, critics claim that U.S. intelligence agencies are indicting people for minor offenses that have no effect on national security. But some of these offenses have proved to be very real, like researchers failing to disclose membership of the PLA when seeking U.S. visas or professors not declaring that they receive funding from the Chinese regime. In mid-2021, cases against five Chinese academics charged with visa fraud were dismissed, after more than 1,000 PLA-linked researchers decided to leave the U.S.[87] — but later that year Harvard University Professor Charles Lieber was convicted of making false statements and tax offenses after covering up his financial relationship with the Wuhan University of Technology and China's Thousand Talents Program.[88]

The dismissal of the cases against the PLA-affiliated scholars, and the saga of Anming Hu, an engineering professor at the University of Tennessee, Knoxville, who was eventually cleared of wire fraud and making false statements, have been seen by some as a failure of the DOJ's "China Initiative."[89] Such criticism aside, Beijing uses a variety of methods to infiltrate U.S. organizations. Exporting Chinese technology to the U.S. and other countries is a backdoor means which the CCP uses to spy on foreign countries and obtain their data. In November 2022, the Federal Communications Commission decided to begin stripping Chinese components from U.S. telecom networks, because they pose a hacking risk.[90]

---

[86] https://www.brennancenter.org/our-work/research-reports/national-security-profiling-asian-americans

[87] https://www.insidehighered.com/news/2021/07/26/prosecutors-drop-cases-against-scientists-accused-hiding-military-ties

[88] https://www.politico.com/news/2023/04/26/ex-harvard-prof-sentenced-china-00094045

[89] https://www.wilmerhale.com/en/insights/client-alerts/20210805-dojs-china-initiative-falters

[90] https://cyberscoop.com/fcc-huawei-zte-security-risks/

Another means of spying and projecting soft power are sister cities connections. Around 150 U.S. cities maintain such relationships with cities in the PRC, prompting Sens. Marsha Blackburn (R-TN) and Josh Hawley (R-MO) in October 2020 to ask that these partnerships be investigated, as they pose a threat by positioning the Chinese regime to co-opt or influence city-level officials.

The Confucius Institutes, which the Heritage Foundation on May 27, 2021 declared to be a Trojan horse, have been at the center of espionage discussions for a number of years. These institutes — Chinese language and culture centers installed on campuses in the United States — have been accused of spying, censorship,[91] and disseminating CCP propaganda.[92] Following various investigations into their activities, the number had by mid-2023 fallen from well over 100 to just ten.[93]

Spy Balloons

In February 2023, a Chinese balloon flew over the continental United States, with many believing it was gathering intelligence on military bases. Secretary of State Antony Blinken canceled a planned trip to China.[94] Balloons are suitable for this type of missions because they can fly at extremely high altitudes, above conventional fighter jets, and go undetected. Unlike satellites, which pass over periodically, balloons are capable of fixed-point surveillance.

---

[91] https://www.heritage.org/homeland-security/commentary/confucius-institutes-chinas-trojan-horse

[92] https://dailyiowan.com/2018/02/16/fbi-warns-universities-against-confucius-institute/

[93] https://www.nas.org/blogs/article/how_many_confucius_institutes_are_in_the_united_states

[94] https://www.npr.org/2023/02/04/1154473950/u-s-cancels-blinkens-visit-to-china-after-the-appearance-of-a-spy-balloon

When the postponed meeting was finally held, PRC Foreign Minister Wang Yi told Blinken that the U.S. reaction to the balloon had been "hysterical and absurd."[95] The Chinese espionage threat is very real, however real, prompting several states and the Federal Government to ban the Chinese social media app TikTok, and President Biden to expand restrictions on U.S. investment in China's technology sector.[96]

Through a combination of IP theft, accessing U.S. capital markets, and courting U.S. investors, Beijing has been able to accelerate the technological capabilities of the PLA. The U.S. defense community is especially concerned about the PLA's hypersonic missiles, *Financial Times* reported on October 17, 2021. These advanced weapons are extremely difficult to defend against. Killer satellites, magnetic rail guns, nuclear, and hypersonic arms: The weapons in Beijing's high-tech arsenal are very costly, which is why 41 percent of the PRC's official defense budget of $252 billion is spent on R&D. Part of the PLA's R&D costs are defrayed by stealing U.S. technology. Other technology is purchased from American developers, using funding from U.S. investors. The hypersonic test facility, the China Aerodynamics Research and Development Center, for example, relies on a super computer which uses American chip technology, according to an April 9, 2021 *Washington Post* report.

By listing on U.S. exchanges and gaining access to U.S. capital markets,[97] the regime in Beijing benefits from the deep pockets of American investors to fund its development projects. As of early 2023, 252 Chinese companies were listed on the three

---

[95] https://www.aljazeera.com/news/2023/2/19/blinken-meets-chinas-wang-yi-warns-over-russia-spy-balloons
[96] https://edition.cnn.com/2023/04/20/economy/janet-yellen-us-china-comments/index.html
[97] https://www.reuters.com/business/us-extends-ban-securities-investments-companies-linked-china-military-2021-11-09/

largest U.S. exchanges, with a total market value of $1.03 trillion.[98] Eight are state-owned enterprises, while many others have significant state-ownership or are owned by state-owned or controlled companies. About half of them use Cayman Islands shell companies to list on U.S. exchanges, so their true owners are not known. Other firms, such as Weibo Corporation, are not state-owned, but act on CCP orders to carry out surveillance and other operations.

The Biden administration has maintained Trump-era bans on U.S. investment in firms which have ties to the PLA. Under the regulations, U.S. companies and citizens are barred from buying or selling shares in restricted Chinese companies, including top chip-makers, oil producers, and tech companies. The technology companies have become a particular threat, as they are helping China develop its quantum computing capabilities.[99]

As reported by Reuters on December 3, 2021, the SEC now requires Chinese companies listed on U.S. stock exchanges to disclose whether they are owned or controlled by a PRC government entity. These rules extend to companies listing under shell companies such as variable interest entities, a structure often used by tech companies because, under PRC law, tech enterprises cannot have foreign ownership.

Chinese companies involved in quantum computing,[100] as well as manufacturing memory chips and navigation chips, are among the businesses which have been added to the U.S. blacklist by the Biden administration. Washington's entity list contains the names of Chinese companies, most of them state-backed, which

---

[98] https://www.uscc.gov/research/chinese-companies-listed-major-us-stock-exchanges
[99] https://www.cnbc.com/2021/11/24/us-blacklists-dozens-of-chinese-tech-firms.html
[100] https://asia.nikkei.com/Politics/International-relations/US-China-tensions/U.S.-crackdown-targets-China-s-quantum-computing-navigation-tech

the Federal Government wants to prevent from obtaining U.S. intellectual property and defense technology.[101]

Along with the direct threat posed by funding companies which increase the military capabilities of a belligerent state, Chinese law effectively turns every company and citizen into an agent. Under the National Security Law, National Intelligence Law,[102] and Cybersecurity Law, citizens and entities are obligated to aid the regime in intelligence gathering. This includes stealing IP, which is one of the principal reasons for the U.S.-China trade war. A survey reported by CNBC on March 1, 2019 found that nearly one in three North America-based companies had had IP stolen from them at some point during the previous decade. By 2020, the FBI had more than 1,000 China-related IP theft cases open. In 2020, the cost of this ongoing theft was estimated at "nearly $500 billion per year."[103] The DOJ has stated that China is the primary culprit in roughly 80 percent of its economic espionage investigations.[104]

Legal and illegal acquisition of U.S. technology, combined with state subsidies, is driving Chinese technological progress, including in the field of advanced weaponry. From an economic standpoint, stealing technology saves China huge expenditure on R&D, putting Chinese companies in a position to undercut their U.S. competitors.[105] From a defense standpoint, China stealing U.S. technology means that, in the event of a war, the U.S. military could be facing its own weapons, and that the PLA would know

[101] https://asia.nikkei.com/Politics/International-relations/US-China-tensions/U.S.-crackdown-targets-China-s-quantum-computing-navigation-tech

[102] https://www.lawfaremedia.org/article/beijings-new-national-intelligence-law-defense-offense

[103] https://www.asisonline.org/security-management-magazine/articles/2020/07/an-unfair-advantage-confronting-organized-intellectual-property-theft/

[104] https://www.aei.org/articles/the-rising-risk-of-chinas-intellectual-property-theft/

[105] Ibid.

the capabilities and vulnerabilities of U.S. hardware and defense systems

The U.S. has a number of export controls, preventing certain technologies and equipment being sold to certain foreign entities. The ban on U.S. exports to China includes components which could be used in military hardware. The Export Control Reform Act of 2018 included provisions for evaluating and controlling exports of emerging and foundational technologies. This prevents the U.S. sale of fintech, batteries, and AI to China. Export controls are expected to become more stringent. And since the U.S. revoked Hong Kong's special status, the same rules largely apply to trade and investment in Hong Kong that apply to mainland China.

The Hong Kong Sanctions program prohibits Americans from doing business with multiple Chinese and Hong Kong officials.[106] CNN reported on June 21, 2022 that the U.S. was banning all goods produced in Xinjiang due to forced labor issues. There are also prohibitions against investing in securities and derivatives related to Chinese military-industrial companies, and U.S. entities are barred from doing business with Chinese entities that undermine democracy or have been accused of human rights violations.

A way around these rules, however, is for U.S. companies to invest directly in these technologies in China. Compared to the Chinese regime, it is much harder for a democracy like the U.S. to curtail the behavior of citizens. Consequently, U.S. investors determined to directly invest in China are free to do so. According to U.S. trade officials, the U.S. will most likely not crackdown on, or increase scrutiny of U.S. outbound investment.[107] However, the

---

[106] https://home.treasury.gov/news/press-releases/sm1088
[107] https://asia.nikkei.com/Editor-s-Picks/Interview/U.S.-unlikely-to-screen-investments-in-China-ex-Trump-official

fresh export controls announced by Washington in late 2022, aimed at limiting China's access to and progress in advanced computing and semiconductor manufacturing items — including chips, semiconductors, and advanced computing technologies — signify the U.S. commitment to mitigating the rapid growth of China's high-tech capabilities.

In addition to laws limiting U.S. investments into the Chinese tech sector, the Federal Government's interagency Committee on Foreign Investment in the United States (CFIUS) has applied restrictions to Chinese investment into U.S. critical technology, personal data of U.S. citizens, and infrastructure. Additionally, U.S. federal agencies are prohibited from utilizing certain Chinese telecom equipment.

Members of Congress are working to restrict the flow of technology and money to the Chinese regime, but each law is a small Band-Aid on a very large problem. Working together with U.S. allies on a combined program of reshoring domestic manufacturing, restricting investment in China, as well as restricting Beijing's access to Western capital markets, could deprive China of the opportunity to steal or to acquire technology from the West, as well as inhibit their ability to invest in R&D. Additionally, it would create incentives for U.S. and Western nations to redirect their supply chains away from China and to expand their own manufacturing base.

Cyber Threats to U.S. Civilian Sectors

The 2023 Annual Threat Assessment of the U.S. Intelligence Community pinpointed the cyber threat from China as a primary area of concern, saying the PRC, "probably currently represents the broadest, most active, and persistent cyber espionage threat to the U.S. Government and private-sector networks. . . China almost certainly is capable of launching cyber attacks that could disrupt critical infrastructure services within the United States, including against oil and gas pipelines, and rail systems."

This threat encompasses a wide range of activities, including technology and information theft, surveillance, economic espionage, and cyber theft. There is concern that Beijing's hacker capabilities go beyond manipulation of the information space and could be applied to direct attacks on critical infrastructure or military targets, according to *The New York Times* (July 29, 2023). The regime is progressing in its capacity to conduct cyberattacks, believing such actions can be especially effective against technologically advanced adversaries heavily reliant on information systems.

PLA Unit 61398, the CCP regime's official hacker unit, was uncovered in 2013,[108] operating under a number of names, including APT 1, Comment Crew, Comment Panda, TG-8223, Group 3, and GIF89a. It engages in spyware, ransomware, data theft, cyber espionage,[109] and other online attacks against the United States and other governments, as well as against media and critics of the regime. On May 24, 2023, the Cybersecurity and Infrastructure Security Agency issued an advisory regarding activity by a CCP state-backed cyber actor known as Volt Typhoon; it was believed to pose a threat to both infrastructure and private companies.

As Reuters reported on June 15, 2023, a number of U.S. government departments, energy companies, and other organizations, experienced intrusions linked to MOVEit, a file transfer software. A Russian ransomware gang claimed responsibility for at least some of these attacks.[110] A week earlier,

---

[108] https://www.cfr.org/cyber-operations/pla-unit-61398
[109] https://www.justice.gov/opa/pr/us-charges-five-chinese-military-hackers-cyber-espionage-against-us-corporations-and-labor
[110] https://www.wbaltv.com/article/russian-hacker-group-cl0p-cyberattack-johns-hopkins/44213964#

the FBI and the Cybersecurity and Infrastructure Security Agency had issued warnings about vulnerabilities within MOVEit.[111]

This incident, the third in as many years where foreign hackers managed to infiltrate U.S. government agencies, came soon after a separate incident involving Chinese-affiliated hackers targeting essential infrastructure in the U.S. and Guam.[112] Such actions might serve as preparatory exercises aimed at disrupting communication channels between the U.S. and Asia in the event of a conflict. It is worth emphasizing that Guam would play a pivotal role as a strategic transit point for U.S. forces in the event of a conflict between the United States and China.

A major concern of the DHS is the danger of a cyberattack against critical U.S. infrastructure.[113] Another possibility is cyberattacks on U.S. military installations overseas which could prevent the U.S. from responding militarily to a physical threat. Disrupting critical infrastructure services within the U.S., such as oil and gas pipelines and transportation systems, could cause panic and chaos inside the country.

The Department of Energy is among U.S. agencies repeatedly targeted in cyberattacks. One recent victim was Oak Ridge National Laboratory, where nuclear research is conducted.[114] The breach may have compromised the personal information of as many as tens of thousands of Department of Energy employees and contractors. The DHS is aware that the U.S. power grid is old and vulnerable to both cyber and physical attacks, 70 percent of transmission lines being 30 or more years old. In 2022, 10.7 percent of cyberattacks targeted the energy

---

[111] https://www.cisa.gov/news-events/news/cisa-and-fbi-release-advisory-cl0p-ransomware-gang-exploiting-moveit-vulnerability
[112] https://cyberscoop.com/china-critical-infrastructure-volt-typhoon/
[113] Annual Threat Assessment of the U.S. Intelligence Community February 6, 2023
[114] https://www.bloomberg.com/news/articles/2023-06-15/us-national-lab-nuclear-waste-site-hit-by-cyberattack

industry.[115] The Department of Energy and private-sector partners have since established the Energy Threat Analysis Center to enhance protection of key infrastructure.[116]

Advanced and disruptive technologies are being developed which could neutralize U.S. defense assets. An electromagnetic pulse (EMP) generated from a solar flare or from a nuclear weapon exploded in the atmosphere could cause all affected electronics to fail. As militaries around the world become more reliant on cyber and space capabilities, hacking will become a more important weapon, damaging a country's ability to wage war. Both China and Russia have been developing anti-satellite weapons and satellite-jamming capabilities.

Aiding Drug Cartels

Beijing is guilty of killing Americans with illegal drugs, by allowing shipments of precursor chemicals for fentanyl from China to Mexico.[117] According to CDC data, nearly 107,000 Americans died from drug overdoses in 2021; three quarters of those deaths involved opioids, and the vast majority of opioid deaths were from synthetic opioids such as fentanyl. In addition, 2022 saw an estimated 181,000 non-fatal opioid overdoses. Following the Xi-Biden summit on November 15, 2023, it appeared that the Chinese side had agreed to limit the manufacturing and export of fentanyl precursors,[118] but whether this will result in concrete action remains to be seen.

The fentanyl supply chain begins with the cartels that make the illicit and deadly drug and smuggle it into the United States across the southern border. These transnational criminal

---

[115] https://securityintelligence.com/articles/2022-industry-threat-recap-energy/
[116] https://www.energy.gov/ceser/energy-threat-analysis-center-0
[117] https://www.brookings.edu/articles/chinas-role-in-the-fentanyl-crisis/
[118] https://www.axios.com/2023/11/16/biden-xi-agreement-fentanyl-production-china-mexico

organizations include the Sinaloa Cartel and the New Generation Jalisco Cartel.[119] Once in the U.S., it is distributed by street gangs affiliated with the cartels. The Texas Department of Public Safety reported that the Tango Blast group, a Latin gang with as many as 25,000 members, and the Mexican Mafia both have direct ties to the cartels.[120] According to the Drug Enforcement Agency, major Mexican cartels, such as the Sinaloa and Gulf cartels, have factions operating in Chicago and other U.S. cities.[121]

In addition to drugs entering the country through the southern border, the DHS has also noted increasing numbers of individuals in the Terrorist Screening Data Set, also known as the "watchlist," NBC reported on September 15, 2023. Growing numbers of Chinese are using the turmoil at the southern border to sneak into the United States. During a mid-2023 hearing, Rep. August Pfluger (R-TX) of the Homeland Security Subcommittee on Counter-Terrorism, Law Enforcement, and Intelligence, stressed "increasing encounters of illegal aliens connected to the Chinese Communist Party (CCP) at the southwest border."[122]

Bio-Data Collection

The PRC is developing the world's largest bio-database, according to a U.S. national counterintelligence officer for emerging and disruptive technologies, who pointed out: "Once your genetic data is gone, it's gone. It's not like you can change your PIN code or get identity protection."[123] Racing to dominate the bioeconomy, China is compiling a massive database of medical, health, and

---

[119] Office of Intelligence & Analysis: Homeland Threat Assessment 2024

[120] https://www.newsnationnow.com/us-news/immigration/border-coverage/cartels-recruit-american-gangs/

[121] https://www.dea.gov/press-releases/2023/05/05/dea-operation-last-mile-tracks-down-sinaloa-and-jalisco-cartel-0

[122] https://homeland.house.gov/2023/06/21/6560-2/

[123] https://www.linkedin.com/posts/edward-you-1827bb1b_chinas-quest-for-human-genetic-data-spurs-activity-7110942162564907009-9WDH/

genetic information from people around the world, including Americans.

The regime enlists the help of private companies to help gather genetic data, which can be combined with top military supercomputing capabilities, to discover genetic weaknesses in a population.[124] Biological weapons can then be developed which prey on these weaknesses. As part of China's military-civil fusion policy, Chinese scientists, cooperating with the PLA, have been conducting research in the areas of brain science, gene editing and the creation of artificial genomes.[125]

Similar research could be used to enhance the performance of Chinese soldiers. BGI Group (formerly Beijing Genomics Institute), a company with ties to the PLA, leads the PRC's genome project. It is also a major producer of Covid-19 tests. BGI operates the largest pig cloning project in the world, and in 2022 completed the first successful transplant of the heart of a cloned pig into a human being.[126] After manipulating generations of pig DNA, intentionally producing pigs that are smaller or larger, more or less susceptible to certain diseases, China may be zeroing in on the ability to produce "super soldiers." Among the projects currently underway is BGI's attempt to make soldiers of Han ancestry less susceptible to altitude sickness.[127]

BGI's current chief infectious disease scientist, Chen Weijun, was among the first scientists to sequence Covid-19, taking samples from a military hospital in Wuhan. He is also named on the patent on the BGI test kits which have been distributed around the world, including in the U.S. Four of BGI's

---

[124] https://www.reuters.com/article/us-china-genomics-military-exclusive-idUSKBN29Z0HA/

[125] Ibid.

[126] https://www.nytimes.com/2022/01/10/health/heart-transplant-pig-bennett.html

[127] https://www.reuters.com/article/us-china-genomics-military-exclusive-idUSKBN29Z0HA/

researchers have been affiliated with the National University of Defence Technology under China's Central Military Commission. The university has been blacklisted by the U.S. as a threat to national security.[128]

Since Xi took office, private technology companies have been increasingly integrated into military-related research. BGI offered to set up Covid-19 test centers in the U.S., but U.S. officials warned that the test facilities would gain access to American DNA, as the swabs have genetic material on them, NPR reported on February 24, 2021. No U.S. states agreed, but at least 18 other countries allowed BGI to establish centers, and BGI test kits were sent to 180 nations.

Chinese medical testing companies regularly use DNA collected from test subjects for other research. Human rights groups say the regime is using the data for security purposes, such as identifying and tracking Uygher Muslims. Furthermore, PRC police are trying to compile DNA samples for the country's 700 million males, to keep track of future criminals.

Home ancestry testing is another way for China to obtain DNA from Americans.[129] U.S. military personnel have been warned to avoid companies, such as Ancestry and 23andMe, which have ties to China. Tens of millions of Americans have already paid to have their saliva tested for their DNA ancestry.

A PRC company, WuXi Biologics, bought a Pfizer manufacturing plant in China, and established a production facility in Massachusetts. In 2015, the firm also bought a stake in 23andMe. WuXi Biologics now has locations in Pennsylvania, Massachusetts, and New Jersey, as well as a drug plant in Delaware, which was built with a China government grant. This

---

[128] Ibid.
[129] https://rollcall.com/2020/12/24/hey-soldiers-and-spies-think-twice-about-that-home-genetic-ancestry-test/

expansion prompted U.S. officials to warn domestic companies and universities about the risks of working with Chinese entities in biotech as well as fields such as AI and quantum computing, *Washington Post* reported on October 22, 2021.

BGI Group earns part of its revenue by selling genetic sequencing services to universities and health systems around the world. The company has also been purchasing U.S. genomics firms since 2013, and now has multiple partnerships with U.S. companies, related to gene sequencing. In each of these arrangements, BGI gains access to genetic data. Under China's National Intelligence Law, all data obtained by Chinese companies, even abroad, must be turned over to the CCP, upon request.[130] The same law gives the authorities the right to utilize or confiscate hardware, devices, and networks to facilitate intelligence-gathering activities.

CFIUS, which has the authority to block foreign investment in the United States on national security grounds, warned that Chinese firms invest in U.S. companies hoping to gain access to U.S. data. In 2021, CFIUS — the jurisdiction of which was expanded by the Foreign Investment Risk Review Modernization Act of 2018 — stopped a Chinese purchase of a California fertility clinic located near six U.S. military bases.[131] The concern was that not only would the Chinese regime gain access to the genetic data of U.S. soldiers, but also that of their unborn children. Yet, in spite of the obvious dangers, the Biden administration paid iHealth Labs, a unit of the Chinese firm Andon Health Co., $1.3 billion of taxpayers' money for the home Covid-19 test kits which the government sent out, according to *Fortune* (January 21, 2022).

---

[130] https://www.lawfaremedia.org/article/beijings-new-national-intelligence-law-defense-offense
[131] https://www.cbsnews.com/news/dna-genealogy-privacy-60-minutes-2021-01-31/

The 2022 Beijing Winter Olympics provided another opportunity to gather DNA data. Olympic athletes and coaches were subjected to daily Covid-19 tests, while press and other attendees were also tested on a regular basis.[132] This means that the CCP has the genetic material of every person who attended the Games. Attendees were also required to download a government approved health app which proved to have security flaws.[133] Internet security experts warned that the app would be able to collect user data, which — combined with genetic information — could be fed into China's massive AI and genome projects.

A growing number of Beijing-linked and regime-funded biotech, genomics, and medtech firms are operating in the U.S., raising concerns about medical and genetic data security. With more than $1 trillion at its disposal, China's sovereign wealth fund has more than 30 percent of the world's total sovereign-wealth fund assets.[134] Since 2017, money has been flooding into U.S. biotech companies, as part of Beijing's Made in China 2025 industrial policy. Made in China 2025 specifically identifies biotech as a strategic industry entitled to government financial support, and the authorities in Beijing have allocated $100 billion for investment in the sector.[135]

There are suspicions that the PLA is researching bioweapons which target specific ethnic groups. In 2019, half of Chinese investment in the United States was in the health, pharmaceuticals and biotech sectors, according to a May 2021 report by the U.S.-China Investment Project. In 2021, the number

[132] https://www.nytimes.com/2021/07/21/health/coronavirus-olympics-testing.html
[133] https://www.nytimes.com/2022/01/18/technology/china-olympics-app-security.html
[134]
https://www.institutionalinvestor.com/article/2bstmmp9mfkb5efr2mhhc/portfolio/chinas-sovereign-wealth-funds-too-big-to-be-ignored
[135] https://www.nationaldefensemagazine.org/articles/2021/11/17/keeping-chinese-funding-out-of--us-biotech

of filings for FDA approval by Chinese drugmakers was higher than in previous years.[136]

Among China's growing presence in the U.S. biotech scene is Innocube Bioscience Inc. in Texas. It serves as the North American headquarters for China's Lepu Biopharma Co., which is heavily invested by a PRC sovereign wealth fund, the SDIC (State Development & Investment Corporation).[137] BeiGene, a Chinese pharmaceutical and research firm, located in San Mateo, CA, conducts research on molecularly-targeted agents related to gene sequencing. The company's research center in China received significant government funding.[138]

Chinese infiltration of the U.S. biotech and medical industries has been aided by U.S. citizens and even by the government. Andon Health Co. has received a $1.28 billion contract from the U.S. Army to supply Covid-19 self-test kits, Reuters reported on January 14, 2022. And one of its subsidiaries sold $120 million worth of self-test kits to the New York State Department of Health. While these purchases evoked a harsh response from Republican lawmakers,[139] who wanted to ban the purchase of Covid-19 tests from China, CCP mouthpieces touted the contracts as American reliance on China to fill gaps in its supply chains.

The PLA-linked BGI Group, which is part-owned by four of Beijing's sovereign wealth funds, bought Complete Genomics, a California-based company that holds the genetic information of U.S. citizens.[140] In a February 2021 publication, the National

---

[136] https://www.pharmexec.com/view/china-invests-in-building-biotech

[137] https://en.lepubiopharma.com/new/109.html

[138] https://endpts.com/with-a-big-cash-assist-from-local-officials-beigene-is-building-a-330m-biologics-facility-in-china/

[139] https://www.yahoo.com/video/house-republicans-express-outrage-over-001830595.html

[140] https://www.nationaldefensemagazine.org/articles/2021/11/17/keeping-chinese-funding-out-of--us-biotech

Counterintelligence and Security Center warned about Chinese companies like WuXi Pharma Tech, which acquired a U.S. firm in 2015, saying that, "The PRC views bulk personal data, including healthcare and genomic data, as a strategic commodity to be collected and used for its economic and national security priorities." The U.S. has blacklisted units of BGI and other Chinese biotech firms, and is expected to blacklist others in the near future, Reuters reported on March 17, 2023.

PRC Biolabs in the United States

In early 2023, authorities searched an illegal and unlicensed Chinese-owned biolab containing deadly viruses and lab animals in California. When federal and local authorities entered the warehouse in Reedley, Fresno County, they discovered a lab containing bacterial, viral, and parasitic agents, mice, medical waste, hundreds of chemicals, and other hazardous materials. Charges were later filed, Associated Press reported on October 21, 2023.

The illegal biolab raid entangled a labyrinth of geographic and legislative jurisdictions requiring cooperation among various law enforcement and health agencies.[141] Local officials eventually involved the CDC and the FBI, as well as California's Department of Toxic Substances Control, Department of Health, and Department of Public Health. The warehouse was divided into rooms, some of which contained thousands of samples of human blood, tissue, and other bodily fluid samples and serums.[142] Authorities discovered biological agents such as coronavirus, HIV, hepatitis, and herpes. Additional vials were found containing chlamydia, E. coli, streptococcus pneumonia, hepatitis B and C,

---

[141] https://www.nbcnews.com/news/us-news/officials-believe-fresno-warehouse-was-site-illegal-laboratory-rcna96756
[142] Ibid.

herpes 1 and 5, rubella, and malaria.[143] They also found medical devices including Covid-19 test kits and pregnancy test kits which were believed to have been manufactured on site.

The warehouse belongs to a Nevada-registered company that was not licensed to do business in California, and which lacked a California address. The addresses linked to their business registration were empty offices in the U.S. or addresses in China which could not be verified. U.S. authorities believe the lab had been operating illegally since October 2022.[144]

Biolabs, including biological weapons, are an area where the FBI warns that Beijing poses a threat to the United States. Beijing is pushing for primacy in the fields of biology and biological research, utilizing talent acquisition programs to attract American scientists to work on PRC-funded projects.[145]

So far, the operator of the Fresno lab faces charges of manufacturing and distributing misbranded medical devices and making false statements to federal agencies. It is possible other charges will be added. This incident raises the questions: Just how many of these labs exist across the United States? And how long will they operate before finally being shut down?

---

[143] https://californiaglobe.com/articles/mysterious-chinese-covid-lab-uncovered-in-city-of-reedly-ca/
[144] Ibid.
[145] https://www.fbi.gov/investigate/counterintelligence/the-china-threat/chinese-talent-plans

2

What is National Power and How is it Measured?

National power refers to the ability of a nation-state to influence and shape the outcomes of events, both domestically and internationally, according to its interests.[146] It is a multidimensional concept that encompasses various elements and capabilities. Political scientists and national security analysts employ a number of standard frameworks for the evaluation of national power, each of which considers an array of elements and capabilities, such as:

The PMESII-PT framework: Political, Military, Economic, Social, Infrastructure, Information, Physical Environment, and Time.

The DIMEFL framework: Diplomatic, Information, Military, Economic, Financial, Intelligence, and Legal.

The Composite Index of National Capability (CINC) examines Military Capability (MIL), Economic Capability (ECON), Population Size (POP), Resource Inputs (RES), Technology (TECH), Diplomatic Capability (DIP), Geographic Location (LOC), Transportation Infrastructure (TRAN), Government Stability (GOV), and Comprehensive National Power (CNP).

---

[146] David Jablonsky, "National Power," Parameters 27, no. 1 (1997), doi:10.55540/0031-1723.1815.

The Global Competitiveness Index (GCI) weights institutions, infrastructure, macroeconomic stability, health, primary education, higher education and training, goods market efficiency, labor market efficiency, financial market development, technological readiness, market size, business sophistication, and innovation.

By combining various elements and avoiding redundancy, this book will evaluate China's national power across the following dimensions:

1. Geopolitical Position. A nation's geographic location can be an advantage or a liability in terms of its national power, as it can affect access to resources, trade routes, waterways, and strategic positioning. This includes its relationship with its neighbors as well as its strategic significance in regional and global contexts. A country's geography is directly related to its resource position, particularly food and energy resources. The need to import food and energy can be a detriment during wartime, when supply routes may be blocked or when embargoes and sanctions would prevent other countries from supplying resources. Access to and control over energy resources, such as oil and natural gas, can significantly influence a nation's power in the global arena.

2. Political Power. This refers to the strength of the country's internal governance and political stability. This political dimension helps military planners and strategists consider the internal political landscape when devising military and strategic plans, as it can affect the feasibility and success of combat operations. It is distinct from the diplomatic aspect, which deals with a country's external relations, foreign policy, and its interactions with other nations.

3. Military Power. This encompasses a nation's armed forces, their size, capabilities, readiness, and technological sophistication. A deeper analysis of military power can include considerations of nuclear capabilities, force projection, defense budgets, and alliances. Having a strong military serves as a deterrent against attacks on the homeland, while also projecting power abroad. The military is one of the primary tools at the disposal of national leaders when carrying out foreign policy objectives.

4. Economic Power. This focuses on the broader economic conditions and factors within a country or region. It encompasses macroeconomic indicators, trade, industry, labor, and economic policies. It also involves a comprehensive analysis of a nation's economic health, structure, and performance. Key considerations under the economic dimension may include GDP, inflation rates, employment levels, trade balances, economic growth, and industries. An economic analysis also examines long-term economic trends, fiscal and monetary policies, and the impact of economic conditions on the population. Economic strength is a crucial component of national power; the more powerful the economy, the more money a nation has available to fund its military and to implement foreign and domestic policy. An unstable or poor economy may incite civil unrest or starvation among the general population.

5. Diplomatic Power. Assessing the effectiveness of a country's diplomacy requires an examination of its international relationships, its ability to negotiate, and its ability to influence international politics and shape global agendas. The formation of alliances and leadership of international organizations are both key elements of diplomatic power. A network of alliances and partnerships can increase a country's reach and influence. Alliances can also be a force-multiplier in the event of war. One form of diplomatic power is crisis response and humanitarian aid. By responding to global crises, providing humanitarian aid, and participating in peacekeeping efforts, a country can contribute to its global leadership.

6. Soft Power. This is the ability to attract and influence other nations through culture, values, education, and ideology can enhance a country's standing and influence in the world. Soft power includes factors like educational institutions and global media presence. Furthermore, cultural exports, film, music, and sports all contribute to a country's soft power and global appeal. A willingness to comply with green standards and participate in global initiatives on climate change are additional elements key to a country's international reputation.

7. Financial Power. The financial dimension is distinct from the economic, as it hones in on more specific financial issues, such as monetary systems, banking, currency, and financial institutions. It delves into the management of financial resources, currency stability, and the functioning of financial markets and institutions. A country with a great deal of financial power is able to control or influence the financial behavior of other nations.

8. Technological Power. Advanced technology and innovation contribute to a nation's power, as they can impact economic, military, and global influence. Technological advancement is a function of innovation, which can be assessed by analyzing a country's R&D capacity, academic publishing, patents filing, and its leadership in emerging technologies.

9. Human Capital. The population's education, skills, and health can contribute to its national power by enabling innovation, productivity, and social stability. Human development indicators can be used to measure the country's education, healthcare, and poverty rates. The UN's Human Development Index (HDI) considers indicators like life expectancy, education, and per capita income to assess the overall development of countries. Another component of human capital is pandemic response: in light of global health crises, a country's ability to manage and respond to pandemics, its healthcare infrastructure, and its medical research and innovation capabilities can affect its global standing.

The Geopolitical Position of the PRC

The People's Republic of China, it is now the world's second most populous country, with an official population of 1.4 billion. It is the third-largest by land area, measuring 9,388,211 square kilometers (3,624,807 square miles). Located in East Asia, it shares borders with 14 countries. China also has a significant maritime presence, with coastlines along the East China Sea, to the east, the South China Sea, to the south, and the Yellow Sea to the north. These coastal regions play a crucial role in China's geopolitical and economic strategies. China's relationships with its neighbors are diverse and complex. While it has peaceful and cooperative ties with some countries, it has experienced wars and territorial disputes and regional tensions with others. China's relationship with the United States is particularly influential, shaping its interactions with neighboring countries and the global community.

China's land borders and disputes are worth examining in some detail:

1. Russia (to the north) — "No limits friendship," a member of Belt and Road Initiative (BRI, China's global infrastructure project), and a member of both BRICS and the Shanghai Cooperation Organization (SCO), a Eurasian political, economic, international security and defence organization.

2. Mongolia (to the north) — Mongolia's economy is 80 percent dependent on China. Mongolia is a BRI member and has

observer status in the SCO, while strengthening ties with the U.S. so it is now a strategic partner of Washington.

3. Kazakhstan (to the northwest) — A member of both SCO and the BRI. This former Soviet republic is a member of the Russia-led Collective Security Treaty Organization (CSTO), a Russia-led intergovernmental military alliance in Eurasia. The Central Asian republics tended to trust Russia over China before the Ukraine War began. China is now intensifying its diplomatic efforts to draw them into China's orbit.

4. Kyrgyzstan (to the west) — This SCO and CSTO member's relationships to Russia and China are very similar to those of Kazakhstan.

5. Tajikistan (to the west) — A SCO, BRI, and CSTO member, it has ties to Russia and China akin to those of Kazakhstan.

6. Pakistan (to the southwest) — "The Iron Brotherhood" links Pakistan and China, as well as SCO and BRI membership.

7. India (to the south) — While a BRICS and SCO member, India and China fought two wars in the 1960s, and have a longstanding border dispute in the Himalayan region. This dispute led to violent border clashes in the Galwan Valley in 2020 and 2021. New Delhi has raised concerns about China's naval incursions in the Indian Ocean. India is a member of the Quad, an informal strategic forum that is largely seen as opposition to China.

8. Nepal (to the south) — SCO dialogue partner and BRI member.

9. Bhutan (to the south).

10. Myanmar (formerly Burma, to the south) — A BRI member and a member of RCEP, an Indo-Pacific free trade agreement. Since the coup in 2021, China has been the primary

investment and trade partner of the junta, as most G7 countries have applied sanctions.

11. Laos (to the south) — RCEP and BRI member.

12. Vietnam (to the south) — RCEP and BRI member; Vietnam and China fought a short war in 1979. Overlapping territorial claims in the South China Sea have periodically escalated to violence between China and Vietnam, involving confrontational actions like Chinese vessels violating Vietnamese waters, ramming, and harassing Vietnamese vessels. In 2014, during the "oil rig crisis," anti-Chinese riots damaged Chinese-owned businesses and factories in several Vietnamese cities.[147] There were reports of some casualties. In 2023, Vietnam upgraded its relations with the U.S. to a comprehensive strategic partnership, which includes expanded trade and defense agreements.

13. North Korea (to the northeast) — The Sino-North Korean Treaty of Friendship, Co-operation, and Mutual Assistance is the only official defense agreement either country has. North Korea is almost totally dependent on the PRC, both diplomatically and economically.

14. Afghanistan (through a narrow border in the Wakhan Corridor, a part of the wider region) — A SCO observer and a BRI member, China has appointed an ambassador to Kabul and invited the Taliban to the 2023 BRI event in Beijing.

China also has territorial and maritime disputes with countries sharing its sea borders:

1. Taiwan — China considers Taiwan part of its territory and does not recognize its sovereignty. Taiwan, however, views itself as a separate, self-governing entity and maintains its own

---

[147] https://www.theguardian.com/world/2014/may/15/vietnam-anti-china-protests-oil-rig-dead-injured

government, military, and foreign relations. The U.S. provides Taiwan with arms to defend itself against a Chinese invasion.

2. Japan — A member of RCEP. China and Japan have a territorial dispute over the Senkaku/Diaoyu Islands in the East China Sea. Both countries claim sovereignty over these uninhabited islands. Under the Treaty of Mutual Cooperation and Security between the United States and Japan, Washington is committed to providing Japan with security and defending territory administered by Japan.[148] Most experts take this to include disputed territory controlled by Japan. If China attacks Japanese territory, the U.S. must go to war.

3. Philippines — A member of RCEP and the BRI, the Philippines also has territorial disputes with China in the South China Sea. Manila brought a case to the Permanent Court of Arbitration in The Hague. The 2016 ruling was in favor of the Philippines,[149] but China rejected it. Chinese ships have repeatedly violated Philippine waters and harassed Philippine vessels. On May 3, 2023, Manila and Washington signed the Bilateral Defense Guidelines, reaffirming "that an armed attack in the Pacific, including anywhere in the South China Sea, on either of their public vessels, aircraft, or armed forces – which includes their Coast Guards – would invoke mutual defense commitments under Articles IV and V of the 1951 U.S.-Philippines Mutual Defense Treaty."[150] In short, if China attacks the Philippines, the U.S. will go to war.

---

[148] https://www.mofa.go.jp/region/n-america/us/q&a/ref/1.html
[149] https://www.rappler.com/nation/137202-philippines-china-ruling-case-west-philippine-sea/
[150] https://www.defense.gov/News/Releases/Release/Article/3383607/fact-sheet-us-philippines-bilateral-defense-guidelines/

4. Malaysia — A member of RCEP and the BRI, Malaysia has territorial disputes with China in the South China Sea, particularly related to the Spratly Islands.

5. Brunei — A member of RCEP, Brunei has maritime disputes with China in the South China Sea in the region surrounding the Spratly Islands.

6. Indonesia — A member of RCEP and the BRI, Jakarta has disputes with Beijing over overlapping claims in the South China Sea, particularly near the Natuna Islands.

China also has internal flashpoints in Tibet, Inner Mongolia, and Xinjiang where ethnic minorities oppose restrictive policies as well as linguistic, cultural, and religious repression. As recently as 2016, there were terrorist attacks in Xinjiang, committed by Uyghur Muslim separatists, retaliating for systematic abuse by the Chinese regime. Extremist attacks likely continue, but reporting is suppressed or they are officially described as criminal rather than separatist activity. Beijing has implemented strict control and surveillance measures across the country, but particularly in Xinjiang, in response to these separatist movements.

3

The Political Dimension

The PRC operates as a one-party socialist republic, where the Chinese Communist Party (CCP) is the sole ruling party. The eight minor parties must all concede to the leading role of the CCP. Since the founding of the PRC in 1949, the CCP — which in 2022 had just over 98 million members[151] — has had a monopoly on power.

The president, who is also the general secretary of the CPC, is the head of state. The premier is the head of government. The highest organ of state power is the National People's Congress (NPC), which is the top legislative body. The NPC convenes once per year, generally for about two weeks, to enact laws, amend the constitution, and make important policy decisions. The State Council, led by the premier, administers and implements these laws.

Direct elections are only held at the lowest level of local and village representatives,[152] but the CCP controls the candidate selection process and ensures that its members are elected to these positions. Under the PRC Constitution, Chinese citizens have certain legal rights, including the right to vote in local elections, the right to education, and certain legal protections. However, these rights are often subject to restrictions and limitations. Freedom of speech, freedom of the press, freedom of religion, and

---

[151] https://www.statista.com/statistics/281378/number-of-chinese-communist-party-ccp-members-in-china/
[152] https://freedomhouse.org/country/china/freedom-world/2021

freedom of assembly are constrained. The Chinese regime exercises strict control over the internet and censors content. Most foreign media and foreign social media are blocked in China. There are very few foreign bookstores and they are heavily monitored. Political dissent is not tolerated, and human rights issues, including the treatment of ethnic and religious minorities, have been subjects of international concern.

Xi Jinping, the son of a revolutionary, rose through the ranks and became China's leader in 2012. As of 2023, his titles include general secretary of the CCP, chairman of the Central Military Commission, as well as president of the People's Republic of China. Holding the three most important political positions, he has been called the paramount leader of China. Since 2012, he has solidified his grip on both the party and the populace, asserted China's global influence, intensified suppression of ethnic and religious minority groups, bolstered the military, enhanced governmental oversight over private enterprises,[153] and threatened to forcibly annex Taiwan. His consolidation of power involved the removal of internal opposition within the party, with many of these dissenting voices being targeted in his anti-corruption campaign.

Authoritarian regimes often use anti-corruption campaigns as a political tool, and many Western observers believe that Xi is no different, using anti-corruption actions as a means of solidifying his power. Between 2012 and 2023, the CCP regime claims it investigated almost 5 million party members, leading to formal charges against 553 individuals, while approximately 207,000 members have faced some form of punishment.[154]

The first targets were individuals in the PLA and in the party. Later, the real estate sector and officials and regulators at

[153] https://www.cfr.org/backgrounder/chinese-communist-party
[154] https://www.hudson.org/corruption/six-myths-about-china-anti-corruption-campaign

state banks were subjected to scrutiny (Bloomberg, August 24, 2022). Xi's anti-corruption offensive finally reached the healthcare sector in 2023, with investigations into 155 hospital chiefs. According to an August 18, 2023 blog post on the Council on Foreign Relations website, by attacking corruption in the medical sector, the regime "tactically shifts blame onto hospital managers, doctors, and medical representatives. This deflective strategy shields the government from being the primary target of public dissatisfaction, which could challenge its authority and legitimacy."

As the most powerful leader since Mao Zedong, "Xi Jinping Thought" doctrine has become standard reading in political education and communist reading groups in China. In 2017, it was enshrined in the constitution of the CCP. At the 20th National Congress of the CCP in 2022, Xi was given an historic third term. Further consolidating his power, he eliminated the last remnants of opposition, politburo members and cadres associated with the Youth League Faction.[155] This included Premier Li Keqiang, who was replaced, and former President Hu Jintao, who was escorted out of the venue. Their removal suggested that Xi would continue to tighten his grip over the economy.[156] Wang Huning, considered a leading authority on "wolf warrior" diplomacy, was promoted, as was a former foreign minister, Wang Yi (Asia Nikkei, October 24, 2022). The latter warned the UN General Assembly that "any move to obstruct China's cause of reunification is bound to be crushed by the wheels of history."

In his opening speech to the congress, Xi signaled that he was shifting his focus from the economy to national security.[157]

---

[155] https://www.thinkchina.sg/xi-removes-youth-league-faction-new-leadership
[156] https://www.abc.net.au/news/2022-10-24/who-is-on-chinas-politburo-standing-committee/101568850
[157] https://asia.nikkei.com/Politics/China-s-party-congress/China-s-Xi-stacks-new-inner-circle-with-loyalists-for-third-term

With the appointment of "wolf warriors," and with no opposition left in government, a more aggressive PRC can be expected, exerting greater control over its people and more likely to enter into a conflict with the U.S. or its allies.

Political Stability

The Fund for Peace, an independent, nonpartisan, non-profit organization developed the Fragile States Index (FSI) which ranks 178 countries across 12 indicators assessing the risks and vulnerabilities of individual nations.

In 2023, China's FSI score was 65.1,[158] suggesting that China is perceived to have a moderate level of fragility and vulnerability, but it is not among the most fragile or unstable countries in the world according to this index. It indicates that while there may be certain challenges or issues, China's overall stability is relatively high compared to several other countries. China ranks as the 101st least stable country, while the U.S. ranks 141st and Afghanistan ranks 6th.

The FSI identified significant weaknesses that could undermine China's domestic and global ambitions over the long term. Despite an overall reduction in fragility since 2013, certain indicators remain weak, notably state legitimacy, corruption, and human rights. Additionally, the Demographic Pressures indicator has deteriorated as a result of disease, natural disasters, water scarcity, environment, as well as fertility, mortality, and population decline. China had the world's largest population a few years ago, but has since been overtaken by India. The Chinese population is aging and the workforce is beginning to shrink.

---

[158] https://fragilestatesindex.org/country-data/

As the workforce contracts, China will confront mounting social and economic challenges. These may push the government towards a stricter authoritarian approach to maintain control in the face of growing unrest, like the protests against the zero-Covid policy and unresolved debts, or potential political opposition from minority groups. Furthermore, Beijing could adopt a more confrontational stance towards the U.S. and Taiwan as a means of managing internal divisions, potentially setting off detrimental cycles of tension both internally and externally.

Political Indicators

Transparency International's Corruption Perceptions Index (CPI) measures perceived corruption in countries, which can influence a nation's global standing.[159]

1. Rank 65/180: This means that in 2022, China was ranked 65th out of 180 countries and territories. A lower rank is generally considered better in the context of the CPI because it suggests a lower perceived level of corruption.

2. Score 45/100: The score of 45/100 indicates the perceived level of corruption in China. A score of 0 indicates a highly corrupt country, while a score of 100 indicates a very clean, corruption-free country. A score of 45 suggests that China is perceived to have a moderate level of corruption.

The World Justice Project's Rule of Law Index[160] measures the extent to which governments and societies adhere to the rule of law. A strong rule of law can contribute to state legitimacy.

1. Score 47: The Rule of Law Index is typically scaled from 0 to 100, with 0 indicating a weak adherence to the rule of law and

---

[159] https://www.transparency.org/en/cpi/2022
[160] https://worldjusticeproject.org/rule-of-law-index/global/2022/China/

100 indicating a strong adherence. The score of 47 suggests that China's adherence to the rule of law is moderate.

2. Ranking 95/140: The ranking of 95/140 means that, in the context of the 140 countries included in the index, China is ranked 95th. A lower rank generally indicates a lower level of adherence to the rule of law compared to other countries. China thus falls in the lower half of the countries included in the index in terms of rule-of-law effectiveness.

On the Free and Fair Elections Index, China scored zero and is considered not to be a democracy,[161] although Beijing claims that China has a multiparty democracy.

The Human Freedom Index 2022, compiled by the Cato Institute with Canada's Fraser Institute, assesses the degree of personal, civil, and economic freedoms enjoyed by individuals. China scored 5.22. The scale for this index ranges from 0 to 10, where 0 represents the lowest level of freedom and 10 represents the highest level of freedom. A score of 5.22 falls in the middle of this range, moderate freedom. In the personal freedom category — which includes indicators related to individual rights, freedom of speech, freedom of religion, freedom of assembly, and freedom from violence and discrimination — the PRC scored 4.47. China's performance in these areas is relatively low, indicating restrictions and limitations on individual rights, freedom of speech, freedom of religion, freedom of assembly, and protection from violence and discrimination. It implies that there are concerns or challenges in these aspects of freedom in China. As regards economic freedom, such as ease of doing business, access to markets, property rights, and regulatory efficiency, China scored 6.27. A score between 6 and 7 generally suggests a moderate level of economic freedom.

---

[161] https://ourworldindata.org/grapher/free-and-fair-elections-index

Freedom House's Freedom in the World 2022 provides an assessment of China's political and civil liberties and its status in terms of freedom China is categorized as "not free" with a score of 9 out of 100.[162] China is seen as having significant restrictions on political and civil freedoms. For political rights, the score is -2, which indicates a lack of political rights. The negative score suggests that there are substantial restrictions on political activities and rights, such as the freedom to participate in free and fair elections, to organize political parties, and to engage in open political discourse. China has 56 ethnic groups, yet the political scene is dominated by the Han ethnic majority. The central government is implementing strategies to forcibly alter the demographics of minority-majority regions, including Xinjiang and Tibet, by relocating Han Chinese to the area, transporting local young people to other parts of the country, and incentivizing government employees to marry members of ethnic minorities. In Inner Mongolia, for example, Mongolians now make up less than 20 percent of the population.[163]

In terms of civil liberties, China does better, scoring 11 on a scale of 0 to 60, with 0 being the least free.[164] Individuals are afforded some degree of civil rights and freedoms, such as freedom of expression, freedom of the press, and protection from arbitrary arrest or detention.

The Human Development Index (HDI), devised by the UN Human Development Program, is a composite index that covers several dimensions of human development, among them: health, measured by life expectancy at birth; education, measured by a combination of mean years of schooling for adults aged 25 years or older and expected years of schooling for children entering school;

---

[162] https://freedomhouse.org/country/china/freedom-world/2022
[163] https://www.selenatravel.com/blog/the-differences-between-mongolia-and-inner-mongolia
[164] https://freedomhouse.org/country/china/freedom-world/2022

and standard of living, Gross National Income (GNI) per capita, adjusted for purchasing power parity (PPP). The HDI score for a country can range from 0 to 1, with higher values indicating higher levels of human development. China's HDI score of 0.768[165] means that the PRC's level of human development is relatively high.

The Heritage Foundation's assessment of China's government size[166] reveals: a tax burden of 69.5, government spending at 65.1, and fiscal health at 9.8. China maintains top individual and corporate tax rates of 45 percent and 25 percent, respectively. The tax burden amounts to 20.1 percent of GDP, while three-year government spending and budget balance averages stand at 34.1 percent and −7.3 percent of GDP, respectively. China's public debt is recorded at 71.5 percent of GDP. The foundation gives the PRC relatively low rule-of-law scores because enforcement and the courts are vulnerable to political influence and CCP directives, not to mention corruption.[167]

The World Bank's Governance Effectiveness Indicators[168] estimate the perceived effectiveness of the government in terms of formulating and implementing policies and regulations, as well as the government's capacity to deliver public services and enforce laws. In essence, it evaluates how well the government functions and how efficient it is in serving the needs of the public. The score of 0.5 for China indicates that government effectiveness is moderate. The score falls in the middle of the scale, which typically ranges from -2.5 (very low effectiveness) to +2.5 (very high effectiveness).

---

[165] https://hdr.undp.org/data-center/specific-country-data#/countries/CHN
[166] https://www.heritage.org/index/country/china
[167] Ibid.
[168] https://databank.worldbank.org/source/worldwide-governance-indicators/Series/GE.EST

The Gini coefficient is a measure of income inequality within a population. It is expressed as a number between 0 and 100, where 0 represents perfect equality (everyone has the same income or wealth). China's 2022 Gini coefficient of 46.7 exceeds the warning level of 40 for inequality set by the UN.[169] By comparison, that year's Gini coefficient for the United States was 48.8.

[169] https://www.statista.com/statistics/250400/inequality-of-income-distribution-in-china-based-on-the-gini-index/

4

The Military Dimension

Military analysis extends beyond mere troop figures and necessitates a comprehensive evaluation of a country's overall military prowess. This includes its capacity to engage in warfare effectively, mobilize troops and weaponry, both domestically and abroad for support, replenishment, and training. In this assessment, the quantity and caliber of weaponry, including advanced technology, become paramount. Furthermore, the country's alliances, military budget, capability to recruit and train troops, the quality of its armed forces, the technological advancement of its arsenal, and its nuclear capabilities are pivotal components that must be taken into account.

The Global Militarisation Index (GMI)[170] examines various factors and compares a country's military expenditure and its GDP, as well as its health expenditure. It also assesses the balance between the total number of military and paramilitary forces within a country and the number of physicians available. Additionally, the GMI scrutinizes the quantity of heavy weapons in possession of a country's armed forces.

The GMI ranks 155 countries and a higher score is better. China's militarisation rank is 98 out of 155. The militarisation score of 119 suggests that China is moderately militarized. The score is an aggregate of various factors that contribute to militarization. The military expenditure index score of 1.3 suggests

---

[170] https://gmi.bicc.de/#rank@2021

that China allocates a significant portion of its economic resources to military expenditure. It is important to note that a score above 1 usually indicates a level of military spending relative to GDP higher than the global average; there is also the issue of the PRC's hidden defense expenditure.

The GMI's military personnel index represents the number of military personnel, such as active-duty soldiers and armed forces personnel, relative to the total population. The score of 0.2 suggests that China has a relatively low ratio of military personnel to its total population. However, the heavy weapons index of 0.8 shows that China has a substantial inventory of tanks, artillery, and other heavy military equipment.

Overall, China's GMI score and ranking suggest that the country is moderately militarized. It allocates a significant portion of its economic resources to military expenditure, has a relatively low ratio of military personnel to its population, and possesses a substantial inventory of heavy weapons.

The U.S. ranks first in the world for defense spending, allotting $816.7 billion to the DOD.[171] China ranks second with $224.8 billion, according to the regime's State Council Information Office. The defense budget is directly correlated to a country's ability to purchase and develop new technologies and next-generation weapons and to make the latest equipment available to the largest percentage of its troops. For overall firepower, the U.S. is ranked first of 142 countries, while China is third, behind Russia.[172]

China has nearly double the available manpower, with roughly 148 million military capable citizens who could potentially

---

[171] https://www.defense.gov/News/News-Stories/Article/Article/3252968/biden-signs-national-defense-authorization-act-into-law/

[172] https://www.globalfirepower.com/countries-comparison-detail.php?country1=china&country2=united-states-of-america

serve in the military. China has 2 million active-duty troops, to the U.S. 1.39 million. For reserve troops, the numbers are closer, China having 510,000 while the U.S. has 442,000. China also has 624,000 paramilitary personnel, whereas the U.S. has no significant militia forces.

In terms of air power, the U.S. leads with 13,247 aircraft to China's 3,285. For fighter aircraft, the U.S. has 1,957 to China's 1,200. The U.S. also leads in helicopters, including attack helicopters, as well as combat drones.[173]

According to the 2023 Department of Defense Report on Military and Security Developments Involving the People's Republic of China, the PLA Rocket Force is actively progressing with its long-term modernization strategies, aiming to strengthen "strategic deterrence" capabilities. China is in the process of creating new intercontinental ballistic missiles (ICBMs) that will significantly enhance its nuclear-capable missile arsenal, prompting an increase in nuclear warhead production. This expansion is partly attributed to the introduction of multiple independently-targetable reentry vehicle (MIRV) capabilities. What is more, Beijing appears to be exploring the development of conventionally-armed intercontinental range missile systems. Should these systems be successfully developed and deployed, they would grant the PRC the ability to pose a conventional threat to targets within the continental United States, as well as Hawaii and Alaska.

On land, the U.S. has more tanks (6,612 versus 5,250) and armored vehicles (45,193 versus 35,000), but China has significantly more self-propelled artillery, towed artillery, and mobile rocket projectors. The PRC may have focused more on the development of this aspect of its military, because it borders 14

---

[173] Ibid.

foreign countries, all of which have to be defended against, whereas the U.S. has only two land borders, which are both only minimally defended. Most of the PLA is deployed near China's borders. It is estimated that China has the transportation capacity to redeploy only about 20 percent of its ground forces within the country.[174]

Comparing U.S. and Chinese Personnel

The PRC's military modernization has concentrated on employing new technology, but all wars eventually come down to soldiers fighting soldiers, and U.S. troops are much better suited to combat than Chinese military personnel. The Chinese regime realizes there is a need to improve the soldiers it commands, and has identified the PLA's shortfall in cultivating quality personnel.[175] Consequently, one of the primary focuses of the PLA's transformation into a "world-class military" is to attempt to recruit, train, indoctrinate, and retain talented personnel, particularly officers. The existing officer corps grew out of a Cultural Revolution-era military which detested the educated while stressing political indoctrination.

To improve the quality of its soldiers and officers, the PLA needs to attract and retain educated people. One enticement on offer is fast-track promotion. The result of racing young officers up the ladder, however, is that the PLA has managed to thin-out the experience in its higher ranks. Not only do these fast-tracked officers lack combat experience, they have very limited military experience — and now they occupy higher positions.

---

[174] https://www.brookings.edu/articles/chinas-hollow-military/
[175] https://thediplomat.com/2021/04/chinas-military-has-a-hidden-weakness/

Salary is an obstacle which the PLA seems unable to overcome. Military cybersecurity specialists earn just a fraction of what they could make by working in Alibaba or another of China's tech firms. As recently as 2019, a colonel in the PLA only earned about $24,000 per year (*South China Morning Post*, January 23, 2021), while his counterpart in the U.S. Army can earn up to $162,000.[176] Even after the recent 40-percent pay hike for PLA personnel, a colonel will earn just over $36,000 per year. A PLA recruit, after the raise, will earn about $1,900 a year, while a U.S. Army private earns about $20,000 per year.

An important point, when comparing U.S. reserves to the reserves in other countries, is that the U.S. reserves and National Guard are trained to the same standards as the regular military. They attend basic training and Military Occupational Specialty job school, alongside active-duty soldiers, sailors, marines, and airmen, but then return home to serve one weekend a month and two weeks per summer, rather than going on active duty. U.S. reserve and National Guard units are equipped with the latest weapons and are given numerous opportunities to go on active-duty training. Additionally, they are frequently deployed overseas. National guard troops made up about 45 percent of the soldiers deployed to Iraq and Afghanistan, and suffered 18 percent of the casualties.[177] This is not true of China's reserve forces.

The Chinese regime has spent a great deal of money, modernizing the military, buying the best and most advanced equipment, battleships, and fighter planes. According to a former Japanese Self-Defense Force officer who worked in the Defense Intelligence Headquarters of Japan's Ministry of Defense, the proficiency of PLA personnel operating this advanced equipment is poor (Asia Nikkei, September 19, 2021), owing to an inability to

---

[176] https://www.federalpay.org/military/army/colonel
[177] https://www.military.com/national-guard-birthday/national-guard-service-in-the-war-on-terror.html

train them properly. This is one reason why Beijing has stepped up its investment in unmanned aircraft and ballistic missiles. China has built up a considerable arsenal of both ballistic and cruise missiles, but it is quite telling that the CCP has to tailor its war plans, based on an inability to train PLA troops to use sophisticated weapons.

"Good steel does not become nails," goes a Chinese saying, meaning talented people do not become soldiers. The one-child policy — more than 70 percent of PLA soldiers are only children, and Confucian culture puts tremendous pressure on an only child to care for their parents — a cultural lack of respect for soldiers, poor pay, a deficiency of combat experience, and a need to protect the borders makes the PLA troops much less effective than American land units.

What is more, the PLA remains a conscript army.[178] Those who join may be doing so against their will. The U.S. army, by contrast, has been purely voluntary since 1972, with roughly 150,000 volunteers joining each year. In terms of education, 67 percent of U.S. soldiers have completed a high school diploma and/or some college, 8.9 percent hold an associate degree, 13.6 percent have a bachelor's degree, and 8.3 percent have attained an advanced degree.[179] And while many jobs in the U.S. armed forces do not pay quite as well as their civilian equivalents, the difference is not as dramatic as it is in the PLA.

Higher salaries may help attract better people, but they will also drive up the cost of maintaining the army. It is no wonder that the announcement about the PLA pay increase was accompanied

---

[178] https://warontherocks.com/2020/07/people-win-wars-the-pla-enlisted-force-and-other-related-matters/

[179] https://www.statista.com/statistics/232726/education-levels-of-active-duty-us-defense-force-personnel/

by a cut of 300,000 personnel (*South China Morning Post*, January 23, 2021).

Another significant difference between the PLA and U.S. forces is that 2.77 million American military personnel were deployed in combat zones between late 2001 and early 2018, according to a *Forbes* infographic (March 20, 2018). Since 1991, the U.S. military has been in almost constant combat operations. China's military, by contrast, has no combat experience. China fought a minor naval skirmish with Vietnam in 1988.[180] The PLA defeated Tibet in 1959, a miniscule country compared to China. And the PLA was thwarted during its invasion of Vietnam in 1979. Chinese soldiers engaged in brawls with Indian forces in the Galwan Valley in 2020. The last major battles the PLA took part in were against the U.S., in the Korean War, which ended in 1953.

This lack of combat experience is obvious even during peacetime. In 2018, a Chinese submarine, on a covert patrol near the disputed Senkaku Islands, was detected by the Japanese Self-Defense Force. The submarine immediately surfaced, raising the Chinese flag. This confirmed to Japan and the world that a Chinese war boat had violated Japanese territory, leaving Beijing no plausible deniability.[181]

The Japanese have speculated that the PLA boat surfaced so quickly, because it feared being attacked with depth charges. Under international law, the Japanese forces have the right to attack "unidentified submarines" intruding in their waters. By raising the Chinese flag, the submarine avoided destruction, but divulged its secret mission.

---

[180] https://www.rand.org/pubs/commentary/2018/11/chinas-military-has-no-combat-experience-does-it-matter.html
[181] https://www.dw.com/en/chinese-attack-submarine-lurking-near-disputed-waters-angers-japan/a-42164137

The Chinese regime needs to maintain troops on its Afghanistan border to protect from possible terrorist incursions. They also need to keep a large number of troops stationed on the Indian border. In the past, China fought two limited border wars with India and has recently fought several skirmishes. Additionally, India is part of the Quad, a U.S.-lead defense pact designed to counter China. So, the CCP regime cannot remove troops from that border.

The PRC has fought a war against Vietnam, and Vietnam is now a U.S. ally, so China cannot take troops from there. Although Pakistan is a relative client state, troops are still needed on that border, because of the threat of terrorism. Moscow is only a sometimes-ally, one that Beijing has never trusted. Therefore, the troops on the border with Russia must remain. Furthermore, China shares maritime borders with Japan, South Korea, the Philippines, and Taiwan, all of whom are U.S. allies.

The U.S., by contrast, has two, largely undefended land borders, leaving the vast majority of its forces available for overseas deployment. Additionally, the U.S. troops are better educated. The officer corps have more command experience. And the U.S. military has more combat experience than the PLA.

Chinese Sea Power

The PLA Navy is now the largest in the world, and its land-based missile force is believed to have the capability to target U.S. ships at sea.[182] China has 777 vessels to the U.S. Navy's 484, but the U.S. has 11 aircraft carriers and China only 2. The U.S. has the

---

[182] https://www.nytimes.com/2022/05/27/opinion/biden-taiwan-defense-china.html

advantage in helicopter carriers and submarines, but not destroyers, frigates, or patrol vessels.[183]

The PRC also deploys People's Armed Forces Maritime Militia, which pose as civilian vessels, but carry out military missions. Despite Beijing's disclaimers, the militia is very real. It is composed of ships that look like civilian fishing boats, but are tasked with supporting the PLA Navy in controlling the seas.

Seafood is key to China's food security. China consumes 65 million tons of fish per year, 45 percent of the global volume. China could have as many as 187,000 fishing boats,[184] including 17,000 vessels in distant-water operations. At least 100 of these vessels and 1,800 sailors operate under the command of the maritime militia, Radio Free Asia reported on May 18, 2021. This subcomponent of China's armed forces is trained and equipped to support the PLA in laying claim to islands, features, and waters in disputed areas. Their vessels have automatic weapons and reinforced hulls, and can achieve top speed faster than around 90 percent of the world's fishing boats.[185] Additionally, the vessels are outfitted with BeiDou Navigation Satellite System hardware, so as to be independent of the West's GPS.

An investigation by Radio Free Asia discovered that many of the militia's boats belong to a state-owned enterprise, Sansha City Fisheries Development Co, Ltd., which has managed government projects involving classified national security data. Moreover, the boats carry cutting-edge communications systems, transforming them into mobile communications and surveillance platforms which can gather and transmit intelligence back to authorities in a remote location. The militia — which can be used

---

[183] https://www.globalfirepower.com/countries-comparison-detail.php?country1=china&country2=united-states-of-america
[184] https://edition.cnn.com/2021/04/12/china/china-maritime-militia-explainer-intl-hnk-ml-dst/index.html
[185] Ibid.

to track foreign vessels and U.S. aircraft, as well as surveil shorelines — is thought by experts to play a significant role in the CCP's plan is to establish control over the entire South China Sea.

In 2021, the Philippine Coast Guard became suspicious when they observed the same 200 Chinese fishing boats, sitting idle in the same location, near the Spratlys' Whitsun Reef, a Philippine possession, for several weeks.[186] According to the International Institute for Strategic Studies, the Whitsun Reef incident was the single largest gathering of Chinese fishing vessels ever.

The boats were not fishing, and it is unlikely that legitimate fishing boats would just sit, for a protracted period of time, doing nothing. As a result, the Philippine Coast Guard reported their suspicion that these boats were actually on a covert military operation. Confronted by Manila, the PRC Foreign Ministry and embassy in Manila denied the accusation that the suspicious boats were on a mission from China's Maritime Militia.[187] The embassy actually issued a statement saying that there is "no Chinese maritime militia as alleged."

Under the Xi Jinping regime, the militia's responsibilities have expanded tremendously. In 2013, Xi visited one militia base, recognizing the role they played in the seizure of Scarborough Shoal. Addressing militia personnel, PLA Major-General Gai Longyun, said "the maritime struggle is growing more urgent" and that the state was exploring ways to strengthen the maritime militia. Additionally, military authorities called for the "mobilization forces," such as militia, to participate in the "struggle" at sea.[188]

---

[186] https://foreignpolicy.com/2021/04/19/manilas-images-are-revealing-the-secrets-of-chinas-maritime-militia/

[187] Ibid.

[188] Ibid.

The Maritime Militia, supported by the Chinese Coast Guard, are used to enforce China's territorial claims to 90 percent of the South China Sea, particularly around the Paracel and Spratly Islands. China has also built 3,200 acres (around 1,300 hectares) of new land, to further extend its territorial claims.[189] China's military operations in the Scarborough Shoal in 2012 are an excellent example of the regime's maritime strategy, using the militia as the front line, while reserving the Coast Guard and the PLA Navy as the second and third lines.[190]

The militia poses a particularly difficult problem for the U.S. First, they are civilian vessels, so any actions against them by the U.S. or its allies would be considered an attack on civilians. For the claimants of the South China Sea and other disputed waters, the militia represents a military force which they may not be able to defeat. Additionally, by engaging with the militia, they would be risking retaliation by the PLA Navy. From a pure military and strategic standpoint, a U.S. Navy flotilla could destroy any number of boats it encounters. However, the sheer numbers of these small vessels would make them elusive. While the U.S. is engaging in one place, the Maritime Militia could be active in another. There is also fear that the Philippines — the country most threatened by the militia — might engage with one of the boats, dragging the U.S. into a war with China.

Nuclear Weapons

The U.S is the only country to have used a nuclear weapon in war. Since 1945, the U.S. has conducted more than 1,000 tests of

---

[189] https://www.rfa.org/english/news/southchinasea/china-artificial-islands-10312022043801.html
[190] https://foreignpolicy.com/2021/04/19/manilas-images-are-revealing-the-secrets-of-chinas-maritime-militia/

atomic weapons, while China has done fewer than 50. Currently, the U.S. has around 3,708 warheads with about 1,744 deployed.[191] China currently has 350 nuclear warheads in total.[192]

When dealing with the China nuclear threat, it is essential for the U.S. to also account for other nuclear threats from Beijing-aligned nations. The four major threat nations — Iran, North Korea, China, and Russia — each require tailored deterrence strategies.

There is a connection between China's nuclear posture and that of Russia. It is thought that Moscow has a low threshold for nuclear weapons use, because it maintains the right to deploy nuclear weapons in response to attacks on itself or its allies. It also reserves the right to use nuclear weapons in the face of conventional attacks of sufficient scale, which threaten the national security of the Russian Federation. The question is whether or not Russia considers China an ally, or if Xi might push Putin to deploy nukes, so China could maintain plausible deniability. The PRC's expansion and modernization of its nuclear force further complicates U.S. response strategy. When addressing arms control and risk reduction policies vis-à-vis Russia, developments in China's nuclear capabilities must also be considered. For this reason, Washington is adopting a flexible strategy against the Chinese regime.

The 2023 Annual Threat Assessment of the U.S. Intelligence Community asserts that Beijing is expediting the development of critical capabilities it deems necessary for the PLA to confront the United States in a protracted, large-scale conflict. Enhancing and modernizing the PLA's nuclear, WMD, and

---

[191] https://thebulletin.org/premium/2022-05/nuclear-notebook-how-many-nuclear-weapons-does-the-united-states-have-in-2022/

[192] https://www.armscontrol.org/act/2021-12/news/pentagon-sees-faster-chinese-nuclear-expansion

advanced-weaponry capabilities comes at a financial cost, and there exists a clear correlation between defense expenditure and the pace of expansion. In simpler terms, China's defense spending is directly linked to the timeline for the PLA's readiness to engage with the U.S. — and a 2023 analysis of China state-spending revealed that China's military spending goes beyond the defense budget, bringing the total much closer to U.S. spending.

China's Hidden Military Budget

Previously, it was believed that China's defense spending was a fraction of the U.S. military budget. However, the U.S. intelligence community recently discovered that China may be spending as much as $700 billion,[193] allowing China to challenge the U.S. for military supremacy much sooner than originally believed. This new revelation has lawmakers concerned.[194]

One of the ways Beijing disguised its spending was by directing money into the military-civil fusion,[195] whereby the central government provides money to private companies to develop dual-use technology. Some of the most important areas of military development are funded in this way, such as shipbuilding, information technology, and aerospace. These three domains are expected to play the largest role in any war between the U.S. and the PRC. A special danger regarding information technology and aerospace is that the ability to dominate cyberspace or to damage or disable satellites will be crucial in 21st-century warfare. It could leave ships and planes unable to navigate or communicate, or

[193] https://foreignpolicy.com/2023/09/19/china-defense-budget-military-weapons-purchasing-power/

[194] https://www.romney.senate.gov/romney-manchin-sullivan-king-introduce-legislation-to-expose-chinas-defense-spending/

[195] https://www.aei.org/foreign-and-defense-policy/setting-the-record-straight-on-beijings-actual-military-spending/

prevent the U.S. from guiding its missiles to targets. Furthermore, China's Coast Guard[196] and People's Armed Forces Maritime Militia are not covered by the defense budget. These two forces have been aggressively pushing China's territorial claims in the South China Sea, as well as conducting spying in the Bay of Bengal. They carry weapons and enforce Beijing's foreign policy objectives,[197] but are not considered part of the PLA Navy.

China is one of the five largest arms importers in the world, and in recent years Russia has been the number one supplier (*South China Morning Post*, July 4, 2021). China primarily imports weapons and technology that cannot be produced domestically, such as long-range strike capabilities, combat aircraft, and missiles. These imports do not count in Beijing's official defense spending figures.[198] R&D are other large expenditures which are not charged to the country's defense budget.

Purchasing power parity is another reason why China's spending may be amplified. Because labor and many basic products and services are much cheaper in China than in the U.S., with a smaller budget Beijing can buy more of them. Soldiers' salaries are much higher in the U.S. than in China. According to *The Economist* (May 1, 2021), a private in the PLA has a starting salary of $108 per month. In the U.S. Army, it is $1,918. On a similar note, the U.S. has been plagued by inflation, with prices rising by an average of nearly 18 percent since the start of the Biden administration. China, by contrast, is facing deflation. While prices are going up in the U.S., they are going down in China, making it possible for the CCP to buy more goods and services for the PLA.

---

[196] Ibid.

[197] https://www.aljazeera.com/news/2021/11/19/china-supports-maritime-militia-to-assert-south-china-sea-claim

[198] https://www.wsj.com/articles/china-defense-spending-senate-bill-angus-king-dan-sullivan-u-s-beijing-military-c3b64ba

Although China's defense budget has increased steadily, year after year, China's arms exports have been in decline. In 2022, PRC weapons exports dropped by 23 percent.[199] One reason for this may be that China is stockpiling weapons, in preparation for war.[200] As *Asia Nikkei* explained on September 12, 2023, the PLA Navy and PLA Air Force have increasingly threatened the sea and air space around Taiwan. In response, Washington is strengthening its defense ties with Taiwan, India, Australia, and other nations. In a February 9, 2023 article on its website, the DOD clarified that it is trying to prevent a war in the Indo-Pacific, but that it wants to be ready, if war breaks out. Secretary of Defense Lloyd Austin said that growth in the U.S. defense budget in 2023 was "driven by the seriousness of our strategic competition with the People's Republic of China."[201] Now it appears that China is spending more than originally believed, the stakes have been raised.

In remarks delivered on September 19, 2023, Senate Minority Leader Mitch McConnell (R-KY) recognized the importance of stepping up U.S. preparations for a possible war with the PRC, saying that: "closing the gap with China — and outcompeting our biggest strategic adversary — will require more than innovation theater or speeches about revolutions in military affairs. Real progress will require real investments in long-range strike capabilities. Real expansion of our defense production capacity. Real defense technology cooperation with our closest allies who increasingly share our concerns about the PLA."[202]

---

[199] https://www.dw.com/en/sipri-us-arms-exports-skyrocket-while-chinas-nosedive/a-64948062

[200] https://www.scmp.com/news/china/military/article/3213383/fall-chinas-military-exports-sign-stockpiling-home

[201] https://www.defense.gov/News/News-Stories/Article/Article/3343663/competition-with-china-drives-fy-2024-budget-request/

[202] https://www.republicanleader.senate.gov/newsroom/remarks/china-competition-requires-serious-investments-in-defense-industrial-base

The CCP's Military-Civil Fusion

Another means of stretching China's defense budget is by combining the interests and capabilities of private companies with the needs of the PLA through military-civil fusion (MCF). "Joint research institutions, academia, and private firms are all being exploited to build the PLA's future military systems — often without their knowledge or consent," reads a State Department one-pager on MCF. Xi Jinping is expected to expand the program in his third term.[203]

Under PRC law, in order to gain access to Chinese markets, American companies are often required to enter into joint ventures with Chinese companies, which are then in a position to obtain American technology.[204] A November 2022 European Parliament report asserted that forced technology transfer and other forms of Chinese coercion are so cleverly masked by Beijing that they are difficult to prosecute at the WTO. Acts of economic coercion are frequently carried out through private companies rather than by government agencies; and the foreign companies which are the victims are often hesitant to report the incidents for fear of losing market access. The report's authors expect economic coercion to intensify during Xi's third term.

Washington is intensifying restrictions on both U.S. investment in China and Chinese investment in the U.S. One of the primary reasons for these restrictions is MCF. According to a November 8, 2022 White House briefing, MCF boosts the regime's "military-industrial complex by compelling civilian Chinese companies to support its military and intelligence activities." For American investors, this means that by investing in

---

[203] https://www.aspistrategist.org.au/ccp-constitutional-change-strengthens-xis-power-but-avoids-total-personality-cult/
[204] https://academic.oup.com/jla/article/13/1/127/6180583

private or state-owned Chinese companies, they may be funneling money into the PRC's weapons development programs.

The CCP has said that it aims to develop the PLA into a "world class military" by 2049, and this goal can only be achieved through an expansion of MCF. As chairman of both the CCP's Central Military Commission and the Central Commission for Military-Civil Fusion Development, Xi personally oversees the strategy's implementation, according to the State Department's one-pager.

China believes that advanced technology such as AI will drive the next evolution of warfare, and MCF is critical to Beijing's goal of transitioning to "intelligent warfare." Apart from AI, other technologies which U.S. regulators are trying to prevent Beijing from acquiring include quantum computing, big data, semiconductors, and 5G, as well as advanced nuclear and aerospace technologies.

Intelligence gathering, espionage, and theft are not the only ways by which the CCP acquires American technology. The regime also recruits U.S. scientists and experts, funds U.S. academics and researchers, and collaborates with U.S. research and educational institutions.

By increasingly allowing private companies to carry out military research, the Chinese regime is blurring the lines between private and government entities, making it more difficult for U.S. regulators to prevent funding or technology from flowing from U.S. entities into the PLA. The FBI has identified China as the country which has stolen the most U.S. data and IP. With good reason, the bureau has called for greater scrutiny of Chinese students and researchers in the U.S. Those who receive scholarships from the Chinese authorities are legally required to report on their research work overseas.

The PLA Beyond China's Borders

China's first overseas military base was established in Djibouti in 2016, near the Suez Canal and the entrance to the Red Sea. PRC entities also own significant stakes in 13 overseas ports, including at least 7 in Europe. Worldwide, China owns some interest in over 100 ports in more than 60 nations.[205] China Ocean Shipping (Group) Company (COSCO) has operated and managed 357 terminals in 36 ports from Southeast Asia to the Middle East, Europe and the Mediterranean. Another Chinese port developer, China Merchants Group, claims to have expanded its global port layout to 68 ports in 27 countries.[206]

These ports are designated as civilian but could be modified to accommodate PLA Navy vessels. Although not an official base, China has greatly expanded Ream Naval Base in Sihanoukville, Cambodia, which now acts as a de facto base for the PLA Navy.[207] Nearby Dara Sakor International Airport, which was developed by PRC companies with Chinese money, boasts the longest runway in Cambodia, despite the town having a population of only 100,000. It could easily accommodate PLA Air Force planes. The airport is operated by a Chinese company, which raises additional questions regarding a lack of transparency.

Beijing has invested in container ports in Latin America. These ports potentially serve to facilitate the global operations of the PLA Navy. Additionally, the Chinese National Space Administration, as part of the Chinese Deep Space Network, has established a space monitoring station in Argentina, near the Strait of Magellan.[208]

---

[205] https://www.voanews.com/a/6224958.html
[206] Ibid.
[207] https://asia.nikkei.com/Spotlight/Belt-and-Road/Swallowed-by-China-Cambodia-s-Ream-base-expansion-raises-alarm
[208] https://www.reuters.com/article/us-space-argentina-china-insight-idUSKCN1PP0I2/

In March 2023, the Senate Intelligence Committee issued a statement regarding a suspected PRC spy base in Cuba, just 90 miles (145 kilometers) from the U.S., expressing deep concern that Havana and Beijing appeared to be working together "to target the United States and our people." The White House later confirmed that China has had a spy base in Cuba since 2019.[209] Cuba rebutted the allegations, saying they were just a pretext for the U.S. embargo of Cuba, while China's Foreign Ministry denied any knowledge of the situation.

Around the same time, New Delhi confronted the Myanmar government over satellite images of Chinese workers constructing a listening post and extending an airstrip on the Coco Islands in the Bay of Bengal, *Business Today* reported on April 9, 2023. Myanmar has denied Chinese involvement, but Indian officials are concerned that the facility will enable the PLA to monitor Indian Navy communications and track missile tests. Myanmar's military commander claims there are no PLA personnel on the island, yet he confirmed that Myanmar troops are stationed there. Despite Myanmar claiming otherwise, it is widely suspected that Myanmar has allowed the PLA to use the islands as a listening post since the 1990s.[210]

Myanmar, India, and the Bay of Bengal

From a strategic standpoint, establishing a presence in the Bay of Bengal allows China to encircle India.[211] The economic implications are that the China-Myanmar Economic Corridor (CMEC) allows China to connect its impoverished southwestern provinces to the global economy by accessing the Bay of Bengal

---

[209] https://apnews.com/article/china-cuba-spy-base-us-intelligence-0f655b577ae4141bdbeabc35d628b18f

[210] https://www.chathamhouse.org/publications/the-world-today/2023-04/myanmar-building-spy-base-great-coco-island

[211] https://www.indiatoday.in/india/story/china-encircle-india-string-of-pearls-982930-2017-06-15

via Myanmar. Additionally, the Bay of Bengal provides an alternative for China-bound oil shipments, allowing tankers to bypass the Strait of Malacca, a chokepoint which is heavily patrolled by the U.S. Navy. The strait plays a crucial role in Beijing's energy supplies, as it is the shortest route from the Indian Ocean to Chinese ports on the Pacific Ocean. If a war between the U.S. and China were to break out, the U.S. Navy could easily blockade the strait, cutting off much of China's oil supply. The CMEC is creating a direct route from the China-invested port of Kyaukpyu, on the Bay of Bengal, connecting with the Myanmar-China Oil and Gas Pipeline,[212] which ends in China's Yunnan Province. The gas for the pipeline comes from both onshore and offshore fields in Myanmar's Rakhine and Tanintharyi regions. The pipeline is owned and operated by the Southeast Asia Crude Oil Pipeline Company, a joint venture between China National Petroleum Corporation (CNPC) and Myanmar Oil and Gas Enterprise, in which CNPC is the majority stakeholder.

Beijing has been a major supplier of weapons to Myanmar's armed forces,[213] the Tatmadaw, a way of ingratiating itself and gaining access to the Bay of Bengal. Consequently, over the past few years, there has been increased Chinese activity in the region. In 2018, the Indian Coast Guard apprehended a Chinese fishing boat suspected of engaging in espionage. More recently, the Indian Navy detected a Chinese spy ship docking at Hambantota, the China-owned port in Sri Lanka. In early 2023, a suspected Chinese spy balloon was spotted floating over an Indian Navy base.[214] The Indian Navy says that, at any given moment,

---

[212] https://www.chinacenter.net/2020/china-currents/19-3/a-relationship-on-a-pipeline-china-and-myanmar/

[213] https://thediplomat.com/2022/04/is-the-ukraine-war-boosting-chinas-influence-in-myanmar/

[214] https://moderndiplomacy.eu/2023/03/17/high-altitude-espionage-spy-balloon-and-indias-national-security/

multiple PLA Navy vessels are in the Indian Ocean, *Economic Times* reported on March 4, 2023.

China's expansion into the Bay of Bengal poses security concerns for both the United States and for India. The U.S. is concerned about China establishing overseas bases in the area, including a missile maintenance facility in Bangladesh[215] and ports in Sri Lanka and Myanmar.

The CCP has a long history of circumventing sanctions to support the military rulers of Myanmar; and while Washington and New Delhi appear to be at odds over Russia's invasion of Ukraine, the two have a shared interest in preventing the PLA Navy from gaining access to the Indian Ocean.

India is caught in a balancing act between its long-term ally Russia and long-term adversary China, a *South China Morning Post* op-ed explained (April 12, 2022). Over the past few years, the U.S. has been intensifying its alliance with India through the Quad and other initiatives, but the Ukraine crisis has put this budding friendship to the test. While Beijing may seek to draw India away from the U.S., India's anger about the PRC's border incursions in recent years will not be easily forgotten.

Another dimension to the Indian Ocean situation is that U.S. defense plans versus China tend to focus on the Pacific Ocean, the Strait of Malacca, and the Taiwan Strait, and defense of the Indian Ocean is generally left to India.[216] The U.S. Indo-Pacific Strategy paper confirms that the U.S. counts on India "as a partner in this positive regional vision." Whether or not India is up to the task, however, remains unclear. The Office of U.S. Naval Intelligence estimates that by 2030, the PLA Navy will have 67

[215] https://asia.nikkei.com/Politics/International-relations/India-wary-of-China-setting-up-Bangladesh-missile-maintenance-hub
[216] https://www.politico.com/news/magazine/2022/03/16/india-china-indian-ocean-00017520

new major surface ships and 12 new nuclear-powered submarines, which is enough to control the Indian Ocean.[217] The larger CCP plan is to grow the military so that China will be able to control the seas by 2030 and displace the U.S. as the world's most powerful navy by 2049, according to a *Sunday Guardian* article (June 13, 2020).

There is concern within India that the CCP threat to India's land borders, such as the 2020 incursions in the Himalaya, are distracting the government from building a strong navy. Apart from the fact that India is a peninsula with a huge coastline, security experts, including the CSIS, agree that India should increase its maritime capabilities (The Print, March 23, 2022). This is particularly true now that China has established ports at Gwadar in Pakistan, Hambantota and Colombo in Sri Lanka, and will soon have ports in Myanmar. In August 2021, China shipped cargo from Yangon Port in the Indian Ocean all the way to Yunnan, VOA reported on September 16, 2021. According to Rajeswari Pillai Rajagopalan, director for the Center for Security, Strategy and Technology at New Delhi's Observer Research Foundation, the ports in Myanmar, Pakistan, and Sri Lanka represented the CCP closing in on India.

On January 28, 2022 *Business Standard* reported that there were as many as 125 foreign vessels in the Indian Ocean at any time, and that the Indian Navy might be tracking up to three PLA Navy ships at any given moment. The same report quoted an Indian military expert as saying that, in order to meet the challenge of the CCP, India needs to build up its naval power. Historically, the navy has been the "forgotten service" when it comes to India's military budget, always receiving only a fraction of the funding they ask for.

---

[217] Ibid.

China's total defense spending is at least three times that of India ($72.6 billion in 2023). Finally realizing the need to catch up, New Delhi the Indian government increased the navy budget by 44 percent in 2022. Currently, the Indian Navy only has 130 vessels, many of which are two decades old (*Business Standard*, January 28, 2022). So while the increase in funding is a welcome move in the right direction, the situation is far from resolved.

The U.S. has a number of tools to aid India in improving its maritime defense capabilities. In 2012, the U.S.-India Defense Technology and Trade Initiative was established to foster cooperation between the two countries in R&D, as well as production of defense technologies.[218] Additionally, the U.S. has other programs in place to finance the military of foreign countries and provide them with defense-related equipment, such as the Foreign Military Financing and Excess Defense Articles programs. Both have been applied to Egypt and Israel and could be expanded to include India.

A sticking point in U.S.-Indian cooperation has always been Washington's refusal to provide India with nuclear submarines[219] and other advanced weaponry, forcing India to rely on Russia. Now, in the context of the Ukraine invasion, India's arms trade with Russia is in conflict with the Countering America's Adversaries Through Sanctions Act. As the U.S. will not sell India the latest weapons, India must do without, or maintain its ties with Russia.

Preventing Beijing from gaining control of the Indian Ocean may necessitate the U.S. adopting a new Indian Ocean Policy,[220] and deepening its involvement with India through the

---

[218] https://www.defense.gov/News/Releases/Release/Article/2837908/readout-of-us-india-defense-industry-collaboration-forum-virtual-expo/#:~:text

[219] https://www.indiatoday.in/india-today-insight/story/why-the-us-won-t-give-india-nuclear-submarines-1854818-2021-09-20

[220] https://thediplomat.com/2021/02/the-us-needs-a-new-indian-ocean-strategy-now/

Quad and other programs. Washington is in a position to coordinate with New Delhi by supporting the development of India's economic, political, and military power. To do this, the U.S. will have to evaluate whether India's ties to Russia outweigh the help India can lend the U.S. in countering China. Similarly, India will have to decide if gaining U.S. support against the CCP is worth abandoning its relationship with Russia.

Mixed Results Elsewhere in Asia

Military diplomacy deploys armed forces for foreign policy goals. Interaction between a nation's military and foreign entities can achieve diplomatic goals and bolster security. China is increasingly leveraging its military for engagement and diplomatic advantages. Exercises facilitate overseas training for troops and provide practice in deploying and resupplying at distance. Military exchanges also foster alliances and enhance the PLA's collaboration with foreign forces, boosting China's global military presence.

In September 2023, the PLA concluded its fifth annual joint training exercise with Singapore's armed forces (Xinhua, September 13, 2023). Earlier in the year, the PLA conducted joint training with Cambodia's army, and the PLA Navy joined drills with BRICS members China, Russia, and South Africa conducted joint naval drills (Reuters, February 19, 2023). Symbols displayed on Russian warships docked in South Africa appeared to send a political message that the latter country is slipping into the Chinese-Russian camp.

The South African government justified these wargames by saying they were scheduled long before Russia attacked Ukraine. Of course, this raises the question of why South Africa did not cancel the exercises given the current geopolitical situation, and generated criticism within the country (Business Daily Africa, March 1, 2023). South Africa was one of 35 countries which abstained from voting to condemn the Ukraine invasion at the UN. The ruling African National Congress has ties to Moscow dating back to the Cold War, when the USSR provided training and material support to the movement's armed wing. South Africa, along with 119 other countries, is also a member of the Non-Aligned Movement, as well as a founder of the BRICS alliance.

Joint counter-terrorism exercises, like the ones conducted with Singapore, are sometimes used as a less-threatening way of engaging with the security forces of another nation, which might be wary of hosting a PRC base or participating in joint training. China has conducted similar exercises or training for local forces in Africa.[221]

The First Meeting of the China-Pakistan-Iran Trilateral Consultation on Counter-Terrorism and Security (PRC Ministry of Foreign Affairs, June 7, 2023) was held in the summer of 2023. However, regional security forums like this have had extremely mixed results for China. On the one hand, Beijing is able to convince other countries to participate in such events. On the other, no defense agreements have resulted and almost no country has agreed to host a PLA base.

China's participation in a number of regional security forums and organizations, including the SCO and the ASEAN Regional Forum, are opportunities to engage with other neighboring countries, discussing regional security threats. The irony is that the CCP regime is the largest regional security threat. Taiwan is threatened by a Chinese invasion and is often blocked from attending China-led forums. Vietnam, Brunei, Malaysia, Taiwan, and the Philippines all have disputes with the CCP regime in the South China Sea — and an international tribunal in The

---

[221] https://africacenter.org/spotlight/chinas-policing-models-make-inroads-in-africa/

Hague ruled against Beijing in its dispute with Manila.[222] The Philippines has had numerous run-ins with China's maritime militia, and under President Ferdinand Marcos Jr. Manila has expanded its defense ties with Washington. In late 2023, Marcos ordered the cutting of a barrier that China had installed when laying claim to Philippine fishing grounds (Al-Jazeera, September 25, 2023).

Humanitarian assistance and peacekeeping operations are another means of giving PLA troops operational experience in other countries, while enhancing China's global standing. The PLA has participated in UN Blue Helmet peacekeeping[223] and counter-piracy operations in Africa, as well as UN police operations in Haiti.

PRC military diplomacy incorporates defense cooperation, overseas bases, private security companies (PSC), providing weapons and technology, counterterrorism, humanitarian assistance, and regional security forums. Progress in these areas has been varied, with some successes and some non-starters.

Beijing has had mixed success selling weapons and technology. China was the world's number-four arms exporter in 2022, according to data compiled by the Stockholm International Peace Research Institute, but its weaponry lags behind Russian and American alternatives. U.S.-aligned nations like EU member states, the Philippines, Japan, and Vietnam rarely buy Chinese arms, highlighting the link between diplomacy and arms sales.

[222] https://www.theguardian.com/world/2016/jul/12/philippines-wins-south-china-sea-case-against-china
[223] https://www.brookings.edu/articles/chinas-pragmatic-approach-to-un-peacekeeping/

Chinese Troops and Weapons in the Middle East

According to the CCP's 2016 Arab region policy paper, Beijing seeks to "deepen China-Arab military cooperation and exchange. We will strengthen exchange of visits of military officials, expand military personnel exchange, deepen cooperation on weapons, equipment and various specialized technologies, and carry out joint military exercises."

The CCP's intensifying relationship with the Middle East and North Africa (MENA) extends to military cooperation, arms sales, missiles, and nuclear and surveillance technology. Meanwhile, peacekeeping and counter-terrorism missions have become an excuse to deploy Chinese troops and weapons around the world.

PRC Foreign Minister Wang Yi, speaking at a UN-related symposium, said in mid-2021 that "China has met its responsibilities for upholding world peace…China has taken the side of fairness, upholding equality and opposing interference in other countries' internal affairs..." (Associated Press, June 25, 2021). Suhail Ahmad Khan (September 20, 2021) has written that the CCP claims that, by promoting developmental peace and refraining from supporting democracy or otherwise attempting to improve the human rights or change governmental systems in the region, China is doing more to preserve peace and stability than the United States.

Through participation in UN peacekeeping missions, the CCP regime has been able to place PLA troops in North Africa and the Middle East. The PRC's security engagement with the region began in 2006, when China sent UN peacekeepers to Lebanon. In 2008, the PLA Navy contributed to a UN anti-piracy mission in the Gulf of Aden. In 2012, 700 PLA soldiers joined UN peacekeeping forces in Sudan. And in 2013, the PLA Navy escorted UN ships removing chemical weapons from Syria and Cyprus in 2013.

In 2015, Xi Jinping offered training to 2,000 peacekeepers from other UN member states,[224] as well as a donation of $1 billion to the UN's Peace and Development Trust Fund. By April 2018, 1,800 PLA soldiers and police officers had participated in UN peacekeeping missions in the MENA. Chinese troops have been deployed in Western Sahara, Darfur in Sudan, Lebanon, South Sudan, and Israel-Palestine. By July 2019, China had dispatched 32 anti-piracy convoys to provide security in the waters near Somalia and in the Red and Arabian seas.[225]

Security and surveillance have proved to be additional avenues for Chinese military technology sales and personnel deployment. The CCP pledge to support counter-terrorism efforts in MENA countries, and to help build counter-terrorism capacity, has bolstered sales of AI, smart-and-safe city technologies, and drones.[226] In 2020, Tiandy, one of the world's largest video surveillance companies, sold almost $700 million worth of equipment to Iran's Revolutionary Guard, police, and military, according to MIT Technology Review (December 15, 2021). Surveillance market analysts project that, by 2030, the AI industry in the Middle East could be worth $320 billion, with the largest buyers being Saudi Arabia, Qatar, Bahrain, and the UAE.

PRC security contractors are also becoming more common. As the region's largest foreign investor, Chinese firms and projects often do not rely on local forces for protection. Consequently, Chinese private security firms, many of which have ties to the PLA or China's armed police, have been deployed in the region.[227]

China's arms sales to the region have steadily increased. Because of congressional oversight, the U.S. is restrained from

---

[224] https://ecfr.eu/publication/china_great_game_middle_east/
[225] Ibid.
[226] https://www.washingtoninstitute.org/policy-analysis/rise-chinese-ai-gulf-renewal-chinas-serbia-model
[227] https://ecfr.eu/publication/china_great_game_middle_east/

selling certain types of military hardware to certain countries.[228] The CCP regime, however, is willing and able to meet these demands, selling complete systems, including training and maintenance.

Between 2016 and 2020, China's arms sales to its two major customers in the Middle East, Saudi Arabia and the UAE, respectively grew by 386 percent and 169 percent. The PRC has sold drones to Iraq, Jordan, Saudi Arabia, and the UAE. Since 2017, a Saudi company has partnered with China Aerospace Science and Technology Corp. to produce China's CH-4 Unmanned Aerial Vehicle.[229] Saudi Arabia also has Chinese long-range missiles and has constructed a plant to produce ballistic missiles. Nuclear weapons experts believe that the plant's solid-fuel rocket-engine test-stands are based on Chinese designs.[230]

"China firmly supports Iran in safeguarding its state sovereignty and national dignity," PRC Foreign Minister Wang Yi told Iranian President Hassan Rouhani when Beijing and Tehran signed a $400-billion investment deal that would include discounted Iranian oil shipments to China, Chinese weapons, joint military training and exercises, and joint research projects (*The New York Times*, March 27, 2021).

Defense Diplomacy in Latin America

In the Americas, defense diplomacy is the CCP regime's stealthy move to expand its soft power through arms sales and military education for both autocratic states and democratic allies of the U.S. The PRC is exchanging arms, loans, and investment, for mineral resources and political allegiance. China imports about 75 percent of the world's traded iron ore (Radio Free Asia reported on

---

[228] Ibid.

[229] https://thediplomat.com/2021/06/the-middle-east-an-emerging-market-for-chinese-arms-exports/

[230] https://www.mei.edu/publications/saudi-arabias-nuclear-program-and-china

June 25, 2021) and 60 percent of its copper from Latin America. Beijing repays the favor and strengthens relationships by providing those countries with military hardware and training.

The Bolivarian Alliance for the Peoples of Our America (ALBA), an association of socialist governments which oppose Washington, were the first buyers of Chinese weapons in the early 2000s. ALBA members include Antigua and Barbuda, Bolivia, Cuba, Dominica, Grenada, Nicaragua, Saint Kitts and Nevis, Saint Lucia, Saint Vincent and the Grenadines, and Venezuela. Autocratic regimes prefer buying Chinese weapons, because, unlike the U.S. or Europe, China sells cheap weapons with no strings attached.

Using ALBA states as a springboard, PRC arms sales spread across the continent. Since then, Venezuela, Ecuador, and Bolivia dramatically increased their Chinese arms purchases. PRC weapons sales to Latin America and the Caribbean were just about zero in 2005, but grew to $130 million by 2014.[231] Sales include not only small arms, but also vehicles and aircraft. In 2008, Venezuela's President Hugo Chavez purchased K-8 military training jets and air search radars from China. Chavez, and his successor Nicolas Maduro, also purchased transport aircraft and self-propelled artillery, as well as the armored personnel carriers that were deployed against protesters in 2014. Today, the largest regional purchasers of Chinese arms are Venezuela, Bolivia, Trinidad and Tobago, Peru, and Ecuador. Venezuela alone, accounts for 85 percent of China's weapons sales to Latin America,[232] and regularly sends military personnel to China for education.

---

[231] https://idsa.in/idsacomments/china-growing-arms-sales-to-latin-america_sbmaharaj_200616

[232] https://chinapower.csis.org/china-global-arms-trade/

The Chinese regime has increased its engagement with Latin America and the Caribbean in terms of economics, trade, investment, geopolitics and influence, convincing many countries to switch recognition from Taiwan to the PRC. According to a 2015 white paper published by the State Council Information Office, military cooperation with the region is the next step in China's global influence strategy.

The CCP has increasingly used the military to promote soft power through "harmless" visits and performances. In 2002, the PLA Navy conducted its first circumnavigation of the globe, calling in Ecuador, Peru, and Brazil. The PLA band performed in Grenada. The PLA's acrobatics team conducted shows in Peru, Ecuador, Guyana, Venezuela, and Bolivia, while PLA fighter jets have flown exhibitions in Chile, Argentina, Peru, and Brazil.

Joint exercises have been another excuse for China to temporarily station its soldiers and ships in the Americas. The PLA conducted its first bilateral military exercise in the region in 2010, dispatching the hospital ship *Peace Ark*, to Peru. China has since sent troops to Latin America to conduct training and to participate in humanitarian missions. PRC military police served as peacekeepers in Haiti as part of a UN force from 2004 through 2012.[233]

Uruguay signed a defense cooperation agreement with the PRC in 2016. And the PRC gave them donations of trucks, ambulances, cars, and bullet proof vests.[234] The CCP also sold Uruguay L-15 fighters and Z-9 helicopters. Numerous Uruguayan officers have attended training at China's National Defense

---

[233] https://theglobalamericans.org/2017/06/panamas-recognition-prc-strategic-implications-recommendations-u-s/

[234] https://theglobalamericans.org/2021/06/uruguay-exemplifies-how-to-deal-with-china/

University in Champing, as well as general staff courses in Nanjing.

Officers from 12 Latin American countries have graduated from PLA academies; by opening courses for junior officers, the CCP regime ensures it can begin building relationships with people who will later hold senior posts. The National Defense University of the PLA has hosted officers from Latin America. The Defense Studies Institute, in Changping near Beijing, has a school especially for foreign military. Chile has been sending officers there since 1997, while Uruguayans began attending in 2009. Other countries whose officers were educated there include Mexico, Peru, and Colombia. The Army Command College in Nanjing has been attended by officers from Colombia, Peru, Barbados, and Jamaica. The Chinese Navy Command School, outside of Nanjing, has taught officers from Uruguay and Brazil. Uruguayans also attended a five-month special forces course in Shijiazhuang. Chilean marines trained at the Center of Military Instruction.

PLA personnel are manning at least three Soviet-era monitoring facilities in Cuba: Lourdes, Bejucal, and Santiago de Cuba, and a Chinese company is in the process of purchasing an island, off the coast of El Salvador, where they hope to build a shipping port, NBC reported on September 4, 2021. The PRC's building and acquisition of ports around the work concerns U.S. defense experts, who worry that these harbors could be designed as dual-use ports, large enough to accommodate PLA Navy warships.

The Arms Race in Space

The terrestrial arms race has morphed into Space Wars as China and the U.S. race for control of the moon, satellite orbits, and

Mars. "[China] is the only country with both the intent to reshape the international order and increasingly the economic, diplomatic, military and technological power to achieve that objective," Reuters (November 28, 2022) quoted Lieutenant-General Nina Armagno, then director of staff of the U.S. Space Force, as saying during a presentation at the Australian Strategic Policy Institute.

At the start of 2023, NASA Administrator Bill Nelson II warned that China could try to claim the resource-rich areas of the moon.[235] In a May 17, 2022 report, Malcolm Davis, a space policy researcher at the Australian Strategic Policy Institute warned that "You could have a Chinese company on the moon in the 2030s claiming territory with a resource on it in the same way the Chinese have claimed the entire South China Sea."

There is also a danger of the CCP staking out the most desirable orbits and radio frequencies. Furthermore, Nelson said that he is concerned China could set up scientific research operations on desirable tracts of moon land and claim sovereignty over them. In 2021, the Chinese regime set up an Earth-orbiting space station and has conducted several missions where they orbited the moon and retrieved samples. In 2025, Beijing plans to establish an autonomous lunar research station near the south pole of the moon.

In addition to extracting economic profits, Beijing has strategic reasons for wanting to win the space race. Armagno told the Australian Strategic Policy Institute that she is concerned that China will catch up and pass the U.S., and that they could militarize space. According to the general, the regime is developing military space technology in the areas of satellite

---

[235] https://www.politico.com/news/2023/01/01/we-better-watch-out-nasa-boss-sounds-alarm-on-chinese-moon-ambitions-00075803

communications, reusable spacecraft, and suborbital and orbital spacecraft.

In late 2022, China Aerospace Science and Technology Corporation (CASC) Chairman Wu Yansheng outlined the country's space goals, including concepts for a manned landing on the moon, creating space-transportation infrastructure, on-orbit servicing, as well as their vision for space governance, space law, and space domain awareness.[236]

China's overall moon and space strategy focuses on developing domestic capabilities rather than depending on international cooperation.[237] CASC completed and launched the Tiangong space station in 2022. Over the next 10 to 15 years, Beijing plans to complete three Chang'e robotic landing missions and establish the International Lunar Research Station. One of the unmanned missions to Mars is supposed to return with samples. Beijing is seeking partners for its lunar base, but the U.S. — which is leading the Artemis program of lunar exploration — will not be invited.

Xi Jinping's vision is for China to be the world's number-one aerospace power by 2030 and to become a fully comprehensive space power by 2045.[238] The realization of this vision will require efficient low-cost space transportation, a focus on exploration, and an expansion of national civil space infrastructure combining telecommunications, navigation and satellite constellations with global coverage. Colonizing the moon and Mars is still a long way into the future, but China and Russia

---

[236] https://spacenews.com/china-sets-out-clear-and-independent-long-term-vision-for-space/

[237] https://www.theguardian.com/science/2023/jan/02/china-moon-nasa-space-race

[238] https://spacenews.com/china-sets-out-clear-and-independent-long-term-vision-for-space/

already have killer satellites which can destroy U.S. satellites and wreak havoc among ground forces.[239]

To counter Beijing's space ambitions, the Trump administration established the U.S. Space Force in 2019 as a branch of the United States military. It comes under the U.S. Air Force, with a relationship similar to the one between the Marine Corps and the U.S. Navy. In December 2022, the Space Force activated its first overseas command, in South Korea, to oversee space operations in the Indo-Pacific.[240]

The United States is now locked in a space race with China, rather like the contest with the Soviets several decades ago. For reputation and prestige, the Soviet Union and the U.S. were competing to first put a man in space and later to put a man on the moon. The stakes with China are much higher. The new space race is not about bragging rights, but rather about claiming dominion over the moon and Mars. Dominating space may be the deciding factor in future wars, as modern armies depend on satellites for communication, navigation, and guiding missiles.

The Defense Appropriations Bill for 2023 includes $26.3 billion in funding for the Space Force.[241] The U.S. chip ban has been expanded to cover space technology and Chinese aerospace companies have been added to the blacklist. An August 23, 2022 press release from the Commerce Department's Bureau of Industry and Security quoted Under-Secretary of Commerce for Industry and Security Alan Estevez as saying: "U.S. technologies that

---

[239] https://www.fierceelectronics.com/electronics/how-us-space-force-views-threats-russia-and-china
[240] https://www.spaceforce.mil/News/Article/3249547/space-force-activates-component-field-command-for-us-forces-korea/
[241] https://spacenews.com/congress-adds-1-7-billion-for-u-s-space-force-in-2023-spending-bill/

support space and aerospace activities should not be used to support the PRC's military modernization."

The Final Battleground?

In *Star Wars*, *Flash Gordon* and other science-fiction movies, space weapons are laser cannons, ion guns, blasters, and phasers which shoot impressive rays of light energy and blow up whatever they hit. However, the reality of space wars would be, "low-moving rendezvous robot satellites, ground-based electronic jammers, and cyber weapons and lasers designed to disable satellites without producing space debris," according to the Bulletin of Atomic Scientists.[242]

Unlike in movies, much of the threat in space will come from the ground by way of terrestrial control centers issuing orders to space-based assets. It will probably not entail battles between government spacecraft, but rather utility hardware, owned and operated by private companies, with peaceful missions. A debris-clearing satellite, the property of a company in Palo Alto or Shenzhen, might be commanded from Earth to damage, defuel, or disrupt the trajectory, or operation of a satellite from another country.[243] Rather than firing an ion cannon, a Chinese space asset could simply disable a U.S. or Japanese satellite, making it difficult for allied militaries on Earth to navigate or fire effectively. And the defense against these attacks would be to use bodyguard satellites to gently push the offenders away.

The May 30, 2022 launch of two NASA astronauts into space under the agency's Commercial Crew Program marked a return to the U.S. transporting its own people into space without depending on Russia. Launches to low-Earth orbits can now be carried out by American private firms at competitive prices.

---

[242] https://thebulletin.org/premium/2022-01/a-china-us-war-in-space-the-after-action-report/
[243] Ibid.

Consequently, in addition to no longer being dependent on foreign countries for space assistance, NASA can now focus on its longer-term goal of launching Americans into deeper space.

The Chinese Space Agency frequently captures headlines heralding China's achievements in Space. Apart from the Chang'e-5 landing on the moon, China managed to land a rover called Zhurong on Mars in 2021. However, China is a latecomer to the space race. The U.S. sent its first unmanned mission to the moon in 1962, followed by a manned mission in 1969. Chinese unmanned craft reached Mars in 2020, a feat NASA achieved in 1964, while the first U.S. craft to land on Mars was Viking 1 in 1975.[244] Currently, the U.S. has almost 3,000 satellites orbiting the Earth, or nearly six times as many as China.

Many of the media stories released by the CCP tout grand plans for Chinese landers, space launchers, moon bases, and manned missions to the moon and to Mars.[245] So far, these are just aspirations. The U.S. expects to return to the moon with a manned mission in 2024 or 2025, and have a permanent presence on the moon by 2028.

Washington blocked China's participation in the International Space Station, and a 2011 U.S. law prohibits NASA from partnering with China. The U.S. wants to establish a NATO-like organization to regulate the use of space and space assets. At the same time, U.S. officials have outlined the Artemis Accord, an expansion of the 1967 Outer Space Treaty. Neither Russia nor China have shown any willingness to join the accord; Japan, South

---

[244] https://www.space.com/13558-historic-mars-missions.html
[245] https://www.cnbc.com/2021/06/24/china-plans-to-send-its-first-crewed-mission-to-mars-in-2033.html

Korea, Australia, the UK, Saudi Arabia, and a number of other nations have already signed up.[246]

Even though the U.S is far ahead on some scorecards, China already possesses the capacity to wage a space war, VOA reported on April 2, 2022. Satellites in space can be used to surveil military hardware on the ground, at sea, or even detect submarines in the ocean. Space assets could also help Beijing coordinate missile attacks on Earth. Chinese militarization of space is consistent with the 2019 defense white paper published by the State Council Information Office. Apart from the economic benefits of mining the moon, one of the primary uses of Chinese space weapons could be to aid the PLA Navy in taking control of the South China Sea or invading Taiwan.

Beijing officially opposes the weaponization of space, but it appears to have constructed ground-based missiles that can hit a satellite in orbit.[247] China and Russia have jointly urged an agreement to limit space weapons, yet U.S. experts caution that this proposal is designed to prevent the U.S. from implementing missile defense systems, Asia Nikkei reported on September 9, 2021. Senior officers in the U.S. Space Force have warned that China seeks space superiority through space attack systems, and that the Chinese regime is the biggest threat to security in space.

The CCP regime denies the existence of space weapons, although they used an anti-satellite system to destroy a weather satellite 500 miles (800 kilometers) above the Earth, BBC reported on January 23, 2007. The implementation of dual-use technology is one way in which the PRC can obscure their militaristic intentions in space. Many of the PRC satellites are meant to have

---

[246] https://www.bloomberg.com/news/features/2022-05-17/china-us-are-in-a-space-race-to-make-billions-from-mining-the-moon-s-minerals
[247] https://spacenews.com/pentagon-report-china-amassing-arsenal-of-anti-satellite-weapons/

civilian applications, but can also be used by the PLA. Dual-use technologies include the BeiDou constellation, which allows the PLA to avoid dependence on American GPS systems. This also means that in the event of a war, China would not hesitate to destroy American GPS capabilities, leaving the U.S. military with no means of satellite navigation.

U.S. military operations strategies rely on digital communication and the ability to remotely coordinate and control weapons systems. Aircraft carriers, submarines, fifth-generation fighters, tanks, and missiles are all dependent on digital communications. The outcome of the next war may well be determined in the first few days, when one side takes out the other side's communication satellites.[248]

Because orbital satellites are critical to U.S. operations, U.S. satellite networks are prime targets.[249] Consequently, China's space weapons include satellite jammers and directed-energy weapons, as well as earth-based lasers that can damage or blind a satellite in orbit. China's counterspace capabilities include "kinetic-kill missiles, ground-based lasers, orbiting space robots, and space surveillance" to monitor both earth and space.[250]

The Chinese regime has steadily been increasing spending on space to almost $12 billion in 2022.[251] In addition to building satellites and launch vehicles, the PRC is testing new technologies, such as the world's first quantum communications satellite.

[248] https://asia.nikkei.com/Politics/International-relations/US-China-tensions/China-can-grapple-US-satellites-with-robotic-arm-commander-says

[249] https://interestingengineering.com/us-space-force-chief-warns-china-could-use-satellite-killers

[250] https://spacenews.com/pentagon-report-china-amassing-arsenal-of-anti-satellite-weapons/

[251] https://www.statista.com/statistics/745717/global-governmental-spending-on-space-programs-leading-countries/

Among China's space weapons is a satellite with a robotic arm, which could attack or disable enemy satellites.

China established the Strategic Support Force,[252] which is specifically focused on disabling enemy satellites, and preventing other countries from connecting weapons systems and sharing data and information. China is reportedly building GPS jammers, as well as jammers for communications satellites, to prevent U.S. vessels from linking up or communicating.

The regime claims its activities in space — which in 2021 included landing a probe on Mars and launching the primary stage of what will become China's first manned space station — are peaceful. Yet Beijing has run drills which experts believe simulate co-orbital satellite attacks, and they are suspected of already having satellites armed with lasers. Satellite-attacks are a particular vulnerability of the United States, as the U.S. accounts for roughly 56 percent of all satellites orbiting the Earth. The U.S. military relies on these satellites more than any other military, because of the need to coordinate and communicate with a massive armed forces network deployed across the globe. Attacking satellites is a logical first strike, to prevent the U.S. Army, Navy, and Air Force from being able to respond to attacks on Earth.

In August 2021, China tested its capability to launch a hypersonic boost-glide vehicle (HGV).[253] Such vehicles can achieve speeds of at least Mach 5 (1 mile per second). HGV missiles, armed with ballistic reentry vehicles, are able to change course after being released from their rocket boosters. China has developed an HGV known as the DF-ZF, which it has tested at least nine times since 2014. The DF-ZF could be equipped with a

---

[252] https://asia.nikkei.com/Politics/International-relations/US-China-tensions/China-can-grapple-US-satellites-with-robotic-arm-commander-says
[253] https://breakingdefense.com/2021/10/us-must-build-space-superhighway-before-china-stakes-claims-senior-space-force-officer/

conventional warhead, and its extreme maneuverability may make it capable of evading U.S. ballistic missile defenses. When equipped with the DF-17 booster, it could travel 1,800 to 2,500 kilometers (1,100 to more than 1,500 miles).

The PRC space war plan also includes cyberattacks and ground forces which could knock out U.S. control centers. The PLA is thought to have been behind a 2021 cyberattack which hit 200 Japanese companies and research institutes, including the Japan Aerospace Exploration Agency.[254]

A defensive strategy for the U.S. would be to have many smaller satellites, rather than a few large, expensive ones. Smaller ones would be harder to hunt and destroy. On September 9, 2021, Asia Nikkei reported that the chief of the U.S. Space Force urged allied cooperation and intelligence sharing to counter China. One issue with a coalition strategy is that most U.S. allies fall far behind the United States, China, and Russia in terms of space-wars capabilities. Currently, the U.S. is the only country with an independent military branch dedicated to space operations.

---

[254] https://www.japantimes.co.jp/news/2021/04/20/national/chinese-military-japan-cyberattacks/

5

The Economic Dimension

A country's economic power encompasses its financial resources, budget, industrial base, and economic stability. The economic condition of a country has direct implications for its ability to conduct a war, as it must be able to fund its military while ensuring that citizens have sufficient food and other services. The U.S. economic system is capitalist, whereas the old Soviet Union had a communist-socialist system often referred to as central planning.

A capitalist system utilizes currency as a medium of exchange, a store of value, and a unit of account. Citizens have the right to own property, partake in economic activities, and engage in buying and selling. Furthermore, the market, comprising the total population of buyers and sellers within the country, determines the quantity, types of products, and their prices. The term "free market" is employed because, for the most part, the government allows the private sector to self-regulate. While taxes exist — and some restrictions such as minimum wage, licensing, and insurance requirements are in place — citizens are predominantly free to establish businesses and offer their goods or services at prices they choose. Labor mobility is a key feature, granting citizens the freedom to switch jobs, relocate, or even opt out of the workforce if they so desire. In this system, resources, goods, and services are distributed to the highest bidder within the market.

In a pure communist or socialist system, currency does not exist. Salaries are uniform and are frequently provided in the form of goods or exchange vouchers. The government maintains ownership of all property and enterprises, and exercises control over the means of production, dictating the types and quantities of products produced. Citizens lack the freedom to switch jobs or discontinue work at will. Additionally, the government determines the distribution of goods and the recipients of such products. Until the 1970s, China's system was one of strict communism or socialism. Today, China's economy represents a blend of capitalist and socialist elements.

Market Socialism with Chinese Characteristics

In recent decades, the CCP has boasted about having lifted hundreds of millions of people out of poverty, but they were only able to do this because, for much of its rule, they had hundreds of millions of people living in poverty. From the founding of the PRC in 1949, until the economic reforms of the late 1970s, the economy was nearly 100-percent centrally planned. This meant that the regime controlled the factors of production, determined what products were made and in what quantities and at what price. As a result, the country stayed very poor.

In 1978, China's GDP per capita was $156 per year. That year, GDP per capita in the U.S. was $10,564.[255] Between its economic opening and 2010, China experienced double-digit GDP growth in most years, according to World Bank data. From 2010 to the present, however, the PRC's growth rate has been trending steadily downward. Although China is the world's number-two economy, Chinese people are still relatively poor. The average income in China in 2022 was $12,823,[256] roughly the same as the

---

[255] https://datacommons.org/place/country/USA/
[256] https://www.statista.com/statistics/263775/gross-domestic-product-gdp-per-capita-in-china/

U.S. in 1980. China has worked toward reducing wealth disparity, but roughly half the population still survives on less than $10 per day.[257]

The rule of Mao Zedong from 1949 to his death in 1976 was marked by a strict communist economy with almost no profit incentives nor private ownership. His economic policy, the Great Leap Forward, which lasted from 1958 to 1962, resulted in the Great Famine, which killed up to 45 million people.[258] After Mao's death, Deng Xiaoping, paramount leader from 1978 to 1989, gradually opened up the economy, launching China's exceptional growth.

During China's greatest years of economic development, the economy became more liberal each year. Deng made it clear when he ordered the Tiananmen Square massacre in 1989, however, that economic liberalization and the liberalization of civil society are distinct concepts. The same year, the CCP banned entrepreneurs from joining the party; not until 2001 would business owners be allowed to become members (*Washington Post*, July 2, 2001). Liberalization peaked around 2012, when Xi Jinping, the current leader, took office. Since then, the country has been reverting to a more restrictive form of Market Socialism.

Xi Jinping — who holds the three highest positions in the regime, including president of the PRC — has been recognized by the CCP as the nation's paramount leader. After term limits for the presidency were removed, he was in 2022 given a third term as party secretary, president,[259] and chairman of the Central Military Commission. Presumably, he will have an option of ruling for life,

---

[257] https://chinapower.csis.org/china-middle-class/
[258] https://www.investopedia.com/terms/g/great-leap-forward.asp
[259] https://apnews.com/article/xi-jinping-china-president-vote-5e6230d8c881dc17b11a781e832accd1

although the CCP denies this. In 2013, Xi launched his vision for a China-led world order, through the Belt and Road Initiative (BRI). This global infrastructure development program now encompasses 148 nations as well as China.[260] BRI projects include roads, seaports, airports, telecommunications, hospitals, energy, and mineral extraction.

These projects are financed through a variety of sources, including loans from Chinese policy banks such as the China Development Bank and the Export-Import Bank of China, Chinese commercial banks, and investments from Chinese enterprises. Banks and companies associated with financing the BRI are completely or part owned by the government. China's four largest commercial banks — Industrial and Commercial Bank of China (ICBC), China Construction Bank (CCB), Bank of China (BOC), and Agricultural Bank of China (ABC) — are state owned. Smaller and regional banks tend to be part owned and controlled by the state. Additionally, many of the companies involved with these overseas projects are state-owned enterprises (SOEs).

Socialism with Chinese characteristics can be described as state-led capitalism. While the economy has undergone market-oriented reforms, the state maintains significant control. In 1978, Deng Xiaoping established the household responsibility system. Under it, once farmers had met their state quota, they could sell surpluses at a profit. In 1980, private enterprise in non-agricultural sectors began. In the same year, the first special economic zone (SEZ) was established in Shenzhen, Guangdong Province, facilitating trade between China and the outside world. This began China's march toward export-oriented growth, with China becoming the world's factory.

---

[260] https://greenfdc.org/countries-of-the-belt-and-road-initiative-bri/

The next phase of development, from about 1999, was investment-driven growth which relied on government investment. This period was characterized by infrastructure development projects, including the construction of roads, bridges, railways, and airports. Construction projects accelerated as the population urbanized. In 2007, China implemented its first private property law.[261] Combined with the government's investment strategy, it led to a boom in the housing sector. Today, real estate accounts makes up 30 percent of the overall economy

There are no independent labor unions in China, as all unions fall under the CCP-affiliated All-China Federation of Trade Unions. The CCP also maintains SOEs which account for about 25 percent of the GDP.[262] SOEs operate in all sectors, such as manufacturing, mineral extraction, and banking, but the government also owns hotels and restaurants. The CCP appoints managers and supervisors of SOEs and directs their decision-making. In return, SOEs receive a number of benefits such as state subsidies, easier access to capital from state-owned banks, as well as raw materials from state-owned mining companies. SOEs also get policy support, tax benefits, a favorable regulatory framework, and more. With these government-provided advantages, SOEs dominate strategic sectors such as energy, telecommunications, banking, and transportation.

Private companies of a certain size are required to maintain a party cell, a CCP committee responsible for implementing and maintaining party policies, adherence to political ideology, and party discipline. Party committees exert influence over decision-making and strategic planning, as well as the hiring, firing, and promoting of personnel. Even foreign-owned companies and joint ventures and partnerships with foreign companies are required to

---

[261] https://papers.ssrn.com/sol3/papers.cfm?abstract_id=1084363
[262] https://www.lowyinstitute.org/the-interpreter/has-china-given-state-owned-enterprise-reform

maintain a party cell, (CNBC, July 12, 2023). Furthermore, the regime maintains lists of sectors completely prohibited to foreign companies, as well as sectors where foreign companies are permitted, but only within the context of a joint venture with a Chinese partner.

China's entire economy is strategically mapped out through a series of Five-Year Plans. The CCP not only sets annual growth targets, but stipulates through its Five-Year plans how it wants the economy to grow and which sectors will be prioritized. Party control of both domestic and foreign companies means that Beijing can influence investment decisions, resource allocation, and business strategies, to aid the state in achieving its goals.

The 14th Five-Year Plan, which runs from 2021 to 2025, is focused on "innovation and leading high-quality development."[263] With a fertility rate of just 1.705 births per woman,[264] China is facing an aging crisis. The only way the shrinking workforce will be able to maintain the economy is if the country shifts into higher value-added manufacturing and services. At the same time, China is pricing itself out of the low-end manufacturing labor market. Factory workers in China now earn three or four times more than their counterparts in Vietnam or Indonesia. For this reason, the 14th Five-Year Plan is aimed at "upgrading of the industrial base and the modernization of industry chains."

Developing higher-value manufacturing is dependent on receiving foreign investment, which is trending downward. In some sectors, like electronics, FDI was down 56.7 percent between 2019 and 2022.[265] Investors are being scared off by a general economic slowdown, tensions with the U.S., and possible war with

---

[263] https://digichina.stanford.edu/work/translation-14th-five-year-plan-for-national-informatization-dec-2021/
[264] https://www.macrotrends.net/countries/CHN/china/fertility-rate
[265] https://www.investmentmonitor.ai/insights/chinas-fdi-decline-foreign-companies-covid-geopolitics/?cf-view

Taiwan. China's new Counter-Espionage Law is further spooking investors and visitors, as the potential for arbitrary detention has been dramatically increased.

Despite facing economic headwinds, the CCP continues to tighten its hold. The 14th Five-Year Plan contains a reminder of the power of the party, which will "forcefully develop the digital economy," while Beijing aims to use "data-based national governance capabilities and transform the structural advantages of Socialism with Chinese Characteristics into powerful national governance abilities." For all of China's reforms, the country is still largely socialist and veering toward greater state control, even at the expense of prosperity.

Socialist Economic Slogans

In 2012, Xi Jinping told the Chinese people "only socialism can save China." Although it was capitalism that dramatically increased the country's living standards, Xi is leading the country back to the stricter socialism that kept China poor for decades.

Deng Xiaoping said that "to get rich is glorious," which was consistent with his 1978 program of "reform and opening up."[266] By opening its markets to the world, and by allowing the economy to be driven by market forces, the PRC was able to create a tremendous middle class and the largest number of billionaires in the world. The "go out policy," which began in 1999, promoted outward direct investment (ODI).[267] It also encouraged Chinese companies to go abroad and learn from foreign firms, all of which resulted in China becoming the world's second richest country.

Xi's return to greater socialist controls, turning away from the world, and cracking down on market forces suggests that he has forgotten how China became rich in the first place. The

---

[266] https://www.bbc.com/news/world-asia-china-24923993
[267] https://www.cigionline.org/publications/deeper-look-chinas-going-out-policy/

country's economic "miracle" did not come from central planning, but rather from opening the country to free market ideas, basic economic principles, and allowing the private sector to grow organically, Michael Schuman rightly argued in *The Atlantic* (January 11, 2021). This accelerated the country's development, causing incomes to soar. But now, Xi is tightening the CCP's grip over the economy, as he replaces sound economics with socialist slogans. He is pledging to decrease the wealth gap by "dividing the cake well,"[268] rather than by instituting economic policies which help the poor increase their wealth.

Xi Jinping Thought on Socialist Economy with Chinese Characteristics for a New Era is Xi's key work, and he is the first leader since Mao to have his ideas entered into the party's constitution. Even the name of his collected musings is itself an ideological slogan, referring to the country's system as socialism with market characteristics.[269] In practice, the system has become state-capitalism with socialist characteristics, where large state-loyal companies are favored and controlled, while private enterprise and upstarts are restricted and suppressed.

In June 2021, the first Xi Jinping Thought Center was opened. Two others soon followed, to focus on the study of Xi Jinping's economic ideas. At least 18 research centers have been dedicated to facets of Xi's thinking, such as politics, culture, science, education, religion, diplomacy, economics, and national security, *The Economist* reported on August 28, 2021.

Xi Thought promises, "to ensure that the market plays a decisive role in the allocation of resources." This is consistent with a market economy, but it also stresses "the need to strengthen the

---

[268] https://www.washingtonpost.com/politics/2021/10/22/xi-jinping-wants-common-prosperity-china-thats-going-mean-government-crackdowns/
[269] http://www.xinhuanet.com/english/2020-12/21/c_139607721.htm

party's centralized and unified leadership over economic work"[270] which is suggestive of greater central planning and tighter controls. The cornerstone of Xi Jinping Thought is The Four Comprehensives,[271] which together, are meant to build socialism with Chinese characteristics. They are: 1. Building a moderately prosperous society; 2. Deepening reform; 3. Governing the nation according to law; and 4. Tightening party discipline. It is interesting to note that of the four, only one, building a moderately prosperous society, deals with economics. It is also the only one which promises a reward to the populace. The other three are Xi's pledge for more government control.

The version of Market Socialism that Xi promotes has a set of core values: "prosperity, democracy, civility and harmony;[272] societal values of freedom, equality, justice and rule of law; and the citizenship values of patriotism, dedication, integrity and friendship." But in a country with ever-intensifying state surveillance, and where people's lives can be ruined by a downgrade of their social credit score, citizens are steadily losing their freedoms. Similarly, the CCP claims to be dedicated to democracy, but the country is effectively a one-party system.

The mantra of socialism with Chinese characteristics allowed the CCP enough latitude to support business and economic growth, on the one hand, while maintaining restrictions over basic liberties on the other. This system has held up, more or less, since 1978. Xi, however, has clearly decided to rein in, not only the private economic sector, but also the private sphere of citizens' lives. Xi has instituted a three-hour limit for children playing video games. He has banned "sissy looking" boys from TV and other

---

[270] Ibid.
[271] https://journals.openedition.org/chinaperspectives/7872
[272] https://www.scmp.com/news/china/politics/article/3137393/communist-party-jargon-tigers-and-flies-chinese-dream-10

media.[273] And he wants the people to return to a common set of socialist values and morality.

According to Xinhua (November 12, 2020), a government mouthpiece, Xi said, "The advantage of a big economy lies in its advantage of domestic circulation." This is just a euphemism for turning away from the world economy. Rather than exports, Xi is now urging the people to focus on a domestic demand-driven economy, while he is simultaneously impeding that economy from working.

"The economy is a dynamic circulating system that cannot afford a long-term disruption," Xinhua quoted Xi as saying — Xi, the same man who adopted a zero-Covid policy and shut down parts of the Chinese and global economies for nearly two years. The damage Xi is doing to China is spilling over to the rest of the world. Unless Xi releases his grip, the economy cannot recover. Until then, his Market Socialism slogans are just meaningless double-speak.

To commemorate the 72nd anniversary of the founding of the PRC, the CCP issued a letter, extolling "the six fronts (employment, finance, foreign trade, foreign investment, domestic investment and market expectations) and guaranteeing the six priorities (jobs, livelihoods, development of market entities, food and energy security, stable operation of industrial supply chains, and smooth functioning at the community level)." But this comes as Xi is cracking down on the financial sector, restricting foreign trade, and generally moving the Chinese economy away from market influence towards one of social and central planning. Additionally, in spite of the message's guarantees, China is facing supply-chain interruptions, as well as food and energy shortages, largely because of policy decisions taken by Xi and the CCP.

---

[273] https://www.bbc.com/news/business-58579831

Some of Xi's slogans are not particularly unusual. Others, such as "the Chinese Dream," are stolen from the West, but transformed into something quite distinct. The American dream is an individual dream of pulling yourself up by your bootstraps, in the context of having the freedom to make your own destiny. The Chinese dream, by contrast, is a collectivist dream of strengthening the country and "rejuvenation," which Xi claims refers to returning China to its former place as a world leader.[274]

"Common prosperity" is a slogan, defined with another slogan, "successfully building a comprehensive well-off society" (*South China Morning Post*, September 12, 2021). One would imagine that education would be a significant part of common prosperity, but this is one area that Xi is cutting. China's private tutoring sector was valued at $120 billion, but upon the announcement of Xi's crackdown on the industry, $67 billion of stock value was erased in 48 hours.[275] The market for English classes, once the largest component of private tuition, has been decimated. Without these supplemental English classes, China and Chinese people will be even less equipped to engage with the world, one more sign of the country turning inward.

Xi's policy of restricting civil and economic life has mockingly been dubbed "the Red New Deal" (The China Project, September 9, 2021). Aspects of private enterprise and personal freedoms which Xi is limiting include fintech, social media, celebrities and fan clubs, people with "excessively high incomes," gaming companies, ride-hailing and bike-sharing, Bitcoin mining, most aspects of the real-estate sector, virtual reality, and high frequency stock trading. The abolition of these, and other activities which Xi dislikes, are meant to help build a "harmonious society."

---

[274] https://www.bbc.com/news/world-asia-china-29788802
[275] https://www.institutmontaigne.org/en/expressions/xi-jinpings-new-political-economy-part-2

During Mao's time, there was a slogan, "Attack local tyrants, divide up the farmland." Today, Xi calls it "wealth redistribution," a component of "common prosperity," meant to make people more equal in one of the most unequal of the world's major economies.[276] Wealth distribution in practice is a crackdown on billionaires and celebrities who represent "incorrect political positions" (The China Project, September 9, 2021).

Xi said people with high incomes should give back more to society, both through charitable giving and through higher taxes (CNBC, August 18, 2021). To this end, he has curbed, what he considers, "excessively high incomes" and purged high-profile rich people. It remains unclear, however, how arresting, fining, or otherwise punishing the wealthy can make the poor better off.

"Domestic-international dual circulation"[277] is another socialist slogan which, on the surface, seems balanced. In strict terms, it just means focusing on both the domestic economy and global trade. In practice, however, it means focusing less on exports and more on domestic consumption. It is one more euphemism for China turning inward. U.S. tariffs and a general trend of foreign manufacturing firms leaving China may be reasons for this policy.

Whatever the reason for dual circulation, it is ironic that Xi was telling people to focus on the internal economy during the Covid-19 lockdowns, a time when he was restricting all sorts of domestic non-exporting businesses and services, such as restaurants, tourism, hairdressers, gyms, nightclubs, bars, and cinemas. He was espousing the benefits of an economy driven by domestic consumption of services, yet the part of the economy

---

[276] https://www.theguardian.com/world/2021/sep/02/xi-jinpings-drive-for-economic-equality-comes-at-a-delicate-moment-for-china
[277] https://www.atlanticcouncil.org/blogs/econographics/dual-circulation-in-china-a-progress-report/

worst hit by Xi's "crippling" (*Financial Times*, June 2, 2022) zero-Covid policies was the service sector.

"Chief of industrial chains," one of Xi's slogans,[278] means that local and provincial governments are responsible for "streamlining industrial supply chains" particularly those affected by the trade war. In practice, this policy resulted in quotas being thrust upon local governments. And in order to meet those quotas, local governments took any number of shortsighted decisions, many of which added to their debt. China's local government debt, including bonds and "hidden debt" (shadowy opaque loans taken through shell companies) was estimated at $47 trillion as of the end of 2020.[279]

Another Xi-ism is: "Houses are for living in, not speculation." This was meant to discourage people from investing in property. The policy was introduced in 2017 and yet, in 2021, families had 70 percent of their multi-generational wealth tied up in real estate.[280] At the time of writing, the real estate issue was not close to being solved.

"One bank, one policy" could be interpreted as a standardization of policies across banks. In practice, however, it seems to mean that as local banks falter under a mountain of bad debt due to murky off-balance sheet transactions, the government is picking and choosing which banks it will bail out and which it will allow to fail.[281] With bailouts, there is always the risk of moral hazard: By helping out a struggling financial institution, the government is rewarding it for bad or risky behavior. Bailouts send

---

[278] https://www.scmp.com/economy/china-economy/article/3148106/chinas-economic-buzzwords-explained-common-prosperity-dual
[279] https://finance.yahoo.com/news/china-debt-concerns-mounting-beijing-093000830.html
[280] https://www.ncbi.nlm.nih.gov/pmc/articles/PMC4589866/
[281] https://www.bloomberg.com/view/articles/2020-10-27/china-s-failing-small-banks-are-becoming-a-big-problem

a signal to other banks that they need not fear taking imprudent risks, because the authorities will rescue them. In addition to bailouts, the CCP regime has taken other steps, such as mergers allowing banks to restructure and reorganize, and even permitting unlisted small lenders, regardless of their financial distress,[282] to raise capital through private placements of equity.

The overarching economic slogan which steers the new Chinese economy is that the CCP wishes to "guide" private companies to explore "a modern enterprise system with Chinese characteristics" (*The Atlantic*, January 11, 2021). The party wants greater control over decisions taken by companies, to ensure they follow a correct, state-determined line. As a result, state-owned enterprises are expanding, consuming a greater proportion of resources, including bank loans, while gobbling up private companies, and decreasing the private sector's share of economic output.

One reason for the hype that has surrounded "Xiconomics"[283] is to convince the Chinese people that Xi is an all-knowing master of many fields, including public policy, rule of law, diplomacy, state-craft, and economics. Yet the exact details of what the CCP believes is a new economic discipline are not yet known. *People's Daily* (March 19, 2018) lauded Xi's work on supply-side structural reform as a driver of growth. So perhaps this could be Xiconomics, except that it makes very little sense. Supply-side economics seeks to increase output and employment by decreasing government involvement in the economy and giving more financial and business freedom to the private sector. In short, this is the exact opposite of Xi's approach, which is characterized

---

[282] Ibid.

[283] https://www.scmp.com/economy/china-economy/article/3140057/economic-thought-chinas-xi-jinping-be-immortalised-newly

by tighter controls on the private sector and a growing role for the public sector.

So far, Xiconomics seems more like a publicity stunt than an actual economic theory. It is reminiscent of North Korea's Juche economics, one of many areas of unrivaled expertise attributed to Eternal Leader Kim Il-sung. Comparing North Korea to South Korea, one could arrive at the conclusion that Juche did not work very well.

PRC Economic Data

China is an upper-middle income country with a population of 1.4 billion (according to official data), a GDP of about $17.3 trillion,[284] foreign reserves of over $3 trillion,[285] and a per capita GDP in 2022 of $12,823. The country's development is extremely uneven, however, with nearly a quarter of the population still living on less than $5.50 per day[286] and 40 percent remaining poor. Urban dwellers earn more than double the rural dwellers.

The 8-percent GDP growth which China enjoyed most years from the 1980s until the pandemic has slowed dramatically, with 2022 recording approximately 3 percent, and the IMF (November 10, 2023) projecting 5.4 percent for 2023. It is worth noting that a significant psychological threshold for GDP growth in China has traditionally been set at 5 percent, along with an expectation that the currency should not reach a valuation of 7 Chinese yuan (CNY) to 1 U.S. dollar (USD). As of November 2023, the exchange rate for the yuan stands at 7.14 CNY to 1 USD, a notable shift since 2019 when it was consistently in the very high

---

[284] https://datacommons.org/place/country/CHN/
[285] https://tradingeconomics.com/china/foreign-exchange-reserves
[286] https://www.statista.com/chart/25138/people-under-poverty-line-china/

6s or above 7. China's central bank has been selling off its U.S. dollar holdings in record amounts,[287] prompting speculation about whether China is de-dollarizing or if Beijing is trying to prop up the yuan.

Global Comparisons

The IMD World Competitiveness Index (WCI) measures the competitiveness of countries based on 333 criteria, grouped under the broad categories of economic performance, government efficiency, business efficiency, and infrastructure. The 2023 WCI ranks the United States at 9th and China at 21st in the world (IMD Communications Department, June 20, 2023).

The Heritage Foundation has awarded China an economic freedom score of 48.3, positioning it 154th out of 178 countries assessed.[288] This places the PRC's economic freedom significantly below that of many other nations. This assessment is based on four key categories: rule of law, government size, regulatory efficiency, and open markets.

Within the regulatory efficiency category, business freedom is scored at 68.3, labor freedom at 55.2, and monetary freedom at 72.5. China's regulatory framework as a whole continues to be complex and inconsistent. Business-related regulations and labor codes are often arbitrary and subject to frequent revisions, leaving the private sector vulnerable to the regime's unpredictable decisions. In terms of open markets, trade freedom gets 73.6, investment freedom 20, and financial freedom 20. The trade-weighted average tariff rate imposed by Beijing stands at 3.2 percent, and various layers of non-tariff measures are in effect. The approval process for foreign investment, marked by

---

[287] https://finance.yahoo.com/news/china-sells-most-us-assets-223331094.html
[288] https://www.heritage.org/index/country/china#regulatory-efficiency

protectionist tendencies, remains stringent and lacks transparency. The government maintains a firm control over the financial system.

The Economist Intelligence Unit has reported that China's ease of doing business experienced one of the most significant deteriorations in 2023, dropping 11 positions in the second-quarter rankings compared to a year earlier.. This deterioration is attributed to increased policy uncertainty, escalating Washington-Beijing tensions, and a more challenging long-term growth outlook. In the latest rankings, China lags behind other markets, including Malaysia, Thailand, Vietnam, Mexico, and India, which are actively seeking manufacturing investment relocation from China. Vietnam and Thailand, offering favorable conditions for foreign investors, are benefiting from the "China Plus One" strategy, which involves diversifying supply chains across both China and another Asian market to manage geopolitical risks. Although easing of the zero-Covid policy is positive for business, regulatory changes stemming from the regime's statist economic direction and increasing local costs pose challenges and limit opportunities for international investors.

Despite China's overall tariff level being reduced to 7.3 percent in 2023,[289] the U.S. Department of Agriculture Economic Research Service (ERS) reported on March 30, 2023 that non-tariff barriers caused substantial price disparities. For instance, domestic prices in China surpass the prices of U.S. imports by significant margins: 57.5 percent for beef, 64 percent for corn, 213 percent for pork, and 42 percent for wheat.

According to the ERS, non-tariff measures hinder China's trade in two primary ways. Initially, they directly curtail the quantity of imports and constrain the availability of goods within the PRC. Moreover, these measures contribute to elevated

---

[289] https://www.china-briefing.com/news/china-import-export-tariffs-in-2023/

domestic prices, thereby stimulating increased domestic production as a substitute for imported goods. As a result of these import restrictions, a common outcome is a "price wedge," in which domestic commodity prices exceed international prices. Price wedges frequently serve as an indicator of the presence of non-tariff trade barriers, particularly when these barriers are hard to detect by other means.

The Made in Country Index, which evaluates a nation's commitment to domestic manufacturing and production, places China 49th, with a score of 28. It assesses the extent to which products are created within a country's borders, and measures the economic impact of manufacturing on GDP and the job market. This index often reflects the effectiveness of government policies and incentives in promoting domestic production and examines the quality and standards maintained in the manufacturing sector. Furthermore, it provides insights into a country's export performance and its integration into global supply chains, making it a valuable tool for assessing a nation's industrial and economic strength.

Debt

China's private debt was 193.69 percent of nominal GDP in June 2023, according to CEIC Data, while the IMF-calculated government debt is 83 percent of GDP. Foreign debt stands at $2.43 trillion. State-owned firms make up 71 percent of Chinese firms on the Global 500 List.[290] SOEs and the government itself together account for 40 percent of the country's GDP, while SOEs are responsible for between 50 percent and 60 percent of total corporate debt (Liberty Street Economics, September 26, 2022). As a result of the current economic slowdown, the smallest 90

---

[290] https://www.csis.org/blogs/trustee-china-hand/fortune-favors-state-owned-three-years-chinese-dominance-global-500-list

percent of companies by revenue have had to borrow money to service existing loans.

The real-estate sector accounts for 63 percent of household debt and 36 percent of GDP (Liberty Street Economics, September 26, 2022). Real estate sales plunged by 30 percent in 2022; since 2021, 40 percent of Chinese home sales have defaulted on their debt obligations,[291] threatening the banking sector and the economy at large. Similarly, more than 30 of China's property firms have defaulted and over 29 percent of real-estate loans have gone bad, according to a Bloomberg report (September 19, 2022). A collapse of the real-estate sector is likely to cause China's stock markets to lose 20 percent in value.[292] The banking sector's non-performing loans ratio was 1.65 percent at the end of the third quarter of 2023, Reuters reported (October 20, 2023). Somewhere between 13 percent and 28 percent of Chinese firms were expected to end 2022 cash-flow negative.[293]

In 2022, local government debt amounted to 92 trillion yuan ($12.58 trillion), or 76 percent of the country's economic output, up from around 62 percent in 2019, Reuters reported on October 17, 2023. (Other tallies put the total much higher.) Local government debt is normally repaid through real estate sales, but the sector's grave problems are increasing the risk of default.

China has made about $1 trillion worth of investments in foreign countries as part of the BRI, *Wall Street Journal* reported on September 26, 2022. Now, the majority of the countries who borrowed from China are facing economic distress. Tens of

---

[291] https://www.reuters.com/world/china/china-property-creditors-face-worsening-restructuring-terms-sector-recovery-2023-10-11/
[292] https://www.cnbc.com/2022/09/02/morgan-stanley-chinese-stocks-could-plunge-if-real-estate-gets-worse.html
[293] https://www.spglobal.com/marketintelligence/en/news-insights/latest-news-headlines/china-s-state-owned-companies-encumbered-by-world-s-biggest-corporate-debt-pile-72199736

billions of dollars' worth of loans have had to be written off, and more requests for loan forgiveness are expected.

Foreign Direct Investment

During the period of peak growth, China's rapid economic expansion relied on the export-led growth model, heavily supported by foreign direct investment. However, the current downward trend in FDI poses challenges for the other key drivers of the Chinese economy, such as exports and real estate. Without effective measures to stimulate FDI or to innovate a new growth model, China's economy is likely to face continued deceleration.

Because there has been a notable reduction in foreign investors' confidence in China and its markets, since May 2023, FDI has been dropping by double digits each month. In the second quarter, it hit a 25-year low (Bloomberg, August 7, 2023), and this downward trend persisted into September, when it plunged 34 percent, *Financial Times* reported on October 29, 2023. Mergers and acquisitions also declined. FDI is down across all sectors: inbound-tourism related investment is down 78 percent[294] while FDI in the food and financial services sectors has declined by 63 percent. What is more, tourist arrivals in 2023 have been just a fraction of the pre-pandemic total. Faced with a myriad of disincentives — notably China's high salaries compared to Southeast Asia — foreign companies are looking for ways to diversify away from China. Countries like India, Malaysia, Indonesia, and Vietnam have benefited from this redirection of foreign investment.

---

[294] https://www.investmentmonitor.ai/insights/chinas-fdi-decline-foreign-companies-covid-geopolitics/?cf-view

Consumer spending remains depressed, not yet having rebounded to pre-pandemic levels, CNBC reported (October 11, 2023). Many workers are still grappling with financial setbacks from the Covid-19 lockdowns. More than 21 percent of young people are unemployed, and even those with spare cash are hesitant to part with their money.[295] Factory prices are flat, but consumer prices are experiencing deflation.[296] Adding to the challenges is the shift of Chinese consumers toward domestic brands over foreign ones.[297] For foreign companies, it may be more advantageous to redirect their investments towards manufacturing and marketing their products in other nations where consumers are more willing and financially able to buy them.

Simultaneously, as the potential rewards of investing in China diminish, the risks are rising. Stringent government regulations, exemplified by the recently updated Counter-Espionage law, have effectively turned routine business activities such as due diligence, auditing, and market research into potential criminal offenses. Consequently, the likelihood of office raids and the risk of arrest for both foreign and domestic employees, as well as the threat of detention or exit restrictions,[298] have increased. These developments both deter foreign investment and impede tourism. Moreover, they pose challenges in attracting foreign talent and experts who bring fresh ideas and innovation to China.

Both tourism and FDI play crucial roles in China's economic growth as they bring dollars into the country, which are essential for the People's Bank of China to maintain foreign

---

[295] https://www.tbsnews.net/worldbiz/china/china-suspends-youth-jobless-data-after-record-high-readings-682882

[296] https://www.reuters.com/world/china/chinas-sept-consumer-prices-flat-factory-deflation-persists-2023-10-13/

[297] https://www.scmp.com/economy/china-economy/article/3236421/chinese-households-opt-domestic-goods-budgets-tighten-national-pride-swells

[298] https://www.wsj.com/world/china/china-blocks-executive-at-u-s-firm-kroll-from-leaving-the-mainland-99c9bd0f

currency reserves and to facilitate international trade settlements. The influx of dollars also boosts demand for the yuan, thereby supporting the currency's value, which is dropping.

For the past three decades, the PRC has been known for its massive exports. And exports are directly linked to FDI. Foreign-invested companies account for over 30 percent of China's exports.[299] Just as FDI has fallen, so have exports. In July 2023, exports plunged 14.5 percent year-on-year,[300] and continued to drop in August and September.

Another positive aspect of FDI is its potential to generate employment. On top of the spike in youth unemployment, there has been a decrease in labor force participation[301] as more young individuals have abandoned their job search, leading to their exclusion from official unemployment statistics. This suggests that the proportion of jobless young adults within the working-age population could be double the official rate (*Fortune*, August 9, 2023). On a broader scale, general unemployment, across all age groups, exceeds 5 percent.[302] Greater FDI would likely alleviate unemployment and boost consumer spending. And if more people had better jobs, they would be able to buy homes, propping up the real estate sector.

Historically, FDI has been associated with the transfer of technology and expertise. As foreign companies invest in China, they introduce fresh and innovative approaches that enhance operational efficiency. FDI agreements, particularly those involving joint ventures, often incorporate clauses related to technology transfer or offer opportunities for industrial espionage, which plays a significant role in China's technology acquisition.

---

[299]

[300] https://tradingeconomics.com/china/exports

[301] https://www.ceicdata.com/en/indicator/china/labour-force-participation-rate

[302] https://www.statista.com/statistics/270320/unemployment-rate-in-china/

The absence of FDI would pose a threat to this vital source of technological input. Advanced technology not only elevates product quality and functionality but also contributes to cost reduction, enhancing the competitiveness of Chinese goods. Deprived of these advances, China risks losing its competitive advantage, potentially impacting the prospects of an export resurgence.

Another significant advantage of technology is its capacity to enhance worker productivity.[303] A worker equipped with even a basic machine can achieve a greater output compared to a manual laborer. Moreover, a worker utilizing advanced technology can further boost productivity compared to one using a basic machine.

China's aging population is leading to a gradual reduction in its overall labor force. To maintain its current level of productivity and, by extension, its living standards, the country must find ways to sustain or even increase its output while using fewer workers.[304] As older individuals retire and are replaced by a smaller cohort of younger workers, continued technological progress becomes indispensable for China to bridge this productivity gap. Without FDI, the PRC will have to rely on its own innovative abilities. Akin to technological Darwinism, China will have to find a way to innovate or face decline.

Capital Flight

During the 2020 to 2022 pandemic period, money flowed into China while almost none flowed out. Now, the trend is reversing. Between 2014 and 2019, China experienced net capital outflows, meaning more money left the country than went in. But beginning in 2020, with Covid-19 travel restrictions, and stricter control

---

[303] https://www.techfunnel.com/information-technology/how-technology-increases-productivity-in-the-workplace/

[304] https://www.axios.com/2023/01/24/workforce-china-population-decline-economy-impacts

exerted by Xi Jinping, more money remained in the country. During the first two years of the pandemic, when the rest of the world was often locked down, China continued to export, enjoying both a trade surplus and net cash inflows. But during the final quarter of 2022, China experienced the first net capital outflow in over two years (Asia Nikkei, February 22, 2023). In September 2023, net capital outflows hit a seven-year high, according to the same outlet's October 25, 2023 report.

One reason for these outflows is that people are seeking higher interest rates abroad. The People's Bank of China has been keeping interest rates low as a means of stimulating the economy. But low rates make Chinese bonds unattractive, particularly when U.S. interest rates have continued to rise. Another reason cash is leaving the PRC is that people hope to protect their wealth from currency devaluation. Furthermore, investment in China is down because the ailing Chinese economy is now a less attractive investment than it was a few years ago.

A key source of foreign capital is exports. China's exports declined in the fourth quarter of 2022, and in 2023 they fell every month between January and August.[305] By early 2023, containers began accumulating at Chinese ports, with stacks six to seven high being reported at some dock facilities. The CCP regime confirmed the container buildup, but attributed it to "normal market adjustment"[306] rather than a decline in exports. The data tells a different story. Following a drop in exports for much of 2023, by October, the situation began to alleviate. Also, raw material imports remained robust (Reuters, October 16, 2023), suggesting that factory activity was higher than previously believed.

With both FDI and exports down, less money is coming in, but more money is flowing out. Chinese citizens are allowed to

---

[305] https://www.cnbc.com/2023/09/07/china-august-trade-data-exports-imports.html
[306] https://www.globaltimes.cn/page/202303/1286454.shtml

travel abroad again for studies, work, business, and tourism. Furthermore, some wealthy Chinese have relocated to Singapore, *Wall Street Journal* reported on February 27, 2023, because of better education and opportunities for their children, lower taxes, or because they do not like the direction of the PRC under Xi's leadership. Now that both China and Singapore are reopened, this trend is expected to accelerate.

So far in 2023, FDI in China has bounced back to some extent, with much of the investment flowing into high-tech manufacturing.[307] However, business confidence remains low. Foreign companies saw an average 10-percent decrease in China profits in 2022. The European Chamber of Commerce in China has repeatedly stated that foreign companies are not leaving China outright, but they are isolating their China business as they shift new investment to other countries in Asia. Investment by Taiwanese firms in China fell to a three-year low, and with the current political tensions, it is unclear if that investment will return. The U.S. chip ban is also forcing companies to relocate part of their manufacturing to nations not affected by the restrictions.

In an attempt to attract investors, China's local governments are launching their own initiatives, including foreign roadshows. In 2022, foreign investors dumped many of their Chinese stock holdings. But early the following year, foreign investors bought up shares in record numbers. The Chinese government bond market, which saw a 15 percent selloff by foreign investors in 2022, does not seem to be recovering, however.[308] As of late 2023, foreign investors were continuing to rid themselves of central government bonds, a record divestment which wiped out four and a half years of gains. Notably,

---

[307] https://www.bloomberg.com/news/articles/2023-02-21/investment-into-china-picks-up-in-january-after-late-2022-drop

[308] https://asia.nikkei.com/Economy/China-sees-first-net-capital-outflow-in-more-than-2-years

international investors are also offloading Chinese stocks[309] at a pace not witnessed in nearly a decade.

Beijing is taking steps to curb capital outflows by enacting legislation that prevents some brokerages from opening new accounts to move Chinese money into foreign stocks. The China Securities Regulatory Commission announced regulations to prevent "illegal cross-border securities businesses," *Financial Times* reported on March 2, 2023. This closed one of the last remaining loopholes that citizens could use to get their money out of China. Foreign and Chinese retail customers are reporting that they are having trouble removing or transferring money from Chinese banks,[310] although officials claim there has been no change in policy. Professional investor Mark Mobius said he was unable to withdraw money from an account in Shanghai.

For the time being, it seems that ongoing low interest rates will likely discourage foreign investors from entering the government bond market. Simultaneously, a decline in exports is expected to reduce the amount of foreign capital flowing into the country. The CCP regime's stricter regulations on capital outflows are also creating hurdles for conducting business in China and repatriating profits. As a result, these factors are collectively making China a less attractive destination for foreign direct investment.

Real Estate and the Financial Sector

Local governments are facing liquidity issues as debt through local-government financing vehicles (LGFVs) stands at about $7.8

---

[309] https://asia.nikkei.com/Business/Markets/Foreign-investors-net-selling-of-China-shares-hits-9-year-high

[310] https://asiamarkets.com/chinese-banks-cause-alarm-as-capital-flight-measures-intensify/

trillion.[311] The debts are usually paid off through sales of real estate, but that sector is floundering. If the central government does not intervene, several local governments may default. In late 2023, Reuters (October 25, 2023) identified 12 regions as having a high risk of default.

In August 2023, Chinese investment firm Zhongrong Trust, which manages $87 billion for corporate clients and wealthy individuals, missed payments to corporate investors.[312] The company released a bizarre statement cautioning customers about fraudulent notifications they might receive from "criminals" falsely claiming that the company had canceled some investment products. An August 18, 2023 CNN report speculated that this might be "China's Lehman moment."

Zhongrong is part of a large conglomerate, Zhongzhi, which manages $138 billion. The missed payments sparked panic on social media, and investors speculated whether the rest of the conglomerate is also facing financial difficulties. As the CNN report noted, there was real fear about a possible collapse of China's investment trust sector, which is worth $2.9 trillion.

As of October 2023, $124.5 billion worth of property-sector bonds were in default.[313] The financial sector's heavy exposure to real estate could spark a chain of defaults and lost investments. For years, analysts have been calling China's overinflated and debt-ridden real estate market a bubble, and predicted dire consequences when it finally bursts. On August 13, 2023, CNBC reported that major Chinese property developer Country Garden would suspend trading of onshore bonds until debt

[311] https://www.bloomberg.com/news/articles/2023-08-20/china-local-govts-to-sell-206-billion-of-financing-debt-caixin
[312] https://www.businessinsider.com/china-real-estate-crisis-zhongrong-trust-misses-payments-country-garden-2023-8
[313] https://www.reuters.com/world/china/chinas-troubled-property-sector-face-more-debt-defaults-2023-10-20/

restructuring could be arranged. In the first half of 2022, Country Garden turned a healthy profit. In the first six months of 2023, it lost $6.7 billion, having lost 99 percent of its stock-market value over the past three years, *The Guardian* reported on August 31, 2023.

Country Garden may just be the tip of the iceberg. It is estimated that the entire property sector has $390 billion in unpaid bills (*New York Times*, August 21, 2023). Since mid-2021, when the real-estate debt crisis began, the companies accounting for 40 percent of all home sales in the PRC have all experienced defaults. Many offshore bonds of Chinese real estate developers are selling for pennies on the dollar while their share prices have crashed. The People's Bank of China granted property developers a 12-month extension to repay loans due in 2023.[314] By late October 2023, Country Garden was declared to be in default and required restructuring to remain in existence.[315]

The turmoil in China's financial industry is just one example of how turbulence in the property sector extends to other industries. In the United States, the stock market is often used to gauge the overall health of the economy. In China, that gauge is the real estate sector. With a total value of $62 trillion, real estate is the largest repository of wealth in the country and the most common investment vehicle. So, when the real estate sector falters, people become cautious about spending their money — and this caution is driving the current decline in consumption.

On top of local consumers buying fewer products, the rest of the world is also demanding fewer Chinese exports. Reduced demand means less factory activity and fewer jobs. Pessimism is rising and fixed asset investment has fallen. When businesses and

---

[314] https://edition.cnn.com/2023/08/01/economy/china-real-estate-country-garden-intl-hnk/index.html
[315] https://edition.cnn.com/country-garden-default-debt-what-next/index.html

governments reduce their investments in long-term capital goods like buildings, machinery, and infrastructure, fewer new jobs are created, and unemployment is expected to increase.

The rise in unemployment suggests that the Chinese economy is in a great deal of trouble with no recovery path in sight. While it is unlikely that the Chinese economy will collapse, some analysts expect growth to decline to as little as 2 percent by 2035.[316] This will hinder Xi Jinping's goal of surpassing the United States as the world's greatest economic and military power by 2049. The Chinese dream for the future may just remain in the future forever.

Access to Natural Resources and Food

As one of the world's two largest trading countries, China is also one of the world's largest importers of raw materials and energy. Additionally, China is a net importer of food. Crucial resources for China include coal, which is the primary source of its energy production, and rare earth elements, which are critical in the manufacturing of electronics and high-tech products However, China faces limitations in terms of freshwater resources, arable land per capita, and certain high-value resources like oil. These limitations have driven China's foreign policy focus on securing overseas resources through trade, investment, and infrastructure development in regions such as Africa and the Middle East.

A primary reason for the conflicts in the South China Sea is that China wants to control access to fishing which is crucial to China's food security. Additionally, by constructing manmade islands, which the PRC claims as sovereign territory, Beijing hopes

---

[316] https://www.wsj.com/world/china/china-economy-debt-slowdown-recession-622a3be4

to secure rights to undersea minerals. Similarly, China's lending to poor countries in Africa, Asia, and other parts of the world is part of a strategy to obtain metals and other resources.

While China has focused its foreign policy on securing these resources for itself, China has also striven to control global supplies, putting Beijing in a better strategic position. In 1987, Deng Xiaoping said "The Middle East has oil, China has rare earths." It seems that decades ago, the CCP had already recognized the importance of controlling raw materials. Beyond mining and extraction, China's efforts to hold power over the global raw materials' market have included domination of processing and smelting. This processing-based strategy, combined with government monopolies, and lax environmental regulations have allowed China to become the world's largest producer of critical raw materials.

China dominates the global supply of 21 of the 35 minerals recognized by the U.S. government as critical.[317] This means China either accounts for the largest exports of these minerals to the U.S., has the world's largest deposits, or is the largest producer. A good example in the minerals sector is that there are only two operating cesium mines in the world, and China controls both.[318] Another example is arsenic, which is needed for the manufacture of electronics; the U.S. now imports all its arsenic from China.[319]

By dominating the processing of raw materials, and through soft loans from state banks, China is able to undercut its competitors and dominate supply. The country also commands the global manufacture of electric vehicles, by holding dominion over the chemicals needed to make the batteries, as well as the

---

[317] https://www.dw.com/en/how-chinas-mines-rule-the-market-of-critical-raw-materials/a-57148375

[318] https://www.theglobeandmail.com/business/article-china-sinomine-tanco-mine-manitoba/

[319] https://www.visualcapitalist.com/charted-americas-import-reliance-of-key-minerals/

manufacture of cathodes, and anodes, which are core building blocks of lithium-ion batteries. China accounts for 99 per cent of world output of LFP batteries, *Financial Times* reported on August 14, 2023.

China's lock on the industry has been compared to an arms race. Beijing dominance of metal refining, as well as the production of battery-grade chemicals, restricts the world's ability to produce EVs.

A walk along the global supply chain reveals the CCP's footprints at every level. In the upstream supply chain, lithium, cobalt, nickel, graphite, and manganese are extracted from the ground, and the PRC has worked strategically to control both mining and processing. China has increased its presence in the extractive stage of the value chain through BRI loans and soft power campaigns in Africa, Asia, and Latin America. The midstream supply chain includes two areas that China dominates — refining and production of battery grade chemicals — as well as the production of cathodes and anodes. Downstream consists of the production of lithium-ion battery cells, another area where China is the world's largest producer. Lithium-ion batteries are essential components in a wide range of advanced weapon systems, including missiles, drones, and other military equipment. China has 73 percent of lithium-ion battery cell manufacturing. Of the world's 136 lithium-ion battery plants, 101 are in China.

China alone accounts for 40 percent of the global chemical market.[320] While only 23 percent of all battery raw materials come out of China, 80 percent of battery-grade chemicals are produced there. The PRC also owns 66 percent of the world's cathode and anode production. CCP-linked companies have invested heavily in the refining of lithium carbonate and hydroxide, cobalt sulfate,

[320] https://www.mckinsey.com/industries/chemicals/our-insights/chinas-chemical-industry-new-strategies-for-a-new-era

manganese, and uncoated spherical graphite. This means that global supply chains flow toward China for crucial value-added stages.

The regime's disregard for human rights and democracy gives it an advantage in obtaining raw materials from conflict zones, where payments for minerals go into the hands of dictators who use the money to buy weapons to oppress the populace. Many of the countries which have raw materials are plagued by civil unrest, corruption, and a lack of democracy.[321]

These countries typically lack independent courts and have lax enforcement of environmental protection and human rights laws. The Democratic Republic of Congo is an excellent example. It accounts for 60 percent of the world's cobalt supply.[322] According to the Human Rights Watch 2020 Report on the country, 4.5 million people have been displaced, 13 million are in need of humanitarian assistance, and 140 armed groups are active. Congo's $6-billion minerals-for-infrastructure deal with Chinese investors gave rise to concerns that the deal gave away too much with little benefit to the country.[323] Despite an estimated $10 billion of PRC investment in Congo's mining sector, with Chinese companies now running 30 of the region's 40 mining companies, at least 60 percent of the country's 112 million people live on less than $2.15 per day, according to the World Bank's website.

Corporate social responsibility norms, international laws, and public opinion are making it more difficult for Western democracies to obtain what are often called "conflict minerals." The CCP is unperturbed by public opinion or international convention, and continues to import from conflict zones. The

---

[321] https://www.dw.com/en/how-chinas-mines-rule-the-market-of-critical-raw-materials/a-57148375

[322] Ibid.

[323] https://www.miningweekly.com/article/congo-to-hike-stake-in-copper-cobalt-venture-with-china-2023-05-24

regime has positioned itself to control the world's supply of vital inputs for countless consumer and defense-related products. Global supply-chain disruptions in the past few years have largely been the result of China's command of the flow of raw materials, and Beijing's power to dictate who can access which raw materials and in which quantities.

Rare Earth Elements

On July 18, 2023, an article published by the CSIS identified China's control over gallium (a rare earth element, or REE) as a national security threat. REEs are crucial to the U.S. military, but China is holding the key. Some 36 percent of the world's known REE reserves are in China, but the PRC controls over 70 percent of the world's extractive capacity and 90 percent of processing capacity.[324] This dominance in extraction and processing gives China a commanding position in the global REE market, raising concerns about resource security and international dependency.

REEs are critical to defense technology as modern weapons cannot be built, repaired, or maintained without them. Everything from F-35 fighter aircraft and cellphones depend on rare earths[325] as do critical space technologies, electronics and semiconductors. Of the 50 minerals designated as critical by the U.S. Geological Survey, 17 are considered REEs. Although the supply of rare earths is sufficient to meet defense needs, extracting a small amount of REEs produces a large quantity of waste materials.[326]

Acknowledging the crucial role of these minerals in many modern technologies, in a February 2022 White House Fact Sheet the Biden administration outlined steps it is taking to secure the

---

[324] https://www.heritage.org/defense/commentary/rare-earths-supply-chains-and-confrontation-china
[325] Ibid.
[326] https://hir.harvard.edu/not-so-green-technology-the-complicated-legacy-of-rare-earth-mining/

U.S. supply chain. Yet the problem remains unresolved, in large part because of the stricter environmental regulations in North America and elsewhere in the West. These make the mining of REE extremely difficult and expensive.[327] The U.S. has just one REE mine, at Mountain Pass, California.

In 2022, the White House granted $35 million to process REE from Mountain Pass, but the mining company still sends its REE feedstock to China for advanced processing.[328] Similarly, the U.S. provided funding to Australia's Lynas Corporation for REE mining, but Lynas continues to outsource processing to China.

One apparent contradiction in the environmental regulations that govern REE mining is that the same amount of pollution is added to the Earth's atmosphere whether the mining and processing are done in the U.S. or in China. Furthermore, green technologies are heavily dependent on REEs. Wind turbines, solar panels, and EV motors require REEs. Unless the U.S. and other nations dramatically increase REE mining and processing, the world can never achieve the Paris Agreement's climate change goals.

To meet President Biden's emission-reduction targets, the U.S. will have to increase electricity generation 60 percent by 2030. Sales of electric vehicles and wind turbines are growing, and Boston Consulting Group published an estimate on July 6, 2023 that demand for REEs will increase from 170 kilotons in 2022 to 466 kilotons by 2035. Given the size of the average REE project, this means that 30 new projects will have to start operations by 2035. A shortfall could result in electricity outages and reduced living standards for many Americans.

---

[327] https://www.heritage.org/defense/commentary/rare-earths-supply-chains-and-confrontation-china
[328] Ibid.

It could take years for the U.S. to build sufficient REE mining and refining operations. Under current regulations, it takes an average of 16 years for a permit to be awarded. Once given the greenlight, REE projects are capital intensive and take a long time to turn a profit. Due to the uncertainty of earning a positive return, most established mining companies have steered away from REEs. Boston Consulting Group estimates that keeping up with increasing demand would require an investment of $100 billion per year for the next 12 years.

Environmentalists suggest recycling REEs already above ground as a partial solution.[329] The Heritage Foundation recommends that private industry and the DOD should stockpile processed and semi-processed REEs.[330] To rebuild American capacity to mine and process REE, Congress must reduce environmental restrictions. Federal and state agencies must also follow suit, reopening Federal land to mining.

Furthermore, the U.S. should collaborate with its defense partners around the world to establish mining and processing operations so allies can mitigate dependence on China. Finally, the United States International Development Finance Corporation (DFC) should be empowered to provide financing to corporations in the U.S. and friendly nations to establish mining and processing operations.

Under the Sea and in Space

China's control of global supply chains may eventually extend to the sea and the moon. A laptop purchased in the United States bearing a "Made in China" sticker was assembled in China, and many of the components were sourced from China. That is the easy

---

[329] https://www.greenbiz.com/article/climate-solutions-depend-rare-earths-heres-how-they-can-be-sourced-responsibly
[330] https://www.heritage.org/defense/commentary/rare-earths-supply-chains-and-confrontation-china

part of tracing global supply chains, and most consumers know that components of many everyday products come from or are assembled in China. Many people do not know, however, the reason why China is able to dominate global supply chains so thoroughly: The small things — the metals and elements that are crucial to making electronics work — are also dependent on China.

The CCP's 11th and 12th Five-Year Plans encouraged Chinese companies to invest overseas, while the regime pledged financing and support from its state-owned banks. One of the goals stressed in the 12th Five-Year Plan (2011–2015) was to strengthen China's position in metals.

The 13th Five-Year Plan, spanning 2016 to 2020 — dubbed a "decisive battle period" by the CCP[331] — sought to control the global nonferrous metal industry. This strategy is coupled with "Made in China 2025," which seeks to dramatically expand the PRC's strategic industries and national defense, as well as science and technology. To this end, an action plan for China's metals industry to achieve world-power status was announced in 2016 by the Ministry of Industry and Information Technology. These five-year plans, Made in China 2025, as well as achieving world status in metals, all included directives for state-owned enterprises — funded by state-owned banks — to purchase and control mines in resource-rich countries around the globe. To further ensure its domination of mineral markets, Beijing imposes export restrictions on elements produced in China. These restrictions have been the subject of WTO complaints filed by the U.S., the EU, Japan, and Mexico, citing unfair competition.

Several laptop brands advertise themselves as "not made in China," although this is a bit of a mislabel, because even these laptops are dependent on inputs from China. The typical laptop

---

[331] https://foreignpolicy.com/2019/05/01/mining-the-future-china-critical-minerals-metals/

contains many or all of the following elements that originate from countries spread out across the world, but that are controlled by the Chinese regime: graphite, cobalt, lithium, chromium, vanadium, magnesium, antimony, and copper.

China supplies or controls half of the raw materials used across the world. Graphite used in rechargeable batteries is found in China, Mexico, Canada, Brazil, and Madagascar, but 69 percent of it comes from China. Cobalt originates in the Democratic Republic of Congo, where Beijing controls 35 mining companies. China controls 86 percent of the global supply of magnesium, although this element can be found in the U.S., Israel, Brazil, Russia, Kazakhstan, and Turkey.

Around 90 percent of the world's lithium comes from Chile, Argentina, and Australia. Through investment in local companies, China now controls 59 percent of the global supply.[332] And it is not only developing countries that are giving up their resources in exchange for Chinese cash. In Australia, China now controls 91 percent of all lithium mining, as well as 75 percent of the country's reserves.

Two of the principal sources of vanadium are Kazakhstan and South Africa, both of which are members of China's BRI. In Kazakhstan, the China Development Bank is heavily funding the mining sector, while in South Africa, Beijing is now planning investments in vanadium mines.[333] PRC companies also bought significant stakes in the largest copper mines in the Democratic Republic of Congo. In total, China owns 30 overseas copper projects in the operating stage, and an additional 38 in the exploration stage.

---

[332] Ibid.
[333] Ibid.

Zimbabwe has the world's second-largest chromium reserves, accounting for about 12 percent of the global total. China is the world's largest consumer of chrome and chromium, and secures its supplies by investing in extraction in Cuba as well as Zimbabwe. Over the past five years, China has invested billions in Zimbabwe's metals sector, and is a major owner in one of the country's largest chrome-mining companies, Zimbabwe Mining and Alloy Smelting Co. (ZIMASCO). Locals describe the China–Zimbabwe relationship as exchanging mining equipment and technology for ore. This is a strategy that Beijing has used in resource-rich countries across the globe. Namely, that China provides construction and technological services to the local mines. In exchange, the mines agree to sell a percentage of their output to Chinese companies at an agreed-upon price. Other tools used by the Chinese regime include mergers and acquisitions, whereby Chinese companies — often state-owned and funded by state-owned financial institutions — purchase a controlling interest in local mining companies. A traditional leader in northern Zimbabwe accused China of looting the country's mineral resources, and local miners have complained that Chinese firms exploit workers. In a June 2020 incident, a Chinese manager of a mining company shot two Zimbabwean employees over a wage dispute.[334]

The PRC also controls 90 percent of global antimony supply, and until recently owned 100 percent of the world's antimony processing plants. Once antimony is extracted from the ground, it must be processed into ingots in order to be used in the manufacture of other goods. Although antimony is found in Russia, Australia, and Tajikistan, nearly all of it is sent to China for processing. In 2018, for the first time in 30 years, the

---

[334] https://edition.cnn.com/2020/06/27/africa/zimbabwe-mine-shooting-intl/index.html

construction of an antimony processing plant, called a roster, began outside of China.

In addition to investing in other countries, the CCP is now scrambling to dominate the newer sector of undersea mining. Approval for seabed mining comes from the International Seabed Authority (ISA). Chinese companies have already filed 30 requests with the ISA for various undersea mining projects.

After conquering the seas, China plans to mine the moon. In 2020, the PRC's Chang'e 5 lunar probe landed on the moon and brought back 2 kilograms of samples. This mission discovered a crystal containing helium-3 which could prove incredibly valuable as an energy source. Scientists believe that these tiny crystals may have the ability to power nuclear reactors and that they are abundant on the moon. To put the power of helium-3 in perspective, about three tablespoons of helium-3 could replace 5,000 tons of coal.

U.S. space analysts suggest that China is building up its lunar research experience in order to support future moon-based mining projects, and former NASA Administrator Jim Bridenstine has said that he believes mining the moon will be possible in this century. There is evidence and speculation that the moon contains many critical materials.[335] Beijing hopes to achieve a manned moon landing by 2030 and then build a lunar research station. One PRC space official has proposed creating an "Earth-moon Special Economic Zone" by 2050.[336]

At the rate China is expanding its control of laptop inputs, it is likely that, 20 years from now, not only will most or all of the

---

[335] https://www.popularmechanics.com/space/moon-mars/a41171205/china-plans-three-moon-mining-missions/
[336] https://www.china-briefing.com/news/china-proposes-establishing-moon-based-special-economic-zone/

inputs lead back to Chinese companies, but some will originate from under the sea or from the moon.

Food Security

China has long been a net food importer. The country is only slightly larger than the United States, but must feed a population more than four times the size. What is more, China has less than half as much farmland as the U.S. Between 2013 and 2019, its arable land shrank by 5 percent,[337] making the country even more dependent on food imports. In 2000, China's self-sufficiency ratio was 93.6 percent, but by 2020, that number had dropped to 65.8 percent.[338] The increase in imports is the result of several factors, including a larger population and higher standards of living. Chinese are eating more food in total, especially more meat and processed foods that have to be imported.

The dearth of agricultural production in China and the increase in food demand has made China the world's largest importer of food.[339] By contrast, data from the UN's Food and Agriculture Organization show that the U.S. is the world's largest food exporter. The U.S. has never needed a push to increase domestic food production, and exports make commercial farming profitable. Additionally, Washington takes comfort in knowing that food supplies could not be threatened in wartime. Beijing, on the other hand, is concerned that in the event of war, the country could face widespread hunger. The issue of food security has implications for national defense and for any potential invasion of Taiwan. If war breaks out, the U.S. Navy could cut off food and energy shipments to the PRC. Establishing food security is thus part of Xi's preparations before trying to seize Taiwan.

---

[337] https://foreignpolicy.com/2023/02/27/china-xi-agriculture-tax/
[338] https://www.cfr.org/article/china-increasingly-relies-imported-food-thats-problem
[339] https://www.lowyinstitute.org/the-interpreter/china-s-food-dilemma

In 2020, as a result of the pandemic, flooding, and a number of other factors, China faced shortages and food prices shot up. At the same time, the CCP warned that skyrocketing energy prices would decrease the supply of fertilizer,[340] negatively impacting food security. Consequently, the government redirected chemicals and raw materials to fertilizer manufacturers, to ensure that supplies would not run out. China uses 30 percent of the world's fertilizers and pesticides on just 9 percent of global cropland.[341]

The situation became so dire that the Chinese authorities cracked down on hoarding and price gouging of urea, a chemical used in fertilizer production. Urea producers were struggling because they used coal-powered processing plants which were being stifled by pollution controls, imposed as part of Xi Jinping's climate pledge.

A CCP propaganda video explained how agriculture management systems created as smartphone apps can help farmers modernize their farms.[342] One of Beijing's goals is that, by 2035, every region in the country should achieve agricultural and rural modernization. This is just one component of ongoing reforms. China's farmers are still under a household contract responsibility system, and cannot own the land they work on. Instead, it is owned by rural collectives, which allocate land-usage rights to eligible households.[343]

The country must maintain a "red line" of 120 million hectares of farmland which is permanently planted with food, so

[340] https://www.bloomberg.com/news/articles/2021-09-23/china-warns-on-food-security-as-energy-crunch-hits-fertilizers

[341] https://earth.stanford.edu/news/overuse-fertilizers-and-pesticides-china-linked-farm-size

[342] https://www.chinadaily.com.cn/a/202109/23/WS614c3135a310cdd39bc6b066.html

[343] https://news.cgtn.com/news/2020-11-02/Xi-Jinping-stresses-deepening-rural-land-system-reform-in-new-era-V5rnLGD98A/index.html

that the country can be self-reliant, the PRC State Council Information Office announced on January 13, 2021. The regime plans to use technology, genetic modification of organisms, and subsidies, to improve crop yields. The "red line" also suggests that rural dwellers will be forced to remain in the countryside, to keep those farms planted.

Various policies aim to close the urban-rural divide, stabilize the economy, and help the hundreds of millions of farmers who were unable to work in the cities during the pandemic lockdowns. However, Xi's promises to improve the lot of farmers are made out of fear of food shortages, rather than any true commitment to significantly increasing the wealth of agricultural workers. Altering the household responsibility system, and other rural revitalization programs will not close this massive wealth-gap, nor end the desire to leave the farm and work in factories in the cities. And if it did, China would face a huge shortage of factory personnel.

In 2020, Xi pushed a "finish your plate" campaign. In 2021, China hosted a Conference for Reducing Food Loss and Waste. The CCP adopted a strict campaign of propaganda and censorship to reduce food wastage. Video platforms removed eating shows, and punished users who searched for certain keywords, such as eating shows or competitive eating.

Ironically, because Beijing maintained the Covid-19 lockdowns into early 2023, disrupting transportation and distribution, food waste increased, particularly of perishable agricultural produce. According to *China Daily*, roughly 25 percent of food produced in China was lost or wasted.[344] During lockdowns, crops perished in the fields because they could not be

---

[344] https://www.chinadaily.com.cn/a/202109/10/WS613b0d6fa310efa1bd66eb09.html

harvested. Food also expired when processing plants and factories were shut down.

The threat of food shortages is enough for the CCP regime to swallow its pride and trade with the enemy. In 2021, China and Australia experienced a significant diplomatic rift, triggered by Canberra's accusations regarding the Covid-19 pandemic and its stance on PRC human rights abuses. In retaliation, Beijing imposed import tariffs on Australian coal, wine, and barley. Nevertheless, China purchased nearly two million tonnes of Australian wheat, underscoring its reliance on Australia's food supplies, *South China Morning Post* reported (September 24, 2021). Despite this evident need for Australian food, high-level talks between the two nations did not resume until 2023, when China's food situation was even worse.

"Food security is the most important thing in a country," Xi Jinping said in comments quoted by a regime website on July 20, 2023. "The rice bowls of the Chinese people must be firmly in our own hands. Our rice bowls should be filled mainly by Chinese crops." Hoping to grow more food, he ordered the expansion of agricultural land and domestic food production. For this project, parks and green zones are being destroyed, to allow for the planting of more food.[345] The project is reminiscent of the Great Leap Forward, when villagers melted down finished products made of metal in order to meet iron production quotas.

Xi's handling of the food security issue is a prime example of the inefficiency of central planning. From a market economic perspective, the best farmland would already be used for agriculture, while land not being used for farming is most likely unsuitable for growing food. When food demand outstrips supply, the price of food should increase, making less productive land

---

[345] https://www.rfa.org/english/news/china/china-greenery-04282023152513.html

economically viable. However, if imported food is cheaper than reclaiming land, then food will be imported. This is why China and every other country, including the U.S., imports certain kinds of food. Countries grow the quantity and type of food that is cheapest and most productive, while importing those foods and quantities that would be too expensive to produce locally. This is why pineapples in Canada are imported, not grown locally. And while they are more expensive than domestically produced foods, they are cheaper than domestic pineapples would be.

Xi wants to keep food prices at the same level or lower than imports, but is ordering the least fertile land to be converted to farmland. In some cases, this reclaimed land is as much as 70 percent less productive, but still requires the same or greater amounts of labor, chemicals, and water to produce a smaller quantity of food, *South China Morning Post* reported (10 May, 2023). Because the new land is not profitable to farm, the government is providing farmers with subsidies. Meanwhile, as part of Xi's carbon neutrality agenda, the authorities are trying to boost China's forest coverage through a program of tree planting.[346] Consequently, some land that could have been used to grow food is being planted with trees. At the same time, because local governments are being pressured by the central government to show that they have increased farmland, some are clearing forests to plant crops.

Large sums of public money went into building the parks and planting the forests that are now being turned into fields. Additional public money is being used to clear the land. And public money will have to subsidize farmers growing food on this unproductive land. In the end, China will gain a small quantity of very expensive food.

---

[346] https://www.prnewswire.com/news-releases/cgtn-china-steps-up-tree-planting-efforts-to-reduce-carbon-emissions-301515077.html

Why China's Growth has Stalled

China's economy is slowing and the old growth model will not work. FDI is down, the yuan is losing value, and exports are in decline. The burden of regulations is increasing, making it more difficult for the private sector to operate. There is tremendous youth unemployment. The population is both aging and shrinking. Tourism and arrivals are down. The banking sector is facing a major debt bubble, centered around overpriced, oversupplied, and unsold real-estate. Moreover, China is facing food insecurity. If Xi is to restore the economy, he will have to dramatically change the existing system, something he is unlikely to do.

The Chinese growth model which previous leaders depended on during the heydays of rapid growth, from 1980 to 2010, will not work. At that time, only about 20 percent of the population was urban.[347] Moving hundreds of millions of farmers to the cities and putting them to work in factories caused China's economy to explode. But the country is now about 63 percent urbanized,[348] so, there are fewer people to move to the cities. Additionally, some of them will have to remain in the countryside and grow food, to ensure China's food supplies.

Another issue with urbanization as a means of growing the economy is that China already has roughly 295 million migrant workers.[349] These are countryside people traveling to the cities to work in factories. Moving them to urban areas will not significantly increase the GDP, and any talk of growing the economy through urbanization presupposes there being jobs for the

---

[347] https://www.statista.com/statistics/270162/urbanization-in-china/
[348] Ibid.
[349] https://www.statista.com/statistics/234578/share-of-migrant-workers-in-china-by-age/

newcomers when they arrive. But exports and manufacturing are trending down; the cities are now full of jobless youth.

FDI was one of the engines of growth during China's economic rise. FDI would bring in foreign currency and create jobs. The problem is that foreign companies and investors no longer see any advantage in investing in China. Meanwhile, the slowing economy offers less of an upside potential for foreign companies, while the demographic crisis means there are fewer young people to sell to. In 2022, China's population fell for the first time in six decades[350] — and some observers believe the demographic picture is even bleaker than official statistics suggest.[351] Between 2023 and 2028, roughly 27 percent of the population will reach retirement age.[352] The shrinking workforce is one factor why investment is increasingly being redirected toward places like Vietnam and India.

When China was growing at its fastest pace, the central government invested in infrastructure. Debt was used to build roads and railroads connecting major cities. Domestic economic activity increased and people became richer. Today, first-, second- and third-tier cities are already connected. Some existing highways could be upgraded, and stretches of standard rail could be replaced with high-speed railway lines, but this will not have much impact, if any, on GDP. Linking small and remote cities with high-speed railroads makes little economic sense.

Increased infrastructure investment would add to China's debt. The country's debt-to-GDP ratio is close to 300 percent.[353]

---

[350] https://www.bbc.com/news/world-asia-china-64300190

[351] https://www.project-syndicate.org/commentary/china-2020-census-inflates-population-figures-downplays-demographic-challenge-by-yi-fuxian-2021-08

[352] https://www.statista.com/statistics/1101677/population-distribution-by-detailed-age-group-in-china/

[353] https://www.wsj.com/world/china/china-economy-debt-slowdown-recession-622a3be4

Real estate accounts for 25 percent of the debt held by Chinese banks,[354] with the sector's total debt standing at $8.4 trillion, according to *Financial Times* (August 24, 2023). Creating more debt will not help rescue the economy. After years of unbridled lending and building, the real estate sector is plagued with defaults. One of the country's largest developers, Evergrande, filed for bankruptcy protection in the U.S. in the summer of 2023, Reuters reported (August 19, 2023).

The old way is clearly not working. If he wants to save the economy, Xi will have to come up with a new paradigm. Repealing draconian restrictions and anti-spying laws might help increase investor confidence. Removing government protections and allowing market forces to tear through the property sector would help to simultaneously burst the debt bubble and make homes more affordable. Furthermore, a lack of government intervention in banking would force banks to make responsible lending decisions, which would improve the country's future economic health. But reducing his control of the economy does not seem to be an option that Xi is even considering.

Xi's Loyalists Rise to the Top

Xi's reshuffle at the top of the CCP regime represents an intensification of government control over the economy, Asia Nikkei reported on May 23, 2023. Appointments like those of Vice Premier He Lifeng and at several new party-led bodies will ensure the country's financial system stays in line with CCP principles. Infusing CCP values into banking and financial systems is the latest step backward to a time of more orthodox central planning.

---

[354] https://www.washingtonpost.com/world/2023/08/31/china-country-garden-default-warning/

He, a close ally of Xi, has experienced the shift from full communism to market socialism, to liberalization, and now to a greater consolidation of CCP control under Xi. As vice premier, he will oversee industrial policy and trade negotiations. He spent the past five years as the leading central planner for China's economy, and will now have even more influence to ensure Xi's plans and edicts are followed. This approach includes a return to reliance on SOEs and CCP supervision of companies. This also means increasing China's huge debt.

Several new financial supervisory bodies have been set up. These bodies, which will be overseen by the CCP Central Committee, include the State Administration for Financial Regulation (SAFR), the Central Financial Commission (CFC) and the Central Financial Work Commission (CFWC) (Asia Nikkei, May 23, 2023).

The SAFR will oversee the financial sector, excluding securities, and report directly to the State Council and Premier Li Qiang. According to its 2023 budget, the SAFR plans to inspect 2,500 banking institutions and 800 non-banking financial institutions across the country. A reform plan published in March 2023 stated that the purpose of the CFC is to "strengthen the party's Central Committee's centralized and unified leadership over financial work." The CFWC, which will be led by a politburo member, is responsible for overseeing the ideological and political role of the CCP within the Chinese financial system, Reuters reported on March 1, 2023. As a party-building commission, the CFWC will ensure that the financial system is aligned with the goals and theories of the CCP, as well as the party's morals and discipline.

Technically, the CFWC is not a new organization but a rebirth of the original CFWC which existed from 1998 to 2003.

The old CFWC was meant to ensure the separation of the CCP, the government, and business. Under Xi's leadership, the CCP and the government have merged, and the CFWC will add the financial sector into this amalgamation. With the reestablishment of the CFWC, Xi and his allies will be able to more quickly restructure elements within the financial industry, purging the last holdouts from previous administrations, and filling positions with Xi loyalists.

As the Federal Reserve was raising interest rates and China was adopting expansionary policies, the People's Bank of China appeared to be losing its ability to enact independent monetary policy. In the U.S., political parties, government, and business are separate entities. And within the government there is a division of powers, with checks and balances. Furthermore, the Federal Reserve is independent of the government. In China, Xi holds the top posts in both the party and the government. His loyalists, appointees, and politburo members will now have more direct control over banking and finance. Xi instituted the Belt and Road Initiative — and now it seems that all roads lead to Xi.

The Middle-Income Trap

China's annual growth rate has declined, and Xi Jinping's complete lock on power means the country will be steered toward his vision of the future, which is one of greater security and forcible unification with Taiwan. Improving economic growth is not as high of a priority, despite Xi's call for China to become an upper middle-income country by 2030.

To achieve Xi's goal, the economy would have to grow at an average rate of 5 percent per year. Given recent slow growth, the generally poor state of the economy, extreme debt, a massive budget deficit, and a demographic crisis, this seems unlikely. In fact, given current trends, it seems likely that, in terms of sheer size, China's economy will never surpass the American economy.[355]

The PRC appears to be caught in what is referred to as the middle-income trap, in which a middle-income country fails to transition to a high-income economy due to rising costs, declining competitiveness, and stagnating investment. As low as factory wages are in China, they are much higher than those in India or Vietnam. This means China is no longer competitive at low-end manufacturing. At the same time, China lacks the capital, investment, technology, and human capital to replace the low-end factory jobs with a similar number of high-end manufacturing jobs.

China is faced with the need to increase the productivity of its aging workforce in order to maintain growth. But productivity growth has fallen by roughly 50 percent over the past decade.[356] Given the rate at which the workforce is shrinking and China's dismal current productivity growth, the country will just about break even. Productivity is only just growing fast enough to offset the decline in the size of the workforce.

The CCP's Expanded Role in Companies

Through the infiltration of CCP members, China is able to place loyal eyes, ears, and hands in companies and research institutions around the world. Since 1993, both foreign and domestic companies in China have been legally obliged to establish CCP units.[357] Jiang Zemin, PRC president from 1993 to 2003, called for the party to represent the entrepreneurial class, who were once considered enemies of the people. More recently, CCP branches in

---

[355] https://finance.yahoo.com/news/chinas-economy-may-never-eclipse-americas-202222283.html

[356] https://www.ft.com/content/cff42bc4-f9e3-4f51-985a-86518934afbe

[357] https://www.institutmontaigne.org/en/expressions/influence-without-ownership-chinese-communist-party-targets-private-sector

the private sector have increased dramatically. Under Xi Jinping, it seems the country is moving to an old-style economic policy, in which the party plays a larger role in enterprises.

When the CCP revised its charter in 2017, language was added to expand their sphere of control: "Party, government, army, society and education, east, west, south, and north, the party leads on everything."[358] To form a party unit, a cell of three party members must be employed by the company. Many private businesses are too small to comply, but, as of 2021, about 48.3 percent of private companies and 92 percent of China-500 companies host party units. In 2018, it became mandatory for all companies listed on the stock exchange to host a party unit.

The original role of such units was to recruit new party members, provide welfare assistance, and organize study and training sessions, as well as social gatherings. More recently, the party unit's mandate has been expanded to recruiting entrepreneurs into the CCP.[359] They also maintain databases with profiles of employees and managers to know who is loyal. Additionally, the unit must educate entrepreneurs, ensuring that they do not lose their socialist values. This includes instructing entrepreneurs to work and behave in such a way that pleases the CCP. Private companies are also required to recognize the leading role of the party in their charter.

Large companies must hire a party secretary and workers, allowing these party representatives to have significant influence on hiring and other decisions. These rules apply to SOEs, private Chinese companies, listed companies, and foreign companies. To increase its control over the private sector, the CCP acts through the UFWD (Bloomberg, September 16, 2020), which is charged with increasing the party's influence and control both within China

---

[358] Ibid.
[359] Ibid.

and abroad. The UFWD is building a database of private citizens, entrepreneurs, state employees, even investors and stakeholders. It seems that Xi favors the state sector, but will give priority to companies that assist in realizing the goals of the CCP, rewarding them with financial and policy resources.

In 2020, the UFWD published a paper titled, "Opinion on Strengthening the United Front Work of the Private Economy in the New Era," which called for the creation of "a modern state-owned enterprise system with Chinese characteristics" (CSIS, October 8, 2020). This echoed the words of a 2016 speech by Xi, in which he explained that "Chinese characteristics" means incorporating the party into each company's management and decision making. The vice chairman of the All-China Federation of Industry and Commerce then extended this call to private companies, encouraging the building of a modern private sector with "Chinese characteristics." This would mean allowing the party to not only control hiring and firing, but also to carry out audits and to monitor internal behavior.

The CCP has determined that overseas Chinese projects should also have party cells (*The Economist*, June 23, 2021), which should raise concerns in other countries about foreign political influence. In the PRC, joint ventures are expected to maintain a party cell; the foreign partner must accept that the party may be influencing or outright making decisions for the Chinese side. Meanwhile, China's Cybersecurity Law requires all companies, including foreign companies, to turn over data to Chinese authorities.[360] This raises real issues of data security and customer and employee privacy. For a wholly foreign-owned enterprise, it seems strange to have to host and pay for a CCP cell.

---

[360] https://thediplomat.com/2017/06/chinas-cybersecurity-law-what-you-need-to-know/

According to a list of 1.95 million party members that was leaked to the Inter-Parliamentary Alliance on China (*New York Post*, December 13, 2020), companies and research institutions around the world — among them Boeing, Qualcomm, and Pfizer — are riddled with CCP members, all of whom have sworn an oath to never betray the party, and all of whom are obligated to further the interests of the state and party when called upon to do so.

The Foreign Relations Law

The Law on Foreign Relations which came into effect on July 1, 2023 increases government control and creates risk for foreign companies. The law intensifies Xi Jinping's power over private-sector enterprises, and so will likely restrict China's economic development during a time when its economy is slowing.

The danger that foreign businesses could be accused of espionage has increased. Recently, the CCP regime has been leading a campaign against foreign consulting and auditing firms, accusing them of prying into state secrets (BBC, May 9, 2023). With tighter legislation, normal business activities such as conducting market research could be seen as spying. In China, all sorts of sectors, from agriculture to energy, are considered to be components of national security (CNBC, July 10, 2023). This leaves foreign companies little room to operate without stepping into allegedly sensitive areas.

Beijing claims that the purpose of the law is to "safeguard China's national sovereignty, national security and development interests, and uphold international fairness and justice."[361] The term "national sovereignty" generally refers to a possible invasion of Taiwan and is often used to vilify the United States or other nations that support or engage with the island nation. The law

---

[361] https://www.whitecase.com/insight-alert/law-foreign-relations-peoples-republic-china-became-effective-1-july-2023

empowers Xi to act against entities that are "detrimental" to the interests of the CCP.

However, as is typical of laws in China, these interests are not spelled out. Similar to the PRC's new Counter-Espionage Law, the ambiguity in the verbiage dramatically increases risk for companies and people working in China, as nearly any actions they take could be identified as a violation. For example, Article 32 of the Foreign Relations Law states that it applies to "foreign-related fields," which suggests that the law may apply to companies and entities beyond China's borders.

Other PRC laws also carry extraterritorial authority, such as the Data Security Law, which applies to data processing and storage activities the regime feels could threaten national security or national interests. That law places nearly all data-related activities under government scrutiny. Chinese officials' fears about the possible transfer of sensitive data abroad is creating challenges for international companies trying to conduct business in China. In late 2021, local providers of ship-tracking data ceased sharing information, citing concerns related to the Data Security Law (*Wall Street Journal*, December 6, 2021).

Following his announcement in October 2022 that he would now be prioritizing national security over growth, Xi told the CCP's National Security Commission to prepare to meet "complex and grave" national security threats.[362] While obsessing over national security — and doubling down on his goal of supplanting the United States as the preeminent economic and military power — he is stressing the importance of socialism, CCP leadership, and remaining true to "the guiding role of Marxism in the ideological domain."[363] Xi wants the CCP to exert even more

---

[362] https://edition.cnn.com/2023/05/31/china/china-xi-national-security-meeting-intl-hnk/index.html
[363] http://my.china-embassy.gov.cn/eng/zgxw/202210/t20221026_10792358.htm

control over the economy and to rein in civil society, preempting any movement or action which might challenge his or the party's authority. He has even abandoned his oft-repeated phrase "strategic opportunity period" (*Washington Post*, October 21, 2022) as the window of opportunity for foreign investment and economic expansion is closing and a new era of security and militarization is beginning.

Xi's new security-related restrictions can only serve to impede economic growth. The raids, investigations, and detentions to which Western consulting companies have been subjected has created a perception among analysts that doing business in China is becoming much riskier. Consequently, numerous firms are shifting production out of China; others are considering doing so. For the first time in 20 years, Goldman Sachs predicted that net foreign direct investment in China will be negative (*Wall Street Journal*, July 13, 2023).

Counter-Espionage Law

Under China's revised anti-spying law, passed in the summer of 2023, espionage can now include "organizations or individuals [that] collude, to steal, pry into, state secrets, intelligence, and other documents, data, materials."[364] While the definition of spying in most countries would apply to attempts to steal state secrets, prying into state secrets would generally not be a crime. This type of broad and ambiguous language is concerning for Westerners who might assume it is acceptable to ask sensitive questions. Now, merely asking appears to be illegal. This imperils everyone from foreign journalists to auditors.

The law purports to protect national security interests, but the definition could extend to any information that is related to documents, data, and materials related to state organs or

---

[364] https://www.chinalawtranslate.com/en/counter-espionage-law-2023/

infrastructure. The law also empowers investigators to access data, electronic equipment, and information on personal computers and phones. Investigators have the authority to prevent people under investigation from leaving the country.

Agence France-Presse (July 1, 2023) quoted Jeremy Daum, a senior research fellow at Yale's Paul Tsai China Center, as saying that the revised law uses a "whole-of-society approach to dealing with anything that is a risk to this broad definition of national security," enlisting private companies and persons as agents for the CCP regime. Article 7 of the law states: "Citizens of the People's Republic of China have an obligation to preserve the nation's security, honor, and interests." Article 8 reads: "All citizens and organizations shall support and assist counter-espionage efforts."

This approach is consistent with Article 7 of the PRC's National Intelligence Law (as amended in 2018). It stipulates that, "All organizations and citizens shall support, assist, and cooperate with national intelligence efforts." Article 24 of the law states that, in addition to public security and civil affairs, sectors expected to aid in intelligence-gathering include "civil affairs, finance, health, education, human resources and social security, veterans affairs, and healthcare security, as well as state-owned enterprises and public institutions."[365] It is important to note that the law does not say that these intelligence-gathering responsibilities are limited to within China. Effectively, the two laws turn all Chinese companies and individuals into agents of the CCP.

The Counter-Espionage Law puts PRC citizens working for foreign companies in a particular predicament, as they could be convicted of "Activities carried out, instigated or funded by foreign institutions, organizations, and individuals other than espionage

---

[365] https://www.chinalawtranslate.com/en/national-intelligence-law-of-the-p-r-c-2017/

organizations and their representatives, or in which domestic institutions, organizations or individuals collude."[366] The regime's repression of Christianity has often been justified as preventing citizens from colluding with foreign entities. But the wording of the revised law could be applied to any PRC national working in a foreign company or representing a foreign company.

The revised law explicitly applies to foreigners, and states that violators can be deported. The law goes on to say that foreigners considered to have been in violation of the law may also be banned from entering the country. Barring entry suggests an extraterritorial dimension to the law, as the violation may have occurred while the person was in another country. Even more concerning, however, is a potential exit ban on foreign nationals. Article 33 empowers state security organs "at the provincial level or above may notify the immigration management bodies to not allow persons suspected of acts of espionage to exit the country."[367]

The 2023 police raids on the PRC offices of management consulting firm Bain & Company and due diligence firm Mintz Group raised fears that the normal operations of management consulting companies could run contrary to the Counter-Espionage Law, as they involve asking sensitive questions and obtaining data and information (*Financial Times*, July 23, 2023). The revised law could also be exploited as a pretext for the regime to gain access to a company's trade secrets or proprietary data, or information about clients.

The U.S. National Counterintelligence and Security Center (NCSC) issued a warning (June 20, 2023) to Americans and American companies in China: "These laws provide the PRC government with expanded legal grounds for accessing and

---

[366] https://www.chinalawtranslate.com/en/counter-espionage-law-2023/
[367] Ibid.

controlling data held by U.S. firms in China. U.S. companies and individuals in China could also face penalties for traditional business activities that Beijing deems acts of espionage or for actions that Beijing believes assist foreign sanctions against China. The laws may also compel locally-employed PRC nationals of U.S. firms to assist in PRC intelligence efforts."

Among the activities NCSC warned about were handling personal data, both inside or outside of China, as well as gathering and retaining personal data. Around the same time, the U.S. State Department advised Americans to reconsider travel to China, Hong Kong, or Macau "due to the arbitrary enforcement of local laws, including in relation to exit bans, and the risk of wrongful detentions."

Since 2020, foreign companies have found the PRC a less attractive place to do business. The new law is just the latest reason for companies to leave China. According to the European Union Chamber of Commerce, business confidence in China is at an all-time low, driving companies to shift investment away from China in record numbers.[368] One in five of the chamber's member-companies have already shifted investment out of China, while one in five are considering relocating their investment elsewhere.

Tighter Controls Impeding Growth

Western analysts used to believe that a country could not get rich if it lacked basic freedoms.[369] Press and speech freedom were thought to be necessary to pursue academic research and to foster the creativity and innovation necessary to grow the economy. Then China came along and posted impressive growth year after year, despite having an authoritarian government. Granted, major

---

[368] https://apnews.com/article/china-foreign-companies-investment-trade-a47887e2c89050d291ebd169b0989cc4

[369] https://www.marketwatch.com/story/chinas-economy-is-rotting-from-the-head-11666974350

growth came after 1978 and was accompanied by an increase in freedoms and an opening of society, but China's growth did seem to defy the Western notion that freedom was necessary for a country to become wealthy.

After decades of unprecedented export-led growth, Hu Jintao (PRC President from 2003 to 2013) recognized that growth had to be more balanced. When Xi Jinping came to power, he also spoke of diversifying the economy and increasing consumption as a percentage of GDP. But rather than liberalizing the economy, Xi began hardening his control, utilizing AI and new technology to control nearly every aspect of people's lives. His crackdown on "disorderly" investment have all but crashed the economy.[370] At a time when China needs to innovate in order to grow, Xi's control measures are stifling development. Academic advancement is slowing in China, as is research and innovation.[371]

In his opening speech at the 20th National CCP Congress in 2022, Xi prioritized security over economic growth (*Washington Post*, October 31, 2022). As security pays no economic dividends, this makes it even less likely that China's economy will recover. The Biden administration is also prioritizing security over trade with China, and working toward cutting off China's access to advanced chips.[372] These two leaders are attacking the Chinese economy from both sides of the Pacific. Beijing needs chips to transition to higher-level manufacturing and save their economy; the chips are also a requirement for the next-generation weapons the CCP regime needs to achieve military supremacy over the United States. And of course, they also need money to fund technology investment, weapons purchases, and armament

---

[370] https://edition.cnn.com/2022/10/14/economy/china-party-congress-economy-trouble-xi-intl-hnk/index.html

[371] Ibid.

[372] https://www.washingtonpost.com/us-policy/2022/10/29/china-us-trade-economy-national-security/

development programs. The chip bans are also causing American and other companies to leave China, which is decreasing opportunities for CCP industrial espionage. Consequently, China will no longer be able to innovate through forced technology transfer as they have previously done.

Moving forward, Xi's tight grip, which is killing the goose that laid the golden eggs, is unlikely to abate. Since the political house-cleaning that followed the 20th National Congress, there is almost no one left in the government who can oppose Xi. And if Xi does not change course, he will not achieve his goals of China becoming an economic and military superpower, or Beijing transforming into the leader of a new and Chinese-led world order that will supplant the United States.

6

Social Dimension

Assessing the social component of national power involves an examination of a country's population, demographics, education, and healthcare, as well as the societal factors that might impact its ability to wage war. This part of the book will also cover China's hukou system, religious and ethnic repression, and other forms of social control.

Human Capital

A country's human capital is usually thought of as a combination of the population's size, health, education, and skills. Less tangible components are creativity and loyalty.

Comparing Educational Achievement

According to the UN Development Programme's Education Index, the United States places first, while China ranks 22nd.[373] This is based on effective implementation, providing quality, comprehensive, and inclusive education, as well as levels of educational attainment across society. The average American has 13.3 years of formal education, whereas in China, the average is 9.

Programme for International Student Assessment (PISA) rankings, compiled every three years by the OECD, suggest that

---

[373] https://www.datapandas.org/ranking/education-rankings-by-country

the U.S. lags behind China. The assessment tests the knowledge and skills of 15-year-old students around the globe in reading, mathematics, and science. The U.S. is number 22 overall, whereas China ranked number 1 both overall ranking and in each category. The U.S. scored number 33 in math, number 16 in science, and number 11 in reading.

Many have taken these results to mean that China has better schools. However, PISA scores do not accurately compare the U.S. education system to China's. For one thing, nearly 100 percent of American kids go to academic high school, whereas in China, high school is not compulsory, so some of the lowest performing students are already weeded out. Additionally, the PRC selected its four richest provinces, with the best education: Beijing, Shanghai, Jiangsu, and Zhejiang. China has 23 provinces, as well as province-level authorities in 5 autonomous regions, 4 direct-controlled municipalities, and 2 special administrative regions — but these lower-performing parts of the country were excluded from PISA. What is more, in the four places selected, the children of migrant workers were excluded from taking the exam.[374]

A Detailed Look at China's Education System

According to a 2021 OECD webpage, more than half of pre-primary children are enrolled in private education. This is a significant financial burden on parents, making it very difficult to afford to have two children. Nine years of education is free and compulsory through the end of junior high school. The quality is often poor, with as many as 38 children per class in elementary and 50 children per class in junior high. Approximately 28 percent of 18 year-olds are enrolled in tertiary education, as well 39 percent of 19 year-olds and 40 percent of 20 year-olds. It is extremely uncommon for adults in China to enroll in tertiary education

---

[374] https://www.brookings.edu/articles/attention-oecd-pisa-your-silence-on-china-is-wrong/

beyond the age of 20. China is the world's largest exporter of students, accounting for 22 percent of the foreign students in OECD countries.

An analysis of education attainment levels across OECD nations reveals that, among those aged 25 to 64, the attainment of upper secondary education in the PRC is strikingly low, ranking 44th out of 45 in 2022, with only 36.6 percent achieving this level. Only 19 percent of people in that cohort have completed tertiary education (university or college), placing China with a rank of 43rd out of 46. Likewise, China has a meager 1.1 percent of 25 to 64 year olds with a master's or equivalent tertiary education degree, ranking 38th out of 41. China is unpopular as a destination for foreign students, who comprise just 0.4 percent of the student body, ranking China 41st out of 44.

When comparing the quality of education in high schools across the United States, various dimensions may be considered, such as the number of Advanced Placement (AP), International Baccalaureate (IB), and Advanced International Certificate of Education (AICE) courses offered. In Chinese public schools, the number is zero. Next, offering more foreign languages is generally seen as a measure of a better high school. In China, apart from schools in ethnic minority regions, English is really the only foreign language taught on an official for-credit basis. Levels of mathematics and science would also be considered. While Chinese high schools offer chemistry, biology, and physics, they do not have labs. In better schools, the teacher may bring lab equipment into the classroom and demonstrate an experiment, but students would never get to experience their own, hands-on practice.

The size of school libraries, defined as the number of books and periodicals they held, used to be an indicator, but now they are being replaced by virtual libraries. However, even during the era of physical books, the typical school in China did not have as large a library as a comparable school in the U.S. They might have had a small collection of books in a closet or an office, and call that the library. Today, because of internet censorship, few schools and universities can access Western media or online dissertation and academic databases.

Activities have always been a large part of American education. American schools generally have a theater arts program or a drama program where students can learn to perform on stage. There is usually a school band, often an orchestra, and a chorus, while better schools might have multiple bands, including a marching band and a jazz band. The scholastics sports system is very well organized in the U.S., and schools offering a wider variety of team sports generally correlates with schools offering better academic programs. Chinese schools have none of these programs. On an individual basis, a headmaster may install some sort of afterschool program, but it would not be part of a national system, as it is in the United States and the reach would be minimal in terms of the number of students participating and in what depth they participated.

China maintains a separate school system for athletes, as well as for performers and musicians, where they spend most of each day on their training and only receive a modicum of general academic education. Roughly 250,000 to 300,000 children are enrolled in live-in sports academies or live-in kung fu academies; these run grades 1 through 12. Whereas American Olympic athletes come from the scholastic and collegiate sports system, PRC athletes come from the sports school system. These students have minimal academic levels and are excluded from PISA scores. Those who fail to earn gold in the Olympics or to turn pro in sports will wind up with no education and no skills to earn a living.

The existence of the two types of schools, all academic or all sport, is evidence of the lack of a holistic approach to education in China. A 2022 paper by researchers at Shanghai University of Sport, published in *Journal of Exercise Science & Fitness*, scored China's youth physical activity as C, organized sport participation as F, school as D, and government as D.[375]

Health in China

On the Global Health Security Index, China in 2021 had a moderate Index Score of 47.5, ranking 52 out of 195 countries and territories. Another index, the Health and Health Systems 2023, awarded China a score of 83.1.[376] Singapore, which ranked the best in the world, had a score of 86.9. The health index evaluates individuals' well-being and their access to essential services for maintaining good health. This assessment encompasses various factors such as health outcomes, healthcare systems, illness prevalence, risk factors, and mortality rates.

In the PRC, unhealthy lifestyles, increasing obesity rates, and the nation's rapidly aging demographic have led to a continuous rise in chronic diseases.[377] Specifically, cancer, heart disease, and cerebrovascular diseases have emerged as the primary contributors to mortality among the Chinese population. This situation has generated an urgent need for long-term healthcare services for individuals with non-communicable diseases, a demand that pushed annual healthcare spending to around 1.2 trillion U.S. dollars in 2021, according to a June 12, 2023 post on the China Briefing website.

China has a system of universal healthcare coverage, which means that all PRC citizens have access to basic healthcare services. Additional costs for certain treatments, medications, and

---

[375] https://www.sciencedirect.com/science/article/pii/S1728869X22000570
[376] https://www.statista.com/statistics/1290168/health-index-of-countries-worldwide-by-health-index-score/
[377] https://www.thelancet.com/journals/lanwpc/article/PIIS2666-6065(23)00127-X/fulltext

procedures may still be incurred by patients. Out-of-pocket expenses are a concern for some, especially for advanced or specialized medical care.

Both public and private healthcare providers are available. Public hospitals and clinics are prevalent and funded by the government. Private healthcare services are also available, and some people choose to use private facilities, especially in larger cities. The government has implemented various health insurance programs, such as the New Rural Cooperative Medical Scheme for rural residents and the Urban Employee Basic Medical Insurance for urban workers. These programs help cover the cost of medical services. The quality of healthcare in China varies widely. Major cities, particularly those in coastal regions, have modern and well-equipped hospitals with high-quality care. In contrast, rural areas may have more limited access to healthcare services, and the quality may be lower.

It is common for people to go directly to hospitals for medical care, bypassing primary care or family doctors. This is partly due to the lack of a well-developed primary care system and long-standing cultural preferences for hospital-based care. The majority of China's top 100 hospitals are clustered in Beijing. Meanwhile, in the western part of the country, key hospitals are predominantly found in cities such as Xian, Chengdu, and Chongqing. Although the south enjoys a relatively advanced economy, its healthcare resources tend to be centered in cities like Changsha, Wuhan, and Guangzhou.

China's Aging Population

In 2022, the population of the PRC declined for the first time since 1961 (Asia Nikkei, January 17, 2023). India has now surpassed

China as the world's most populous country. With a smaller population and a slowing economy, China's aim to surpass the U.S. as the global superpower is now even more remote.

The birthrate in 2022 was at a record low of 1.18 children per mother, well below the "replacement rate" of 2.1 children per mother. The falling birthrate has led to both a diminishing and a rapidly aging population that is inching China closer to a demographic crisis. One fifth of the country's population is already over the age of 60,[378] and by 2035, the total number of seniors is expected to be 400 million, or nearly a third of the population. These trends are likely to jeopardize Xi Jinping's vision of a world-class PLA by 2049 that is capable of "fighting and winning wars." By 2050, China's total population is expected to have shrunk by 100 million, with 52 percent of citizens being over the age of 65.[379]

Reversing a falling birth rate is not easy, and no country has ever succeeded in doing so. Countries like Finland, Estonia, Italy, Japan, Australia, and Hungary have offered citizens cash bonuses for having additional children, but to no avail. The costs of additional children outweigh even the most generous allowances given by the government. One policy designed to reduce the expense of raising children was Xi's decision to crack down on for-profit tutoring businesses. Apart from destroying jobs and wiping billions from share values of industry leaders,[380] the abrupt reform drove a great deal of supplementary education underground. In the long run, the policy will also decrease the overall English level of China's young people, making them and the country less competitive in world markets.

---

[378] https://www.pewresearch.org/short-reads/2022/12/05/key-facts-about-chinas-declining-population/
[379] https://chinapower.csis.org/china-demographics-challenges/
[380] https://thechinaproject.com/2022/08/05/chinas-radically-transformed-tutoring-market-one-year-after-crackdown/

In 2015, facing an aging population and a dwindling workforce, Beijing repealed the one-child policy. The expected birth explosion, however, never materialized. The cost of raising and educating a child in China is just too high to encourage young couples to have more than one child (BBC, May 31, 2021). In Shanghai, a pre-owned, two-bedroom apartment can cost more than $1.5 million,[381] while the average monthly salary is just $1,700, and the minimum wage is $374. Given the cost of housing, few married couples can survive without support from parents or grandparents, completely ruling out having two or more children.

In 2020, 12 million babies were born. In 2022, there were just 9.56 million births,[382] indicating that the government's response so far has been ineffective. China's problem is exacerbated by the fact that it is among the world's top six countries in terms of imbalanced gender ratio. Historically, Chinese people have preferred sons over daughters. The one-child policy, combined with liberal abortion rules, led to the birth of more boys than girls. UN data shows that between 1970 and 2020, China accounted for 51 percent of the global gender imbalance, or "missing" females.[383] After the one-child policy was relaxed, birthrates increased slightly, but not nearly enough to reverse the trend of population decline. Additionally, families still prefer boys. In 2021, the birth ratio was 112 boys to 100 girls; that same year, China had 30 million more men than women.[384]

Immigration has saved the United States from falling into a similar aging crisis. Immigrants tend to be young working people who marry and start a family after getting settled, or they

---

[381] https://www.loveproperty.com/gallerylist/114837/the-heavy-cost-of-housing-in-shanghai-now-the-worlds-most-expensive-city

[382] https://www.statista.com/statistics/250650/number-of-births-in-china/

[383] https://www.pewresearch.org/short-reads/2022/12/05/key-facts-about-chinas-declining-population/

[384] Ibid.

immigrate with their family. Many come from countries where families usually have more than two children; this has helped to keep America's age demographics balanced. However, there is almost no immigration into China to help with balance.

In the 2022 fiscal year, 969,380 immigrants became naturalized U.S. citizens.[385] By contrast, naturalization in China is nearly impossible with the exception of people from Taiwan, Hong Kong, and Macau, and individuals of Chinese descent who can demonstrate they have family living in China. In most years, the total number of applications for naturalization is about 1,500, most coming from Hong Kong. To make matters worse, an estimated 310,000 Chinese leave the country each year.[386] After three years of lockdowns and Xi Jinping's tightening grip on the economy, it seems that even more Chinese are in the process of leaving for good. Many of them are young people with excellent qualifications or successful business people with investment capital (*The Economist*, May 5, 2022). The outflow of young people will further contribute to China's demographic imbalance. It will also decrease the size of China's workforce. The loss of entrepreneurs and the wealthy will reduce the amount of investment capital and know-how, making an economic recovery even less likely.

Japan Survived Aging, China May Not

As the population ages, there are fewer workers to contribute to GDP. Additionally, older people are less likely to buy things like new homes or cars, so consumption usually contracts. Paying pensions and providing care for the elderly increases the tax burden, which is then spread over a smaller population of working taxpayers. Countries like Japan, Germany, and South Korea have been able to manage their diminishing young population by

---

[385] https://www.statista.com/statistics/247069/number-of-persons-naturalized-in-us/
[386] https://www.pewresearch.org/short-reads/2022/12/05/key-facts-about-chinas-declining-population/

increasing their development of technology, which allows more work to be done by fewer people. But China is far behind those countries in technological development, and with the country's most qualified engineers leaving for careers in the West, innovation in the PRC will suffer.

China's GDP growth is slowing. Consumer spending is waning, yet debt and defaults are rising. The real estate crisis shows no sign of abating. The scenario of a previously fast-growing economy, supported by debt and an overinflated real estate market, is similar to Japan in the 1980s. In 1990, the Japanese bubble burst, leading to ten years of economic stagnation. Complicating Japan's recovery from its economic implosion was the fact that Japan's population was aging. (Business Insider, October 16, 2021). Now China is facing a similar aging crisis.

In Asia Nikkei (July 5, 2019), a former governor of the Bank of Japan warned other countries that Japan's sluggish economy is the result of aging, rather than economic policies. In China, the aging population will require an expansion of infrastructure and healthcare which cater to the elderly, as there is a lack of facilities to provide physical and mental care for China's 264 million seniors, *South China Morning Post* reported (November 26, 2021). In the absence of government programs, the burden of caring for aging parents falls on the children. After decades of forced family planning, most couples have only one child who can care for them. Many of the elderly remain in the countryside and their adult children are faced with giving up their jobs in the city, to move back to the village and take care of their parents, or bringing their parents to the city where life is incredibly expensive.

Japan and other countries generally faced an aging population after their per capita GDP had reached between $5,000 and $10,000.[387] China, however, is facing an aging crisis at a much lower per capita GDP, meaning that the PRC simply cannot afford to age. Within five years, the country's old-age pension gap is expected to hit $1.25 trillion to $1.56 trillion.[388]

When the number of people working dwindles, both the government's tax revenue and the country's GDP fall. Japan's workforce peaked in 1995, and has been in decline ever since.[389] The size of China's workforce peaked in 2015.[390] Compared to the median age in Japan (48.6 years), the median age in the PRC (38.4 years)[391] is low, yet still cause for concern.

China is actually aging faster than Japan. Over the next 20 years, the four major indices of an aging population are predicted to be more favorable for Japan than China. Japan's aging rate — the rate at which the median age changes — is expected to increase by only 8.38 percentage points, compared to 13.24 percentage points in China. The elderly dependency ratio (the number of retired people, relative to the number of working people) will rise by 22.52 percentage points (in China, 24.21 percentage points). Japan's oldest-old coefficient will go up by 8.29 percentage points, but China's by 8.33 percentage points. The median age of the population will increase by 6.2 years in Japan, and by 8.47 years in the PRC.[392]

For decades, China has relied on manufacturing and exports to drive the economy. With an aging population, not only are there fewer workers, but those workers are getting older. As the workforce ages, worker productivity drops. Consequently, China

---

[387] https://www.chinadaily.com.cn/a/202111/22/WS619af472a310cdd39bc76a93.html
[388] Ibid.
[389] https://asia.nikkei.com/Spotlight/Society/Japan-s-shrinking-labor-pool-sharpens-quest-for-productivity
[390] https://www.china-briefing.com/news/china-labor-market-hiring-costs-job-preferences-talent-acquisition/
[391] https://www.worlddata.info/average-age.php
[392] https://pubmed.ncbi.nlm.nih.gov/31434814/

will have to promote new industries to capitalize on its older workers (CNBC, February 28, 2021). Capital-intensive industries will have to replace labor intensive ones.

Japan, Singapore, South Korea, and Taiwan are all facing aging populations and declining workforces. However, these countries have been able to survive those demographic changes by increasing the education and productivity of their workers, and moving up the value chain. China, however, is not Japan. With its massive income inequality, urban-rural divide, and low per capita GDP, China is not in a good position to make such radical changes.

Japan provides free healthcare and education. The CCP regime does not. Japan also established a national pension program, which all workers must pay into. This is much easier to do in a country like Japan, which has low income inequality. China, however, is a very unequal society. As recently as 2020, an estimated 600 million Chinese, or about 40 percent of the population, earned around 1,000 RMB ($156) per month.[393] The 2022 per capita GDP, however, was $12,823, which suggests that one half of the population earns dramatically more than the other. It would be problematic to have both classes paying an amount they could afford into a system which would pay a benefit which each could live on.

Japanese cities and towns offer incentives to families who are willing to have a third child, ranging from cash payments to free spots in kindergarten, free cars, and sometimes houses. As a result, Japan's fertility rate in 2022 (1.368) was higher than China's (1.09), according to data published by MacroTrends. The current retirement age in Japan is 65, but the government is planning to raise it to 70. For decades, the retirement age in China

---

[393] https://www.thinkchina.sg/600-million-chinese-earn-1000-rmb-month-so-are-chinese-rich-or-poor

has been 55 for women and 60 for men. It is unclear if the CCP regime will raise it.

Japan's workforce lost as many as a million people in a single year, during the peak of its population decline. No country has ever had as extreme a reduction in workforce, for any reason other than war. A significant difference between China and Japan, however, is that while Japan has the lowest overall GDP growth of the G7 countries,[394] its GDP per worker has increased at the highest rate. This means that Japan is able to sustain more GDP growth with fewer workers.

GDP per hour worked is a measure of worker productivity across countries. In Japan, each hour worked contributes $41.90 to GDP (*Time*, January 4, 2017). In China, by contrast, each hour worked contributes roughly $15 to GDP. Not only are Chinese workers less efficient than their Japanese counterparts, but in December 2022, labor productivity in China declined by 4.82 percent year on year.[395]

One way to increase worker productivity is through education. Better educated workers can do work which is higher up the value chain, contributing more to GDP. Thanks to education, Japan, South Korea, Singapore, Taiwan, and Hong Kong were able to move up the value chain, becoming wealthy and then maintaining their wealth. China, however, is starting at a much lower point than those other countries. The average years of education of an adult in China is 9, while in Japan it is 12.8.[396]

Having a high Human Development Index (HDI) is highly correlated with a country being wealthy and having high worker productivity. Japan's HDI is 0.925, while China scores 0.768. This

---

[394] https://asia.nikkei.com/Opinion/Emerging-Asia-should-learn-from-Japan-s-demographic-experience

[395] https://www.ceicdata.com/en/indicator/china/labour-productivity-growth

[396] https://ourworldindata.org/grapher/mean-years-of-schooling-long-run

puts China and Japan in very different positions. The Economic Demographic Matrix classifies countries according to age and wealth demographics.[397] Japan is classified as rich-old; China is classified as poor-old. Both countries are aging, but the per capita GDP of Japan, $34,135 per year, is almost triple that of China.[398]

China's aging crisis will make it very difficult for the country to pull out of its downward economic trend. Most of the measures that Japan used to cope with its aging population and still maintain GDP are costly and take time. The vast majority of the PRC's people are significantly poorer and less educated than Japanese people were when Japan hit its economic peak in 1989. With only 70 years' experience running a country, and only about 40 years' experience with market economics, it will be interesting to see if the CCP can come up with a solution that more developed countries, like Japan, did not.

China does not have decades. By late 2023, its economy was already close to crisis. When the property bubble bursts, it seems unlikely that an aging population and a diminishing workforce will be able to restore the country to its previous, stellar GDP growth rates.

The Hukou System and Migrant Workers

China's hukou system, also known as the household registration system, is a family identification system that has been in place in China since the 1950s. Based on similar structures used for governance during the country's imperial past, it has in the CCP

---

[397] https://www.weforum.org/agenda/2019/10/what-ageing-china-and-japan-teach-us-about-our-economies/

[398] https://www.worldometers.info/gdp/gdp-per-capita/#google_vignette

era played a significant role in determining a person's residency status and their access to social services and benefits.

The hukou system classifies individuals into two main categories: Those with a rural (agrarian) hukou and those with an urban hukou. The former is applied to those officially registered as rural residents. They live in villages and small towns, and may have limited access to urban social services and benefits. The latter are officially registered as urban residents and live in larger settlements. They have greater access to social services, including better education and healthcare, as well as more employment opportunities. As a CSIS blog post (April 20, 2022) puts it, "The hukou system codifies various social inequalities in China by dividing the population into two classes."

Something like 295 million rural dwellers[399] have relocated to China's cities and manufacturing hubs to seek work, some seasonally, some permanently. The children of these migrants are effectively barred from attending government schools in the cities,[400] because of their hukou status. Even if the children are born in the city, they are assigned the hukou number of their parents. It is extremely difficult to change a hukou number; it generally follows a person through their entire life. Assuming that migrant parents were able to bribe or otherwise cajole a local school into accepting their child, the child would not be permitted to sit the National Higher Education Entrance Examination, through which places at universities are assigned. The children are often sent back to the countryside, to attend subpar schools, far away from their parents, for the final years of high school.

---

[399] https://www.statista.com/statistics/234578/share-of-migrant-workers-in-china-by-age/
[400] https://www.brookings.edu/articles/attention-oecd-pisa-your-silence-on-china-is-wrong/

Religious Repression

The United States Commission on International Religious Freedom (USCIRF) 2023 Annual Report documented a significant increase in religious oppression in the PRC. Government and NGO reports documented nearly one million Muslims in detention centers,[401] organ harvesting from members of the Falun Gong sect,[402] the jailing and torture of Tibetans,[403] Catholics, Protestants, and Buddhists. Additionally, the CCP regime has complete control over the frequency and scheduling of worship services, liturgy, and the appointment of clergy. Religious schools or facilities must have government approval; religious gatherings outside of approved locations and times are prohibited. And the situation has got progressively worse under Xi Jinping.

Despite Article 36 of the PRC Constitution stating that citizens are entitled to the freedom of religion, in practice the authorities have so much control over religion that there is no meaningful freedom. Under Xi, there has been a steady crackdown on religion, infusing the state-recognized religions with socialist principles.[404] Children under the age of 18 are not allowed to participate in religious activities and atheism is required to be taught in schools. Members of the CCP and the PLA are required to be atheists by the party's disciplinary regulations.

Wang Zuoan, director of the State Administration for Religious Affairs, wrote in a CCP journal, that party members must be "unyielding Marxist atheists" (*Economic Times*, July 19, 2017). In 2022, the regime promoted a new textbook for universities and party members, titled *The Principles of Scientific*

---

[401] https://www.cfr.org/backgrounder/china-xinjiang-uyghurs-muslims-repression-genocide-human-rights

[402] https://www.ohchr.org/en/press-releases/2021/06/china-un-human-rights-experts-alarmed-organ-harvesting-allegations

[403] https://freetibet.org/freedom-for-tibet/political-prisoners/torture/

[404] https://www.hrw.org/legacy/campaigns/china-98/religion.htm

Atheism, to disseminate the CCP's religious theory and policy, which are based on "the non-existence of God" and "the harmful effect of religion."[405]

For non-party members, only so-called "normal religious activities" are permitted under Article 36. The regime has the authority to determine what constitutes a religion. Cults, as defined by the CCP, are prohibited under Article 300 of China's Criminal Code, which stipulates that "Whoever forms or uses superstitious sects...or cult organizations...to undermine the implementation of the laws and administrative rules and regulations of the state...shall be sentenced to fixed-term imprisonment of not less than seven years or life imprisonment and concurrently sentenced to a fine or confiscation of property."

Only five religions are officially recognized: The Buddhist Association of China, the Chinese Taoist Association, the Islamic Association of China, the Three-Self Patriotic Movement (Protestantism), and the Chinese Patriotic Catholic Association.[406] All are controlled by the State Administration for Religious Affairs, the UFWD, and ultimately the CCP. Religious activities outside of these state-sanctioned bodies is illegal.

Neither Judaism nor Hinduism have any official status. And because the Three-Self Patriotic Movement is the only Protestant organization which is recognized, all other forms of non-Catholic Christianity — including Lutheran, Episcopal, Church of England, Baptists, Mormons, Seventh-day Adventists, and Jehovah's Witnesses — are prohibited. Uyghurs Muslims and sects of Islam apart from the Islamic Association of China are suppressed. The Church of Almighty God, the Falun Gong

---

[405] https://www.ucanews.com/news/china-promotes-new-book-on-atheism-targeting-religions/95956
[406] https://www.cfr.org/backgrounder/religion-china

spiritual movement, and the Association of Disciples are expressly prohibited.

All Buddhist worship is governed by the Buddhist Association of China which does not support Tibetan Buddhism.[407] Additionally, Tibetan Buddhists are not allowed to recognize His Holiness the Dalai Lama or display his image. All monks and nuns in Tibet have been subjected to re-education.[408] Religious individuals are often barred from traveling abroad as Beijing does not want Tibetans visiting the Dalai Lama or the Tibetan community in exile in India. The CCP also limits the number of Muslims permitted to go on Hajj.

Regulations adopted in 2020 require religious groups to incorporate party ideology in their teachings. To this end, Xi Jinping Thought has been infused into the liturgy of the five approved religions.[409] The CCP's Administration of Internet Religious Information Services has banned unlicensed online groups or ceremonies, prohibiting foreign organizations or individuals from spreading religious content online, *South China Morning Post* reported (December 22, 2021). According to China Aid, a Christian NGO, party censors search for and remove the words Jesus and God from internet posts.

Apart from text, Beijing restricts religious symbols and imagery. In 2015, the regime ordered the removal of 1,200 crosses from churches in Zhejiang (*New York Times*, August 11, 2015). A Protestant pastor was sentenced to 14 years in prison for refusing to remove the cross from his church. Images of Xi have replaced those of the Madonna and the Jesus Child; Xi quotes have been painted over the Ten Commandments.[410] Because the party has

---

[407] https://www.hrw.org/legacy/campaigns/china-98/religion.htm
[408] Ibid.
[409] https://www.cfr.org/backgrounder/religion-china
[410] https://nypost.com/2020/02/01/how-chinas-xi-jinping-destroyed-religion-and-made-himself-god/

decreed that religious organizations must "spread the principles and policies of the CCP." Consequently, both the Bible and the Quran are being rewritten.[411]

In spite of this repression, the PRC State Council Information Office has reported that more than 200 million Chinese practice a religion. Reports by NGOs, however, suggest that the number is much larger — perhaps 350 million — but that many adherents keep their beliefs secret to avoid repercussions. One estimate is that there are 185 million to 250 million Buddhists, 60 million to 80 million Protestants, 12 million Catholics, 21 million or more Muslims, between 7 million and 20 million Falun Gong practitioners, and up to 8 million Tibetan Buddhists, as well as hundreds of millions who follow various folk traditions.[412]

Some foreign observers estimate that there could be as many 100 million Christians in China, with the number worshiping in underground or home churches exceeding the number who attend government-recognized churches. Members and leaders of home churches have been charged with "illegal religious activities" or "disrupting social stability," or under Article 300.

The Chinese Catholic Patriotic Association is not allowed to recognize His Holiness the Pope.[413] The association's chairman has said that the church needed individuals who love the country "and fervently love the socialist motherland." And that the Catholic Church in China cannot have relations with the Vatican, because "the Vatican wants those who are opposed to the Communist Party" (*China Daily*, September 6, 2007). He said that in order for the Catholic church of China to normalize relations with the Vatican, the Holy See would have to rescind its

---

[411] https://www.hudson.org/human-rights/the-attempted-shutdown-of-china-s-christians
[412] https://china.usembassy-china.org.cn/2018-report-on-international-religious-freedom-china/
[413] http://www.cardinalkungfoundation.org/ar/ChineseCatholicPatrioticAsso.php

recognition of Taiwan. By some estimates, about half of China's Catholics worship in illegal churches which tend to recognize the Pope.

The CCP appoints the PRC's Catholic bishops through the party-run Bishops' Conference of the Catholic Church in China. In 2018, the CCP signed an agreement with the Vatican, allowing the Pope to confirm the appointment of bishops for the Chinese Patriotic Catholic Association. In 2023, however, the CCP broke the agreement and unilaterally appointed a bishop without a blessing from the Pope (Radio Free Asia, April 5, 2023). The relationship with the Vatican is such a core element in Catholicism that many Catholics will turn away from the state-sponsored religion and join an underground church. By trying to drag religion into the open and control it, the CCP is driving the religious into worshiping in secret.

The regime has stated that it must have sole authority to select the next incarnation of the Dalai Lama and Panchen Lama, the two highest positions in Tibetan Buddhism.[414] The boy selected in 1995 by Tibetan religious leaders as the next Panchen Lama was whisked away by the authorities; according to Beijing, he was raised by a Han Chinese family, has no interest in religion, and is now a college graduate with a job.[415] Many China watchers, however, believe the boy may be dead. Beijing later appointed its own candidate as Panchen Lama. As part of its efforts to control Tibetan Buddhism, in 2007 the regime instituted a law requiring a "reincarnation application" from all lamas wishing to reincarnate.[416]

---

[414] https://tibet.net/china-is-preparing-the-dalai-lamas-succession/
[415] https://edition.cnn.com/2020/05/20/asia/china-tibet-panchen-lama-dalai-lama-intl-hnk/index.html
[416] https://www.cecc.gov/resources/legal-provisions/measures-on-the-management-of-the-reincarnation-of-living-buddhas-in-0

PRC law says that religions practiced in China must not be subject to foreign administration and influence. This is one reason why the CCP regime has a particular issue with Catholicism and Tibetan Buddhism. Additionally, the perceived connection with outside entities prevents the regime from allowing the Church of Latter-day Saints or the Jehovah's Witnesses from establishing churches in China.[417]

In response to China's systematic repression of religion, Washington has passed laws and set in place limited sanctions. The Tibetan Policy Act of 2001 calls for political and religious freedom in Tibet.[418] The 2021-2022 Congress introduced a human rights bill, H.R.4821, which would hold CCP officials responsible for repression against Christians and other religious minorities.[419] In January 2021, the final legislation of the Trump administration designated the CCP's treatment of Uyghur Muslims in Xinjiang as genocide and crimes against humanity (*Washington Post*, January 19, 2021). This legislation was renewed by the Biden administration,[420] and coordinated sanctions were imposed by the United States, Canada, the EU, and the UK.

The Uyghur Forced Labor Prevention Act, effective June 21, 2022, aims to block the importation of products made with slave labor in China's Xinjiang Uyghur Autonomous Region. Around the same time that law was passed, Beijing imposed sanctions on members of the United States Commission on International Religious Freedom (USCIRF) in retaliation for penalties the U.S. government imposed on PRC officials over human rights abuses in Xinjiang (Al-Jazeera, December 21, 2021).

---

[417] https://www.licas.news/2020/08/18/jehovahs-witnesses-sentenced-to-prison-in-chinas-xinjiang/

[418] https://www.congress.gov/bill/107th-congress/house-bill/1779/text?r=97&s=1

[419] https://www.congress.gov/bill/117th-congress/house-bill/4821/text

[420] https://www.dw.com/en/us-renews-china-genocide-claims-over-uyghur-treatment/a-58245806

Religion holds a central place in Tibetan life, with the majority of the population adhering to Tibetan Buddhism.[426] Monasteries and temples stand as powerful symbols not only of Tibetan religious beliefs but also of the broader culture and identity. Throughout history, these monastic institutions have served as hubs of knowledge, imparting teachings on traditional medicine, crafts, rituals, and various professional trades. Additionally, they have functioned as vital centers for the printing and preservation of sacred texts and sutras, making them indispensable for the continued vitality of Tibetan culture.

Larung Gar Buddhist Academy, also known as Larung Gar Serta Buddhist Institute, situated within Garze Tibetan Autonomous Prefecture in Sichuan, was once the world's largest Buddhist academy. However, in 2016, it suffered extensive damage at the hands of the authorities. Thousands of students, monks, and nuns were forcibly expelled, with many subjected to political re-education. Of the approximately 6,000 monasteries that once existed in Tibet, it is thought that only 13 remain unharmed.[427] Furthermore, in the past three years, two Chinese-style pavilions were erected near Jokhang Temple, a sacred site in Tibet's capital city of Lhasa, representing a desecration of the holiest temple in Tibet.

Mongolians also practice Tibetan Buddhism, and so the systematic repression of Tibetan religion equates to the restriction of Mongolian religion as well. As part of their training, Mongolian monks study in Tibetan monasteries, where they learn to read and speak Tibetan. Under the new laws, this practice will be severely curbed.

The Chinese regime forbids Tibetans and Mongolians from offering prayers to the Dalai Lama and displaying his image in

---

[426] https://undispatch.com/china-is-widening-its-crackdown-on-tibetan-culture/
[427] Ibid.

their temples and homes. It has also prohibited the display of the deeply symbolic Tibetan prayer flags, which are cherished by both Mongol and Tibetan communities, and the celebration of many significant Tibetan festivals. Furthermore, China has intensified its surveillance of religious leaders, practitioners, and individuals attending religious ceremonies and services.[428] Reportedly up to 1.2 million Tibetans have undergone DNA sampling, contributing to the creation of an extensive genetic database. This development enhances Beijing's surveillance capacity, enabling China to closely monitor Tibetan populations, infringe upon their privacy, and potentially subject them to persecution. Thermo Fisher Scientific Inc., a U.S.-based company specializing in analytical instruments, laboratory, pharmaceutical, and biotechnology services, has sold DNA kits to the Chinese regime, which in turn has distributed them to police units in Tibet.[429]

The Inner Mongolia Autonomous Region was originally Southern Mongolia. In the first quarter of the 20th century, China's northern territories, including Southern Mongolia, experienced political and territorial changes following the collapse of the Qing Dynasty. It became part of the Republic of China in the early 20th century. In 1947, the region was designated the Inner Mongolian Autonomous Region within the framework of the PRC. Ever since, Inner Mongolia has witnessed ongoing repression of Mongolian culture, including restrictions on language, education, and traditional customs. Traditionally, Mongolians have been nomadic herdsmen, relying on livestock such as horses, sheep, goats, camels, and yaks for their way of life. However, Chinese government policies have significantly restricted traditional nomadic herding practices. These policies, aimed at sedentarization, have made herding more challenging or, in some cases, illegal, compelling many Mongolians to transition to settled

---

[428] Ibid.
[429] https://tibetandna.org/

ranching or other forms of livelihood. This shift has had a profound impact on the traditional Mongolian way of life and cultural practices in the region. Passports issued by Beijing now say Nei Menggu rather than Inner Mongolia (Radio Free Asia, October 12, 2023). Once again, Beijing is attempting to not only erase the culture, but also remove the place from maps and the consciousness of locals and foreigners alike.

During the 2020-2021 school year, Beijing announced severe curbs on bilingual education in Tibet and Inner Mongolia (VOA, September 13, 2023). Since then, the restrictions have been intensified to the point that no websites in either Tibetan or the Mongolian language are accessible inside the PRC. Books in both languages have largely been banned, and those which exist are heavily censored to support Marxist values. According to the Southern Mongolia Human Rights Information Center (September 6, 2023), the Inner Mongolia Autonomous Region Books and Periodicals Distribution Association has announced the prohibition of both the Mongolian-language and Chinese-language editions of the multi-volume *The Comprehensive History of Mongolian Nationality*. The book disappeared from shelves, and member units of the Distribution Association were ordered to align with the CCP's approved historical narrative. The regime in Beijing wants to rewrite history, to avoid accepting that both Inner Mongolia and Tibet were formerly independent of China.

In 2020, many students and parents protested the change in curriculum in Inner Mongolia. Parents kept their children at home, rather than send them to Chinese-language schools. Beijing's reaction was to threaten the parents with having their bank accounts frozen, loss of their jobs, and loss of access to state services (Southern Mongolia Human Rights Information Center, September 14, 2020). In the end, the parents acquiesced. Schools, including kindergartens, are now forced to use Chinese as the sole language of instruction for every subject.[430] Nearly one million Tibetan children — around 80 percent of all children in Tibet — have been forcibly separated from their parents and placed in boarding schools (*Time*, February 7, 2023), where they are isolated from their families, language, and religion, while being subjected to intense political indoctrination.

Beijing's "second-generation ethnic policy" purports to protect minority cultures, but in reality it forces assimilation.[431] Uyghurs, Tibetans, Inner Mongolians, and other non-Han communities are experiencing an unprecedented level of repression, with the ultimate goal of erasing their languages, religious customs, cultural traditions, and distinct histories. The overarching objective is to assimilate and Sinicize these communities.

The Social Credit System

All Chinese citizens have been subjected to the social credit system since 2020,[432] and a 2023 official report proposed enhancements to the system (China Briefing, March 24, 2023). This system goes beyond mere financial history and transactions; it also takes into account factors like legal compliance and ethical conduct.

Extensive and intrusive methods are used to calculate scores. The authorities employ a mix of surveillance technologies (such as cameras linked to facial recognition software) and data-collection techniques to closely monitor and evaluate the behavior

---

[430] https://tchrd.org/worst-in-recent-years-2022-annual-report-on-human-rights-situation-in-tibet/

[431] https://icds.ee/en/chinas-second-generation-ethnic-policy-from-mass-surveillance-to-forced-sterilization-and-genocide/

[432] https://www.brookings.edu/articles/chinas-social-credit-system-spreads-to-more-daily-transactions/

of citizens. Citizens are required to use various apps and services that gather data on their financial behavior and lifestyle choices. The government has access to databases, including financial records and legal history. Citizens are encouraged to report on the behavior of others, potentially affecting their scores. And assessments conducted in schools or workplaces can influence social credit ratings.

PRC citizens with low scores can incur travel restrictions, preventing them from purchasing plane and train tickets. They can also be banned from attending the best schools, staying in luxury hotels, obtaining government positions, or using dating apps. In some cities, citizens can have their score reduced for parking tickets, but can add bonus points for donating to charity or giving blood.

While having a high score gives citizens certain advantages, some individuals may face structural obstacles that prevent them from improving their score.[433] These barriers may include limited education, a socially isolated network, or the stigma of low trustworthiness due to an initial low score. Moreover, challenging one's score can be viewed as an act of disloyalty, potentially resulting in further score reductions. The system is opaque, somewhat arbitrary, and varies in its enforcement. A social credit score downgrade could remain permanent. As Xi Jinping said of the system, "Once untrustworthy, always restricted."[434]

A similar system is applied to enterprises. The information compiled encompassed elements that determine whether a company is regarded as "trustworthy" or "untrustworthy." Actions such as engaging in anti-competitive or monopolistic practices, involvement in illegal or unethical tax activities, environmental

---

[433] Ibid.
[434] Ibid.

harm, or deceptive consumer behaviors may all become part of a company's record, potentially leading to adverse consequences (China Briefing, March 24, 2023). On the flip side, positive contributions to society, including the establishment of social programs, charitable donations, or corporate social responsibility (CSR) initiatives, can have a favorable impact on a company's score.

7

The Information Dimension

Information warfare and intelligence are essential aspects of modern warfare. A country's information capabilities — including intelligence agencies, propaganda efforts, and cyber activities — will determine who controls the flow of information and what information is allowed to be disseminated.

The PRC has one of the most repressive information regimens in the world.[435] Although the country officially has freedom of speech, restrictions can be made for speech relating to state secrets, subversion, and separatism or speech which is harmful, terms which are loosely defined and strictly enforced by the CCP.

All major media in China are state-owned,[436] and each day they are instructed by the regime what content to cover and which to suppress. The major media for both domestic and foreign consumption are Xinhua News Agency, China Central Television (CCTV), China National Radio (CNR), and the newspapers *China Daily*, *People's Daily* and *Global Times*. Additionally, the state-owned China Global Television Network (CGTN) and Radio China International (RCI) specifically target foreign markets.

China's press freedom ranks close to the bottom of global rankings, 175 out of 177 countries.[437] In terms of internet freedom,

---

[435] https://www.cfr.org/backgrounder/media-censorship-china
[436] https://rsf.org/en/country/china
[437] Ibid.

on a scale of 0 to 40, with 0 being the least free, the PRC scores 8.25 on Obstacles to Access, 2.35 on Limits on Content, and 0 on Violations of User Rights, according to Freedom House.

Due to a lack of freedom of press, speech, or assembly, there are very few protests against the central government. In general, citizens are thought to have approved of Xi's anti-corruption campaign, as well as the regime's poverty-reduction programs. Other Xi policies, such as Covid-19 lockdowns, have been less popular. Additionally, citizens are not happy seeing their standard of living decline, in the face of the worst economy in decades.

Ministries and Agencies

The Ministry of State Security (MSS) serves as the primary civilian intelligence and counterintelligence agency in the PRC. Its responsibilities encompass safeguarding national security, conducting counterintelligence efforts, countering foreign espionage, and investigating entities or individuals within China who are involved in activities that are perceived as threats to national security. Since 2021, the MSS has had explicit legal authority to pinpoint companies and organizations vulnerable to foreign influence or infiltration. These entities are then compelled to implement measures aimed at preventing foreign infiltration.

The MSS is so secretive that, unlike the CIA, it does not even have a website. However, in August 2023, the ministry opened an account on China's largest social media, WeChat, to encourage citizens to help fight espionage.[438] Posting the message "Countering espionage requires the mobilization of all members of

---

[438] https://edition.cnn.com/2023/08/02/china/china-security-ministry-on-wechat-intl-hnk/index.html

society," the MSS offered cash, anonymity, and protection to those who stepped forward and reported cases of suspected espionage.[439] It also encouraged clubs, associations, and companies to enact counter-espionage measures. This was the continuation of a policy begun a year earlier, which offered $15,000 rewards to those who report people engaged in espionage.

The Strategic Support Force

China has officially recognized cyberspace as a vital component of national security, and the regime has expressed its commitment to accelerate the development of cyber forces capable of the synchronized use of space, cyberspace, and electronic warfare as strategic tools to disrupt the enemy's overall operational and command systems at the outset of a conflict. PLA documents acknowledge that other nations have successfully employed cyberspace warfare and other information operations in recent conflicts. They advocate for targeting command-and-control (C2) systems and logistical networks to disrupt an adversary's decision making and actions during the initial phases of a conflict.

PLA assessments explore the potential use of warning or demonstration strikes, which are targeted actions against specific military, political, and economic targets intended to send clear deterrent messages. Consequently, the PLA is likely interested in leveraging its cyber-reconnaissance abilities for intelligence gathering and cyberattack purposes. This includes targeting network-based logistics, C2 systems, communications, commercial operations, and critical civilian and defense infrastructure. Such cyber capabilities may serve as a force multiplier when combined with kinetic attacks during armed conflicts.

Operating at the theater command level, the Strategic Support Force (SSF) was established to centralize the PLA

---

[439] Ibid.

strategic functions, encompassing space, cyberspace, electronic, information, communications, and psychological warfare missions and capabilities.[440] It extends information support through space, cyber, and terrestrial means to all PLA services and the five joint theater commands. During peacetime, civilian reserve and militia units, comprising individuals from various governmental bodies and academic institutions, augment the SSF's cyberspace operations. In wartime, these units are organized into specialized groups to support network defense operations.

The space warfare unit of the SSF is responsible for spy satellites as well as China's alternative to GPS, the BeiDou Navigation Satellite System. The mission of the electronic warfare unit is to disrupt enemy radar systems and communications.

The SSF is known to conduct warning and surveillance alongside information gathering activities in the South China Sea tracking U.S. vessels on Freedom of Navigation tours (Asia Nikkei, February 16, 2023). The unit has a strong presence at Wenchang on Hainan Island, near the launching point for Chinese satellites. According to a PLA news release, the SSF is responsible for "unmanned intelligent equipment."[441] Not surprisingly, the unit is suspected to have been behind the 2023 spy balloon incident.[442]

The PRC Ministry of National Defense says that the SSF is "in line with the strategic requirements of integrating existing systems and aligning civil and military endeavors,"[443] a program the CCP regime calls military-civil fusion. Consequently, the SSF is targeting recruits who would not normally join the military. The SSF has expanded its online presence and is recruiting college graduates and people with advanced education for skilled work,

---

[440] DOD Military and Security Developments Involving the People's Republic of China 2023 Report to Congress
[441] http://eng.chinamil.com.cn/ARMEDFORCES/index.html
[442] https://japannews.yomiuri.co.jp/world/asia-pacific/20230206-89269/
[443] http://eng.mod.gov.cn/xb/MilitaryServices/index.html

while also targeting vocational and high school graduates for low-level tech positions.

The spy balloon is a classic example of military-civilian fusion. It was operated by a civilian company,[444] despite being loaded with sophisticated antennas which may have been conducting military surveillance (*Time*, February 9, 2023). The involvement of a civilian company provides the CCP with plausible deniability. Beijing claimed that the balloon was a piece of civilian hardware on a benign civilian mission.

The SSF was born from the concept of "unrestricted warfare" — *Unrestricted Warfare* also being the title of a 1999 book written by two PLA colonels. The book outlines strategies of asymmetric warfare: how a country at a military, political, and economic disadvantage could take on a superpower like the United States. The book proposes a number of alternatives to direct military engagement, mobilizing competencies from multiple government and private domains. The book essentially spells out how to defeat the U.S. The concept is consistent with military-civil fusion in that it integrates all aspects of society. Everything from politics and economics to culture, ideology, and psychology can become weapons.

This form of irregular warfare would draw on the capabilities of multiple government agencies, including the PLA, the Ministry of Foreign Affairs, the CCP's spy agencies — the Ministry of State Security and the Ministry of Public Security — as well as the Ministry of Industry and Information Technology (to control the flow of information), and the UFWD, which has evolved into a large intelligence and propaganda organ. Other

---

[444] https://japannews.yomiuri.co.jp/world/asia-pacific/20230206-89269/

organizations, such as state and non-state hackers,[445] would also be involved.

Sun Tzu famously said: "Every battle is won before it's ever fought." And this is the SSF's strategy: Bring all of its competencies to bear, activating cyber and public opinion warfare before a CCP invasion of Taiwan. Right now, many Americans approve of U.S. support for Ukraine. If public opinion were to sour on Ukraine, voters would push lawmakers to stop sending money and weapons to Kyiv and the nation would fall. Similarly, the CCP could launch an unrestricted warfare campaign against Taipei in the hopes of undermining U.S. support for the island nation. And this is true of any initiative that the CCP wishes to launch against the U.S. They could use the SSF to soften the American people and weaken our resistance.

The Network Systems Department (NSD), part of the SSF — and sometimes known as the CSF — is tasked with information warfare, encompassing cyberspace warfare, technical reconnaissance, electronic warfare (EW), and psychological warfare. This consolidation of missions within a single organizational framework aims to address the operational coordination challenges that previously hindered information-sharing within the PLA. By combining cyberspace and EW elements, China has taken a significant step toward realizing the operational concept of integrated network and electronic warfare, a vision the PLA has pursued since the early 2000s. The NSD manages five theater-aligned technical reconnaissance bases, multiple signals intelligence bureaus, and various research institutes. It supplies intelligence support to theater commands by utilizing an array of ground-based technical collection assets to

---

[445] https://edition.cnn.com/2023/02/16/politics/china-russia-fbi-us-elections/index.html

provide a unified operational picture for geographically dispersed operational units.

The SSF NSD is also responsible for carrying out missions related to the PLA's "Three Warfares" concept,[446] which includes psychological warfare, public opinion warfare, and legal warfare. Notably, this department is the sole publicly-acknowledged unit within the PLA dedicated to conducting psychological warfare operations. Since the early 2000s, the PLA has seen controlling the information spectrum within the modern battlespace as a crucial means to establish information dominance early in a conflict.

Psychological warfare employs propaganda, deception, and coercion to apply pressure and influence the behavior of the target audience. Public opinion warfare involves generating and distributing information to shape an adversary's public perception and garner support from both domestic and international audiences. The two basic components of public opinion warfare are propaganda and misinformation. Propaganda pushes a desired narrative like, "The CCP is great and has your best interests at heart," whereas misinformation attempts to convince people that something is true, such as: "The U.S. sent spy balloons over China in the past, but China did not complain."

Legal warfare employs domestic and international legal frameworks to construct narratives that promote Chinese interests and undermine those of an adversary. It is likely that the PLA aims to integrate digital influence activities with the "Three Warfares" concept to demoralize adversaries and sway both domestic and foreign audiences, thereby creating favorable conditions for the PRC.[447]

---

[446] Ibid.

[447] https://thediplomat.com/2015/12/hybrid-warfare-with-chinese-characteristics-2/

From China's standpoint, every nation — with particular emphasis on the United States — employing digital narratives to challenge the CCP regime within China is seen as conducting offensive influence operations. Consequently, Beijing regards its influence operations aimed at countering this perceived subversion as defensive measures intended to safeguard the interests of the CCP and the PLA. In addition, they seek to cultivate public backing for the military. On a global scale, Beijing strives to shape an information landscape that aligns with the interests of the PRC and its broader foreign policy goals. To attain these aims, China targets media outlets, businesses, educational and cultural entities, as well as policy circles in the U.S. and other nations, plus international organizations, with the intent of achieving outcomes that serve its strategic and military objectives.

The establishment of the PLA SSF in 2015 underscored the regime's recognition of cyber operations as the primary tool for psychological manipulation. In its pursuit of global influence and information dominance on the battlefield, the PLA is actively exploring the next phase of psychological warfare, known as Cognitive Domain Operations (CDO). CDO integrates traditional Chinese concepts like public opinion and psychological warfare with modern internet technologies and communication platforms. Its objective is to advance strategic national security objectives by influencing a target's cognition, thereby altering their decision-making and behavior. The PLA is also keen on integrating emerging technologies like AI, big data, brain science, and neuroscience into CDO, anticipating that these innovations will profoundly impact their ability to manipulate human cognition.[448]

The objective of CDO is to achieve what the PLA terms "mind dominance," defined as leveraging information to influence

---

[448] https://jamestown.org/program/cognitive-domain-operations-the-plas-new-holistic-concept-for-influence-operations/

public opinion and bring about changes in a nation's social structure. This is aimed at creating a favorable environment for China and minimizing civilian and military resistance to PLA actions. The PLA likely intends to employ CDO as an asymmetric capability to deter potential U.S. or third-party involvement in a future conflict. Alternatively, it can be used offensively to shape perceptions and sow division within a society. Authoritative PLA documents suggest that deterrence, in this context, involves exerting psychological pressure and instilling fear in an adversary to compel surrender. PLA writings on CDO emphasize that achieving "mind dominance" within the cognitive realm, effectively subduing the adversary without engaging in physical combat, represents the pinnacle of warfare.

The CCP Threat in the Global Information Environment

Beijing's digital authoritarianism seeks to reshape and control the global information environment, the State Department warned in a September 28, 2023 special report. Claiming that the CCP regime has invested billions of dollars in a strategic campaign of disinformation around the world, designed to manipulate the information space, the report stated "Beijing seeks to maximize the reach of biased or false pro-PRC content," and argued that the CCP's actions were not merely a matter of diplomatic misstep, but a challenge to information integrity and availability around the world.

China's official reaction was typical of the CCP. The PRC Ministry of Foreign Affairs denied any culpability, and alleged that the State Department report was in itself disinformation as it misrepresented facts and truth. Beijing then accused Washington of having a long history of misinformation, concluding that "more and more people in the world have already seen through the U.S.'s ugly attempt to perpetuate its supremacy by weaving lies into 'emperor's new clothes' and smearing others."

The issue, of course, is that the State Department's accusations are true and firmly supported by years of investigations and public reports. The CCP's United Front Work Department (UFWD) attempts to control the flow of information outside of China by silencing dissent, spying on the Chinese diaspora, and disseminating overseas propaganda.[449] The regime employs influencers, as well as online bot and troll armies,[450] to support its efforts to shape the narrative around Taiwan, Xinjiang, and the South China Sea. Additionally, the UFWD pushes news stories and online information against the U.S. and in support of Beijing's foreign policies. In Latin America and Africa, the State Department report explained, the CCP exploits relationships with local media in order to shape the narrative and dispel criticism of Chinese investment projects and debt-trap diplomacy.

Another tool in the CCP's online arsenal is the "wumao army" (aka "50-cent warriors"), people who are paid 0.5 yuan per post on social media sites such as Twitter, Facebook, YouTube, and TikTok (VOA, October 7, 2016). First documented about 20 years ago, the wumao are believed to number in the hundreds of thousands. They work around the clock, on social media, pushing CCP propaganda or countering content which the regime disapproves of. The wumao were particularly busy around the beginning of the pandemic, when they portrayed China as the world's saviors,[451] while diverting attention away from Wuhan as the origin of the virus. Their focus shifts as China's foreign policy evolves and in reaction to world opinions of China.

---

[449] https://cset.georgetown.edu/article/how-chinas-united-front-system-works-overseas/

[450] https://foreignpolicy.com/2015/06/17/how-to-spot-a-state-funded-chinese-internet-troll/

[451] https://ndupress.ndu.edu/Media/News/News-Article-View/Article/2884217/misleading-a-pandemic-the-viral-effects-of-chinese-propaganda-and-the-coronavir/

Russia is increasingly alienated from the international order, and Moscow is working with Beijing to control the information space (VOA, April 13, 2021). This is evident in online efforts by both countries to support the Kremlin's narrative on the Ukraine War. To achieve this goal, CCP trolls have spread disinformation about the Kyiv government and Ukrainian President Zelensky. In February 2022, China and Russia issued the "Joint Statement of the Russian Federation and the People's Republic of China on the International Relations Entering a New Era and the Global Sustainable Development,"[452] which included numerous references to collaboration in information society and security. The problem with totalitarian regimes discussing information security is that the leaders will determine which information poses a threat and whether information must be protected or censored.

CCP Propaganda at Home and Abroad

The better the CCP's ability to not only promote propaganda, but also to dictate the narrative in other countries, the more powerful China will be. The goal of the regime's propaganda is to trumpet the benefits of the Chinese system, as well as the notion that living under the benevolent protection of the CCP is best. PRC citizens need not yearn for Western freedoms or democracy, as they already enjoy a better life than the rest of the world. Left-leaning Westerners are led to believe that the West should learn from China, adopting its system of socialism with Chinese characteristics, providing an improved and more egalitarian life for all of its citizens.

---

[452] http://en.kremlin.ru/supplement/5770

To win over hearts and minds abroad and at home, the CCP uses a variety of tools: state media, complicit foreign media, self-criticism in the United States, and self-censorship in foreign countries. Through these powerful tools, fueled by social media, Beijing is able to take advantage of the real or imagined shortcomings of Western powers, particularly the U.S., to convince Americans and Chinese alike that Western democracy is failing and that the Chinese system is superior.

The CCP maintains several news media abroad, to act as government mouthpieces, spout party propaganda, and influence Westerners, as well as overseas Chinese. Some of these include China Global Television Network (CGTN), Xinhua, *Global Times*, and *Sing Tao Daily*. U.S. Secretary of State Mike Pompeo warned that these media were owned and effectively controlled by the CCP, and were part of the regime's propaganda effort (Al-Jazeera, October 22, 2020).

PRC state media abroad exploit the failures of democratic countries, while promoting the wisdom, generosity, and heroic selflessness of the CCP. A March 3, 2019 commentary published by Xinhua explains how Chinese democracy is superior to Western democracy. This is a bit ironic, coming from what is effectively a one-party state with little or no media freedom, where citizens do not vote for the country's leader. On June 5, 2020, Xinhua claimed that the police response to the George Floyd riots "lays bare U.S. double standard on human rights"— at a time when pro-democracy demonstrators in Hong Kong were being arrested in the middle of the night and the pro-democracy legislators were being ejected from the territory's parliament.

One *Global Times* headline ran "China urges terrorist crackdown by Taliban, as Kabul deadly blasts exemplify U.S.

failure."[453] The regime mouthpiece was quick to say that
Washington had failed in Afghanistan, while avoiding any mention
of the fact that Beijing had already held high-level talks with the
murderous Taliban regime and that the CCP has financially
supported terrorist organizations in Myanmar and India.[454]

Commentary pieces in Xinhua have lauded Beijing's
approach to Africa, strongly implying that, not only is Chinese
economic engagement with Africa beneficial to Africa, with no
downside, but also that the rest of the world has recognized
China's generosity. Similarly, a *Global Times* story (May 14,
2020), "Quarantined Italians praise Chinese government's Covid-
19 fight," illustrated the gratitude of the Italian people to the CCP
for saving their country amid a pandemic (which had, of course,
emerged from China).

Sing Tao Daily is a Chinese-language pro-Beijing media
based in Hong Kong, with an international edition targeted at
overseas Chinese. In an August 30, 2021 article, it reported on
criticism of President Biden by U.S. conservatives; because
criticism of Xi Jinping is unthinkable in China, the CCP interprets
criticism of the U.S. leader by Americans as evidence that the
country is on the verge of collapse. As well as looking for any
misstep by the American administration, *Sing Tao Daily* takes
every opportunity to espouse CCP sentiments, such as the May 3,
2021 story about a meeting between State Councilor Yang Jiechi
and U.S. Secretary of State Antony Blinken. Yang reportedly told
Blinken: "I don't think most countries in the world recognize the
universal values advocated by the U.S., or agree that U.S. opinions
can represent international public opinion." Beijing's goal is to
displace Washington as the world leader.[455] Part of achieving this

---

[453] https://www.globaltimes.cn/page/202108/1232641.shtml
[454] https://www.thequint.com/opinion/northeast-india-sustained-insurgency-covert-chinese-support-weapons-supply
[455] https://www.globaltimes.cn/page/202108/1230495.shtml

goal is promoting the notion that the world would prefer to be led by China.

In 2019, CGTN was deemed a foreign agent by the Justice Department. The following year, U.S. Secretary of State Mike Pompeo designated six more Chinese media outlets as foreign missions — Yicai Global, *Jiefang Daily*, *Xinmin Evening News*, Social Sciences in China Press, *Beijing Review*, and *Economic Daily* — (Al-Jazeera, October 22, 2020) bringing the total to fifteen Chinese media who were forced to register. As foreign missions, these entities are required to disclose to the State Department lists of staff as well as property holdings. Unlike censorship of foreign media in China, the U.S. does not restrict what these and other foreign media may publish. The U.S. position is that readers are free to read what they wish, but that they have a right to know that these media are part of a CCP propaganda effort, rather than independent or unbiased news reporters.

Sing Tao Daily was added to the list of Chinese media ordered to register as foreign missions in 2021.[456] *Sing Tao Daily* claims to be a privately owned company, but both the current and former owners were members of the Chinese People's Political Consultative Conference, an organization composed of people loyal to and with close ties to the CCP.

Complicity of U.S. Actors

According to the Hoover Institute (May 5, 2021), the CCP regime has been conducting an ongoing propaganda campaign in the United States for some time. This campaign tries to undermine U.S. confidence and policies, while exploiting the freedom of speech and the current wave of Americans' self-criticism.

---

[456] https://www.newsmax.com/newsfront/justice-department-chinese-newspaper/2021/08/25/id/1033730/

Beijing's primary tools have been U.S. social media, classrooms, and mainstream media.

Over 200,000 Twitter (now X) accounts were found to be working directly for the CCP (Slate, August 20, 2019), exploiting the death of George Floyd or claims of systemic racism in the U.S. Meanwhile, in the PRC, ethnic Tibetans, Uyghur, and Mongolians have been the victims of all manner of repression and abuses, including cultural genocide, torture, detention, and crimes against humanity.

American classrooms have been another front where the regime has waged its propaganda war. The Confucius Institutes, placed on U.S. college campuses, were paid for by China, but came with stipulations that students not discuss sensitive topics, such as human rights, Tibet, the Tiananmen Square massacre, or Taiwan.[457] The institutes were also accused of spying and of keeping tabs on the activities of Chinese and Taiwanese students on U.S. campuses.

Xinhua News Agency, a CCP mouthpiece, was allowed to rent a huge billboard in New York's Times Square in 2011.[458] Signage in Times Square is very expensive, and the landlords were happy to accept payment, even from Beijing. Similarly, *China Daily* has paid millions to U.S. newspapers, magazines, and other media for propaganda inserts, supplements, printing, and advertising. Over a four-year period, the payments were estimated to total $19 million,[459] of which *Wall Street Journal* received $6 million and *Washington Post* got $4.6 million. This underscores

---

[457] https://www.npr.org/2019/07/17/741239298/as-scrutiny-of-china-grows-some-u-s-schools-drop-a-language-program

[458] https://www.hoover.org/research/chinas-influence-american-interests-media

[459] https://www.business-standard.com/article/international/chinese-mouthpiece-paid-us-newspapers-19-mn-in-ads-printing-report-120060900514_1.html

the fact that the CCP international propaganda campaign is aided by U.S. citizens and companies which depend on Chinese money.

Many of the CCP payments to U.S. media outlets were for inserts which appear to be news stories, but actually promote the Beijing narrative of world events. One insert, titled "Belt and Road aligns with African nations," espoused the benefits of the BRI in Africa, and how the people of Africa welcomed China's friendship and aid. The article failed to mention negative aspects of the BRI, such as debt slavery, corruption, loss of sovereignty, and Chinese businesses driving locals out of certain sectors. Another story told how U.S.-China tariffs negatively impacted American homebuyers, through the increased cost of lumber. This story was meant to discredit President Trump for enacting the tariffs, and turn voters against him. It did not mention, however, that the tariffs were put in place to save jobs in the U.S. lumber industry or that they were a response to decades of China charging higher tariffs on American products.

The Justice Department revealed that *China Daily* paid for $50,000 of advertising in *The New York Times*, $240,000 to *Foreign Policy*, $34,600 to *The Des Moines Register*, and $76,000 to CQ-Roll Call.[460] The total spent by *China Daily* came to $11,002,628 paid to newspapers for advertising, plus an additional $265,822 paid to Twitter (now X.com). Other recipients of CCP money were *Los Angeles Times*, *Seattle Times*, *The Atlanta Journal-Constitution*, *The Chicago Tribune*, *The Houston Chronicle*, and *The Boston Globe*. Consequently, the DOJ required *China Daily* to disclose its activities, under the Foreign Agents Registration Act.

China's media propaganda campaign is enabled by U.S. mainstream media. Left-leaning media have, at times, promoted

---

[460] Ibid.

Beijing's positions while discrediting conservative media, simply for publishing an opposing viewpoint. One example would be left-leaning media which supported China's claims that the origin of Covid-19 was not the lab in Wuhan, while criticizing other media for publishing evidence to the contrary. At the same time, CCP media in North America attempted to shift blame for the origin of Covid-19 to other countries, including the U.S. (Freedom House, April 20, 2020).

A subtle example of U.S. media's complicity in CCP propaganda is that they often refer to Xi Jinping as president of China, rather than General Secretary of the Chinese Communist Party.[461] By definition, a president is elected. Not only was Xi not elected, but he had the PRC constitution altered, allowing him to remain in power for life.

U.S. self-censorship is another tool in the CCP's toolbox. The fear of losing access to Chinese markets drives many U.S. firms to avoid doing anything that might upset Beijing. American filmmakers are among the worst culprits. Major media including NBC News, CNBC, and MSNBC, are owned by Comcast, which also owns Universal. China is now the most important export market for films, so Universal has edited a number of its films to accommodate the CCP.

A Taiwan flag on the main character's jacket in *Top Gun: Maverick* was scrubbed from trailers, but after uproar reappeared in the film's worldwide release.[462] The remake of *Red Dawn* changed the script, having the United States implausibly invaded by North Korea rather than Communist China. YouTube has been known to defund or delete videos critical of the CCP regime.[463]

---

461 https://www.hoover.org/research/beijings-woke-propaganda-war-america
462 https://www.vice.com/en/article/7kb5wd/tom-cruises-jacket-top-gun-maverick-taiwan-moviegoers-clapping
463 https://intpolicydigest.org/china-s-communist-party-and-its-american-media-enablers/

The general manager of the NBA's Houston Rockets apologized to Beijing, after tweeting in support of the Hong Kong pro-democracy protesters. One of the more bizarre examples of self-censorship was when the EU removed language blaming China in a report on disinformation.[464]

Through its propaganda efforts, U.S. media complacency and U.S. self-censorship, Beijing is able to portray China as a country with a "different" but equal style of government, where citizens enjoy a high standard of living, a great deal of freedom, and there is universal support for the CCP. Of course, if this were true, the regime would hold general elections and would have no need to censor media and social media at home or abroad.

The CCP's Domestic Propaganda

Around the 100th anniversary of the Chinese Communist Party in 2021, the propaganda was stepped up, praising both the party and Xi Jinping. In a China that has become prosperous and where competition in the new economy is fierce, it would be easy for everyday people to turn away from the party which once vilified the wealthy class. Yet, through continued propaganda efforts and a periodic rewriting of the message — which now suggests that becoming wealthy is an act of patriotism — the CCP has not only managed to stay relevant, but to remain supreme. The anniversary slogan was "always follow the party" (*Washington Post*, June 30, 2021).

A previous generation of Chinese school children read a column called "Socialism Is Good. Capitalism Is Bad." This promoted the idea that the CCP took care of its people, while Western governments allowed their citizens to suffer in hunger until they died. True believers wound up pitying Americans who

---

[464] https://www.theatlantic.com/politics/archive/2020/05/china-disinformation-propaganda-united-states-xi-jinping/612085/

were six times wealthier, on average, than Chinese people. Today, convincing PRC citizens that all Americans are poor is much more difficult, but state media does a good job of distorting wealth inequality and homelessness in the United States.[465]

Xi has stated that the task of the United Front Work Department and other propaganda outlets is to demonstrate the superiority of the PRC system through prosperity (*The Atlantic*, May 28, 2020). Chinese-language articles regularly appear in state media about how unfair the U.S. economic system is, and how "inequality kills." However, according to the Gini coefficient, wealth inequality in the United States is only slightly worse than in China. One key difference is that the lowest 29 percent of wage earners in the United States earn a bit more than $25,000 per year (CNBC, September 28, 2019), while China's middle class earn about $10,000 per year.[466] China has nearly as many billionaires as the United States (BBC, 8 April 2021). Even more concerning, 600 million Chinese are still living on $140 per month.[467] The problem of wealth inequality is at least as bad, if not worse, in China.

The CCP propaganda apparatus at home exploited every misstep Western countries took during the pandemic, including the large number of deaths in the U.S. Every mistake in a democratic country becomes one more piece that Beijing exploits to further its interests. These sentiments were espoused in Chinese-language state media, then echoed in English in *Global Times*, for the rest of the world to read. Chinese media also exploited the January 6 breach of the Capitol to show divisions within the United States (*Washington Post*, February 4, 2021). Reports published inside the PRC even went so far as to call the U.S. a failed state. Beijing

---

465 https://www.globaltimes.cn/page/202106/1227255.shtml
466 https://chinapower.csis.org/china-middle-class/
467 https://www.cnbctv18.com/economy/china-has-over-600-million-poor-with-140-monthly-income-premier-li-keqiang-6024341.htm

capitalizes on negative stories about the United States as proof that democracy either does not exist in the U.S., or that democracy is collapsing, and consequently, Chinese citizens should be happy that they live under the CCP regime.

State-controlled TV includes U.S. media reporting as part of its domestic propaganda campaign.[468] Chinese media regularly tell PRC citizens which U.S. media reports support the official narratives of the CCP. One Chinese-language story appearing on the news portal Sina had a title translated as "The U.S. is undergoing a major collapse." The story was supported by a reference to a *Washington Post* article, the Chinese-language title of which translated to "A Great Crash in the United States."

Beijing also uses these American news stories to establish China as an expert that can help other nations, or as the savior of the world. China is portrayed as an expert in stories about the heroic role the CCP took in controlling the coronavirus, praising its first responders and nurses, or trumpeting its aid to Italy in the early days of the pandemic. Not only are most countries not grateful to China, but many wish to hold the CCP accountable for mishandling and lying about Covid-19, as well as for the disappearance of several Chinese whistleblowers.[469]

At other times, state media portrays China as a hapless victim. A story on the Huanqiu website claimed that "FBI agents admitted that they framed the Chinese professor [Anming Hu.]" That scholar was indeed found innocent, but in countless other cases, the regime is proven to have used academics as spies. Other

---

[468] https://intpolicydigest.org/china-s-communist-party-and-its-american-media-enablers/

[469] https://www.heritage.org/asia/report/holding-the-chinese-communist-party-accountable-its-response-the-covid-19-outbreak

academics that have been arrested for spying for Beijing or failing to disclose their connection to the CCP or the PLA.

Whether state media represents the PRC as a hero or a victim on a given day depends on which image best suits the regime's immediate needs. When the CCP falls out with a foreign nation, propaganda is designed to turn public opinion against that country. In 2019, China sanctioned Norway for awarding the Nobel Peace Prize to pro-democracy activist Liu Xiaobo. Later, propaganda fanned citizens' anger against Australia, because Canberra called for an independent investigation into the origins of Covid-19 (*The Guardian*, April 29, 2020).

After a PRC Ministry of Foreign Affairs spokesperson wrote on Twitter (now X) that — if it is so concerned about transparency and discovering the true origin of Covid-19 — Washington should open its biodefense lab at Fort Detrick, Maryland to international inspectors, state media replayed the tweet in reports published in English, Spanish, Arabic, and other languages. CGTN and *Global Times* ran versions of the story, following Xi's edict that the media should promote "positive propaganda" for the "correct guidance of public opinion."[470]

The regime has complete control of all news media and total censorship on social media, while it is able to keep unwanted information out with the Great Firewall. The people see only what the party wants them to see and know almost nothing about what the regime does not want them to know. The average PRC citizen has no idea that in Xinjiang, millions of Uyghur Muslims are being persecuted, tortured, detained, or subjected to forced labor and organ harvesting. Neither do they know of the countless Tibetans who have been murdered or the millions robbed of their religion

---

[470] https://www.theatlantic.com/politics/archive/2020/05/china-disinformation-propaganda-united-states-xi-jinping/612085/

and language. They are unaware of the cultural genocide being committed in Tibet, Xinjiang, and Inner Mongolia. They were, however, aware of the death of George Floyd and the ensuing riots which engulfed the United States.

While the CCP is waging genocide against its own Muslim population, *Global Times* is running stories about America's mistreatment of Muslim-Americans.[471] The outlet went so far as to call the United States "a colonial, expansionist genocidal settler state" (August 11, 2021). The same Chinese readers would be unaware that East Turkestan (now Xinjiang) and Tibet were independent until forcibly annexed after the CCP's military invasion.

Propaganda is the CCP's most powerful control mechanism, Gordon G. Chang wrote in an essay published May 5, 2021 by the Hoover Institution. The regime's propaganda departments employ millions of people, have tremendous budgets, and can access sophisticated technology. The propaganda machine operates on the belief that propaganda is neither lying nor deceitful, but rather, a necessary and virtuous component of building and maintaining the state.

Propaganda Focused on Overseas Chinese

IRSEM, the Strategic Research Institute of France's Military College identified in a September 2021 report the CCP's three-pronged attack as consisting of psychological warfare, public opinion warfare, and legal warfare, all part of a massive propaganda campaign focused on overseas Chinese.[472] The regime claims ownership of anyone of Chinese descent, anywhere in the

---

[471] https://www.globaltimes.cn/page/202107/1228858.shtml

[472] https://www.rfi.fr/en/international/20210922-french-study-warns-of-the-massive-scale-of-chinese-influence-around-the-world

world, and it is working hard to influence, recruit, co-opt, ostracize, or silence ethnic Chinese in other countries.

In 2017, Xi Jinping called for "closely uniting" with overseas Chinese in support of the Chinese dream.[473] The Chinese diaspora, including both Chinese nationals abroad (*huaqiao*) and foreign nationals of Chinese heritage (*huaren*), number about 60 million. Xi sees these people as being integral to achieving "The Great Rejuvenation" of the Chinese state, and China taking center stage in global politics.[474]

CCP overseas propaganda is largely carried out through the United Front Work Department (UFWD), which often targets overseas Chinese communities. Much of the propaganda is subtle, just nudging foreign public opinion in a direction conducive to the interests of the regime. Some of it is more overt, influencing local politics, damaging media integrity, facilitating espionage, and increasing unapproved technology transfer.

Through its propaganda programs in overseas Chinese communities, the CCP also seeks to undermine social cohesion and exacerbate racial tension, raising support for the regime or intentionally causing divisions among the Chinese diaspora. Most Chinese diaspora do not support Beijing and do not wish to be pawns in China's global game.[475] But CCP propaganda serves to drive a wedge between Chinese who are not loyal to the CCP and their local communities.

One of the regime's subtle disinformation programs was the 2021 effort which linked Covid-19 origin theories with anti-

---

[473] https://warontherocks.com/2018/03/beijings-influence-operations-target-chinese-diaspora/

[474] https://ipdefenseforum.com/2021/05/the-ccp-and-the-diaspora/

[475] Ibid.

Asian racism.[476] Much of this campaign was focused on discrediting Yan Limeng, a Chinese virologist, who published a paper claiming that the virus was made in a PRC government laboratory. One of the goals of CCP disinformation campaigns may not be to convince skeptics, but to draw attention away from more authoritative theories. It also helped to shift lab-origin theories away from mainstream audiences, relegating them to the fringes of dark web conspiracy theories.[477]

Another tactic taken by the CCP regime is to spin their interpretation of news from other countries, in such a fashion as to conclude that the party way is best. In 2018, *People's Daily* ran a piece, praising Xi's "systematic elaboration" of the advantages of China's party system,[478] and how he has educated the world on building a better political system. Such commentary will usually be accompanied by reports of some sort of chaos or political turmoil in the U.S. or India or Nigeria, arriving at the conclusion that democracy causes disorder, while the CCP system provides stability for citizens.

The regime claims that Western societies do not want the Chinese diaspora to know that the CCP system is "providing the world with…a China solution…a better political system."[479] And, for this reason, the West discredits Chinese overseas media, in order to prevent the diaspora from finding out the true benefits of a one-party totalitarian regime.

Between April and June in 2021, the hashtags #StopAsianHate and #LiMengYan were tweeted and retweeted 30,000 times, by more than 6,000 suspicious accounts, all posting the same memes, with English phrases. The vast majority of these

---

[476] https://www.aspistrategist.org.au/stopasianhate-chinese-diaspora-targeted-by-ccp-disinformation-campaign/
[477] Ibid.
[478] https://www.aspi.org.au/report/party-speaks-you
[479] Ibid.

tweets were made during normal business hours, Beijing time. This campaign was seen across American social media — Facebook, Instagram, YouTube, Reddit, Google Groups and Medium — as well as non-US platforms such as TikTok, VK and a Russian amateur blog site.

UFWD actions are difficult for democratic societies to address, because some of the programs fall into the category of freedom of speech,[480] while others are covert actions and espionage, which are hard to detect.

Extraterritorial activities of the CCP regime and the UFWD often violate international law, such as the abduction of Swedish national Gui Minhai in Thailand and Lee Bo, a British citizen in Hong Kong. Additionally, they regularly threaten exiled ethnic Uyghurs and Tibetans who speak out against the regime.[481]

The PRC authorities also fund Chinese schools in foreign countries,[482] where party opinions are disseminated and opposing voices are not tolerated. China News Service, the country's second largest state-run media group, operates at the behest of the UFWD to influence the Chinese diaspora.[483] By controlling diaspora media, funding research at think tanks, and using WeChat and other social media to censor, surveil and control discourse, the UFWD facilitates espionage and unsupervised technology transfer.

About 70 percent of the Chinese diaspora live in Asia, particularly Southeast Asia. To win their support, Beijing offers them various incentives, such as money, access to education, support for their businesses, and protection for their intellectual

---

[480] https://www.wsj.com/articles/china-steps-up-moves-to-influence-diaspora-communities-11591645344

[481] https://ipdefenseforum.com/2021/05/the-ccp-and-the-diaspora/

[482] https://warontherocks.com/2018/03/beijings-influence-operations-target-chinese-diaspora/

[483] https://chinamediaproject.org/the_ccp_dictionary/global-chinese-media-cooperative-union/

property. In Malaysia, where nearly 23 percent of the population are ethnic Chinese, CCP officials regularly conduct visits to Chinese communities, endorse pro-China political candidates,[484] and attend meetings of Chinese political parties.

In the U.S., multiple Chinese scientists have been arrested for technology theft, while thousands of other suspected instances of espionage and coercion are under investigation. In Australia, Canada, the UK, and the United States, on-campus organizations have been heavily infiltrated by UFWD, spying on international students, suppressing academic freedom and mobilizing students to protest in support of the interests of the CCP.

During the early days of the Covid-19 outbreak in China, students and other diaspora in Argentina, Australia, Canada, Czechia, Japan, the UK, and the U.S. were told to buy out medical supplies in local pharmacies and ship them back to China.[485] Much of this effort was directed by a UFWD-linked entity, the All-China Federation of Returned Overseas Chinese. Buying up medical supplies in foreign countries created shortages, boosting demand for Chinese products, driving up prices, and ultimately benefiting the CCP regime economically. This also put Beijing in the position of benevolent savior, doling out much-needed medical supplies as part of its international PR campaign.

The PRC does not recognize dual citizenship, claiming full sovereignty over anyone holding a Chinese passport. And much of the rhetoric of Xi and the party is about Chinese blood and the blood of the ancestors, which translates to the CCP believing that they control or should control foreign citizens of Chinese descent, no matter how distant their ties to China.

---

[484] https://warontherocks.com/2018/03/beijings-influence-operations-target-chinese-diaspora/
[485] https://www.aspistrategist.org.au/the-party-speaks-for-you-foreign-interference-and-the-chinese-communist-partys-united-front-system/

The regime has always seen diaspora Chinese as a source of revenue and investment. In more recent decades, they have regarded them as sources of technology transfer, taking part in Chinese-led multi-national technology development initiatives.[486] The diaspora have also been crucial in the Belt and Road Initiative (BRI), facilitating and smoothing Chinese engagement with various countries. Since 2016, the CCP has held an annual business conference for overseas Chinese involved in the BRI.

Since 1999, China has offered two-week-long "birthright tours," which are largely free, for those with Chinese ancestry. Over 400,000 foreign-born Chinese have taken advantage of this opportunity.[487]

According to the IRSEM report, CCP operations are not limited to the U.S., but also take place in Taiwan, Singapore, Sweden, Canada, and other countries. This propaganda push runs parallel to "wolf warrior" diplomacy, in which individual Chinese ambassadors would attack the countries they were posted in, through letters to local media or in television interviews. One of the more egregious examples was former PRC Ambassador to Malaysia, Huang Huikang, who openly supported China's business interests in the country, while attending events held by the Malaysian Chinese Association of the Barisan Nasional government, *The Diplomat* reported on May 8, 2018. This is a clear example of the CCP working through an embassy to not only win support within the diaspora for Beijing's economic interests, but also to support political candidates and parties that may later be in a position to champion the regime.

---

[486] https://warontherocks.com/2018/03/beijings-influence-operations-target-chinese-diaspora/

[487] https://warontherocks.com/2018/03/beijings-influence-operations-target-chinese-diaspora/

Another PRC entity, the Chinese People's Association for Friendship with Foreign Countries (CPAFFC), states its goals as "to enhance people's friendship, further international cooperation...on behalf of the Chinese people, makes friends and deepens friendship in the international...while carrying out all-directional, multi-level and broad-area people-to-people friendship work to serve the great cause of China's peaceful development and reunification."[488]

Western governments need to ask themselves if they should allow organizations which "serve the great cause" of the CCP regime to operate freely in their countries. Additionally, it is unclear here if the term "reunification" means a Chinese takeover of Taiwan or China annexing the Chinese diaspora living in foreign countries.

In addition to trying to influence overseas Chinese through direct contact and trips and conferences, the regime has sought to recruit students who are studying abroad to spy on one another. These goals are often achieved through threats and other strongarm tactics,[489] frequently coming from the PRC embassy or consulate.

The party's overseas activities include: Suppressing dissident movements in diaspora communities, cultivating a cooperative international environment, smoothing the way for a takeover of Taiwan, as well as intelligence gathering, technology theft, and encouraging investment in China.[490] According to IRSEM, there is also evidence of China trying to alter the narrative about the Hong Kong protests, as well as releasing misinformation that holds the U.S. responsible for the Covid-19 pandemic.

---

[488] https://cpaffc.org.cn/index/xiehui/xiehui_list/cate/12/lang/2.html

[489] https://warontherocks.com/2018/03/beijings-influence-operations-target-chinese-diaspora/

[490] https://www.aspi.org.au/report/party-speaks-you

Until recently, the vast majority of Chinese who left China never returned. Nowadays, around 80 percent of those who leave to study abroad go back. This shows that CCP messages being broadcast abroad — namely that the regime provides a better life to its citizens than Western nations do to theirs — is succeeding. To promote this, and other messages, Beijing has been building a massive, global media network.

One of the largest diaspora media is the website Wenxuecity, largely for those living in the U.S. Founded by Chinese exchange students in 1998, Wenxuecity has been accused of having ties to the CCP, which analysts have largely confirmed. A Stanford University investigation published on September 24, 2020 discovered that about 16 percent of Wenxuecity's general articles and 25 percent of stories about Hong Kong and the CCP or Xi Jinping came from Chinese state media or media friendly with the regime.

In addition to influencing diaspora media, the CCP has spent billions of dollars building a global television network which can compete with the BBC and CNN. Meanwhile, Beijing has stepped up its efforts to bring overseas Chinese-language media under its control. At a meeting of Chinese-language media from over 60 countries, a senior official said that the duty of such outlets was to "retransmit" news from CCP state-owned media at "important times" (*The Economist*, September 23, 2021).

8

The Infrastructure Dimension

The United States has been an industrialized economy for far longer than China, as indicated by various infrastructure statistics. There are 13,513 airports around the U.S., while China has 507. The U.S. has 35 ports to China's 22. The U.S. also leads in railways, with 140,000 miles (225,000 km) compared to 83,000 miles (133,000 km) in China. However, the PRC has built around 22,000 miles (over 35,000 km) of high-speed railway, whereas the U.S. has just one short stretch of high-speed rail, with another under construction in California. In terms of merchant vessels, China has 6,662, to the U.S.'s 3,627. The U.S. has far more waterways than China, 25,000 miles (41,000 km) to around 7,000 miles (11,000 km).

The United States produces more oil per day than China, 13.2 million barrels versus around 4.9 million barrels.[491] In 2022, the U.S. consumed more oil than any other country, around 19 million barrels daily, while China was the number-two consumer, using 12.8 million barrels per day. China's proven oil reserves are estimated at 25.1 billion barrels, while those of the U.S. total 35.23 billion barrels.[492] In terms of primary energy consumption, in 2022

---

[491] https://www.worldometers.info/oil/china-oil/
[492] https://www.worldometers.info/oil/oil-reserves-by-country/

the PRC burned 159.39 exajoules, compared to 95.91 exajoules in the U.S.[493]

Technological Power

The CCP regime's pursuit of supremacy hinges on the success of its economy. Currently, China faces economic slowdown, an aging population, and a shrinking workforce. To break free from its economic challenges and sustain growth and modernization, China must prioritize economic liberalization and innovation. The potential for growing GDP lies in the utilization of modern technology, which can outperform manual labor. Any assessment of China's technological progress must consider the Global Innovation Index (GII), investment in R&D, technological progress, patent applications, the presence and quality of scientific research organizations, corporate investment in R&D, and academic publications.

The World Intellectual Property Organization's GII assesses the innovation capabilities of global economies by considering about 80 indicators including institutions, human capital and research, infrastructure, credit, investment, linkages; the creation, absorption and diffusion of knowledge; and creative outputs. In this way, GII aims to provide a comprehensive view of innovation. In the GII 2023 Report, China places 12th out of 132 economies.

In terms of spending on R&D, China devoted 2.43 percent of GDP, the fourth highest percentage in the world. In terms of dollars, China spent $556 billion, ranking it second, behind the United States. Four Chinese companies rank high on the global list

---

[493] https://www.statista.com/statistics/263455/primary-energy-consumption-of-selected-countries/

of corporate R&D: Huawei Investment & Holding ranks 4th with an expenditure of $20.976 billion; Alibaba Group Holding is 17th, spending $8.254 billion; Tencent is 18th with $7.190 billion; China State Construction Engineering is 34th with $5.509 billion (GII 2023 Report).

According to Data Pandas, the U.S. is the world's number two most technologically advanced country, with a score of 78, behind Japan, which scores 80. China ranks ninth with a score of 26. A ranking by *Global Finance* (August 9, 2023) lists South Korea (6.63), the United States (4.94), and Taiwan (4.90) as the top three, with China in 38th position, scoring negative 0.23. Insider Monkey's November 1, 2023 tally of the most technologically advanced countries heading into 2024 put the U.S. in first place and China sixth.

The QS World University Rankings by Subject 2023: Engineering & Technology featured 7 U.S. universities in its top 15; the only Chinese institution was Tsinghua University at 9th.

For patent applications, China ranked first in the world in 2022 with 1.619 million, while the U.S. was second with 594,340.[494]

China now publishes more academic papers than any other country, but different sources give different totals. In most, but not all, rankings, the United States is in second place. As of 2020, the U.S. remained "the most prolific publisher of high-quality natural-sciences research in the Nature Index, but China is closing the gap with remarkable speed" (*Nature*, April 29, 2020). A September 17, 2019 article in the same publication concluded that, of the world's top universities in the best countries for scientific research,

---

[494] https://www.wipo.int/en/ipfactsandfigures/patents

Harvard was number one while China's Peking University was number two. In terms of most-cited papers, China is now first.[495]

It is important to approach these rankings with caution. There are multiple ranking organizations which rank countries and schools in differing relative positions. Additionally, in China, academic practices can inflate publication numbers, as PRC universities often mandate master's and Ph.D. students to publish multiple papers before graduating. Professors receive bonuses based on publication quantity, not necessarily quality,[496] and there is a culture of mutual citation. Additionally, many publications may not be in English, limiting their accessibility. China's prolific publishing and citation rates can be attributed to its large population and a system structured to prioritize academic output, which might not necessarily reflect its true innovation capabilities.

[495] https://www.science.org/content/article/china-rises-first-place-most-cited-papers
[496] https://www.science.org/content/article/china-rises-first-place-most-cited-papers

9

Diplomatic Dimension

Alliances play a pivotal role in bolstering a country's overall military power for a multitude of reasons. Firstly, they foster collective security by uniting nations under a common defense agreement, effectively deterring potential aggressors and enhancing the combined military strength of member countries. The prospect of a collective response from all alliance members in the event of an attack discourages hostile actions, thereby contributing to regional and global stability.

Secondly, alliances combine the defense spending of multiple nations, encouraging resource sharing, allowing member nations to pool their military personnel, equipment, and expertise. Resource sharing and joint training exercises foster interoperability. Common standards and procedures within alliances make it easier for diverse military forces to work together effectively during joint operations or in multinational missions.

Strategic geopolitical positioning is another vital advantage of alliances. The granting of access to overseas military bases, supports combat operations on multiple fronts. It also enhances the ability to resupply ships and deploy troops to destinations. By facilitating intelligence sharing, and offering logistical support, alliances extend a country's reach and influence in global affairs. This positioning is invaluable both militarily and diplomatically, enabling collaborative actions such as UN sanctions and peacekeeping missions. Furthermore, alliances provide essential political and diplomatic support. Member nations are more inclined to assist each other in diplomatic negotiations and often coordinate their positions on various international issues.

The United States is a member of the North Atlantic Treaty Organization (NATO) which combines the budget, hardware, personnel and capabilities of 31 nations. The U.S. and Canada also collaborate in NORAD, the North American Aerospace Defense Command, which provides aerospace warning, aerospace control, and maritime warning for North America. It is responsible for the detection, identification, and surveillance of aerospace and maritime threats in the airspace and waters around North America.

China only has one official ally, having a longstanding defense pact with North Korea.[497] However, China now includes the word "security" rather than defense, as a term of many of its bilateral agreements, as with the Solomon Islands, or its multinational agreements such as SCO. Beijing also maintains "comprehensive strategic cooperative partnerships" with Belarus, Cambodia, Congo, Ethiopia, Guinea, Kenya, Laos, Mozambique, Myanmar, Namibia, Senegal, Sierra Leone, Thailand, Vietnam and Zimbabwe. The next highest level of relationship are the "strategic cooperative partnerships" that China maintains with Afghanistan, Bangladesh, Brunei, India, Nepal, South Korea, Sri Lanka, and Suriname, as well as the African Union.[498] In addition, the Chinese regime has significant economic influence over a number of countries which could, theoretically be coerced into aiding the PRC in a war with the United States.

---

[497] https://www.upi.com/Top_News/World-News/2021/07/07/china-China-North-Korea-defense-treaty/8851625677806/
[498] https://www.newsweek.com/worlds-eyes-beijing-heres-how-china-ranks-relations-across-globe-1679183

Blocs and Groupings

The best known grouping in which China participates is BRICS, a loose alliance which conducts regular meetings focusing on trade, cooperation, and potential de-dollarization.

Also important is the Shanghai Cooperation Organization (SCO), an intergovernmental body founded on June 15, 2001. The organization was established in Shanghai, China by six countries: China, Russia, Kazakhstan, Kyrgyzstan, Tajikistan, and Uzbekistan. The SCO primarily focuses on regional security, economic cooperation, and cultural exchanges in Central Asia and Eurasia. The original member states have been joined by India, Iran, and Pakistan. The four observer states interested in becoming full members are Afghanistan, Belarus, and Mongolia. There are 14 dialogue partners, among them Cambodia, Egypt, Saudi Arabia, Sri Lanka, Turkey (a NATO member), and the United Arab Emirates.

Beijing hopes these organizations can rival the UN, the World Bank, the IMF, and the dollar-based international trade system. The regime's goal is to replace the Washington-led international order with a Beijing-led world order, but avoids actually saying that. However, there are a number of reasons why the SCO and BRICS cannot rival the U.S.-led institutions. First, when the UN charter was signed in California in 1945, there was no alternative. Most nations wanted to join, and the UN counted 51 founding members. Convincing countries that Beijing has a better solution than the 193-strong UN is a hard sell.

The BRI, SCO, and BRICS lack key institutions, trade deals, defense pacts, and a common currency. BRICS has a China-led New Development Bank, mainly funded in U.S. dollars. In contrast, the international system led by the United States boasts well-established institutions like the World Bank, the IMF, and the

Bretton Woods dollar-based global trading system, all of which were established during the same conference at Bretton Woods, New Hampshire, in 1944. The General Agreement on Tariffs and Trade (GATT), which later became the WTO, emerged in 1947. These institutions were integrated into the UN and underpinned the U.S.-led global order.

BRICS

BRICS, an acronym representing the five major emerging economies of Brazil, Russia, India, China, and South Africa, serves as a significant platform for China to advance its diplomatic and strategic objectives while challenging what it sees as the global hegemony of the United States. This international grouping fosters economic cooperation among its members, emphasizing trade agreements, investment opportunities, and infrastructure development projects. The intent of the CCP regime is to build stronger economic ties among BRICS nations, thereby reducing dependence on the Western-dominated global economic system.

Moreover, BRICS offers a forum for these emerging nations to engage in multilateral diplomacy, helping them coordinate positions on critical global issues. China actively works to align BRICS countries on topics such as international trade, climate change, and global governance reform. This unity enables them to challenge Western dominance and have a more substantial influence on international decision-making.

Beijing also takes advantage of BRICS by establishing financial institutions like the New Development Bank. These institutions offer an alternative to traditional Western-dominated organizations, such as the World Bank and the IMF, providing member nations with financing options and more influence in shaping the global financial landscape.

In addition to these initiatives, China views BRICS as a crucial counterbalance to Western alliances like the G7 and NATO. By strengthening relations within BRICS, China aims to diminish the influence of Western powers in shaping global norms and policies. The collective strength of BRICS allows these emerging economies to assert themselves on the world stage and present an alternative to the Western-centric approach to international affairs (NBC News, August 23, 2023).

South-South cooperation is another vital aspect of China's strategy within BRICS. This concept underscores collaboration among developing nations to address common challenges. By working closely with other BRICS members, China claims to champion the interests of developing nations globally. However, the goals of any expanded BRICS grouping would likely be unachievable, given the divergent interests and outright conflicts among the member countries, not to mention their very different economic and political conditions.

Unattainable Goals

At the end of the BRICS Summit in Johannesburg on August 24, 2023, it was announced that the five founding nations had invited six countries to join: Saudi Arabia, the United Arab Emirates, Iran, Egypt, Ethiopia, and Argentina. The expansion in membership, to take effect in January 2024, was called "historic" by Xi Jinping[499] and "a game changer" by some supporters.[500]

The term BRIC, coined in 2001 by Goldman Sachs economist Jim O'Neill, initially excluded South Africa. O'Neill's

---

[499] https://edition.cnn.com/2023/08/24/business/saudi-arabia-brics-invitation-intl/index.html
[500] https://usiblog.in/brics-expansion-game-changer-for-the-global-economy/

later prediction that, by 2041 — a date he later revised to 2039, then to 2032 — the BRICS would overtake the six largest Western economies in terms of economic might,[501] now appears unlikely. This has not stopped Xi from promoting BRICS as a rival to the G7, yet it remains loosely organized with no institutions or common currency. If it can create them, escape what some perceive as U.S. hegemony, and build an alternative to the Western-led system, the result may simply be Chinese hegemony.

China, Russia, and, to some extent, India hold most of the political and economic influence in BRICS. These three nations are also the world's top military powers, after the United States. Both China and Russia are experiencing severe economic downturns. Since the beginning of the Ukraine War, Russia's economy has been deteriorating. As a result, Moscow is steadily becoming more financially dependent on Beijing. At the same time, China is wrestling with declining trade and investment, reduced exports, and record youth unemployment. Beijing may find it difficult or even impossible to underwrite the other BRICS nations. And if it can, then BRICS will just be replacing the Washington-led international order with one led by the CCP regime, which India is unlikely to accept.

Those who believe that BRICS will disrupt the international order can cite a number of impressive statistics. With the accession of the new member countries, the total population of BRICS will increase by 400 million, bringing the grouping to 46 percent of the world's population. It will also have 75 percent of the world's manganese supply, 50 percent of its graphite, 28 percent of the planet's nickel, and 10 percent of the world's copper. However, like the oil-producing members of BRICS, there

---

[501] https://www.ft.com/content/112ca932-00ab-11df-ae8d-00144feabdc0

is no coordination among its mineral producers to control the quantity or price of minerals.

BRICS will now account for 30 percent of global GDP, making it larger than the G7. Additionally, the grouping represents 25 percent of world exports and 42 percent of world oil production, as well as significant percentages of various critical minerals (CSIS, August 25, 2023). And the group is expected to grow; 40 countries have expressed interest in joining.

Xi said that the expansion of BRICS will "inject new vitality into the BRICS cooperation mechanism and further strengthen the power of world peace and development."[502] This is despite the fact that Russia, the second most powerful and developed member of the group, is actively engaged in a war and widely sanctioned by the international order. Proposed member Ethiopia is in the midst of a civil war. Iran is heavily sanctioned for its support of Russia's invasion of Ukraine, as well as its nuclear weapons ambitions. Until recently, Iran and Saudi Arabia were involved in proxy wars in Syria and Yemen.

BRICS heavyweight India has an active border dispute with China, resulting in minor military clashes in 2020 and 2022.[503] The PLA Navy's activities in the Indian Ocean have led India to strengthen defense ties with the United States, Australia, and Japan through the Quad. Just days after the BRICS summit, the PRC Ministry of Natural Resources released its 2023 map, claiming Indian and Russian territory. India promptly lodged a diplomatic complaint (*Times of India*, August 30, 2023). This complicates meaningful cooperation within BRICS for global peace and economic development.

---

[502] https://www.fmprc.gov.cn/eng/zxxx_662805/202308/t20230824_11132358.html
[503] https://www.usip.org/publications/2023/05/why-we-should-all-worry-about-china-india-border-dispute

De-Dollarization

Over the past years, Chinese state media, pro-cryptocurrency media, and other non-mainstream media have been running stories about how the world is abandoning the U.S. dollar as its reserve and trading currency.[504] It is claimed that the yuan is gaining internationalization, or that the BRICS grouping is set to issue its own currency (*Times of India*, April 4, 2023), in order to move away from the dollar. The other claim is that OPEC will either switch to the yuan, a composite currency, or the BRICS currency. These claims are highly exaggerated. Moscow and Beijing have always aspired to move away from the dollar, and many nations resent Washington's currency hegemony. But attempts to de-dollarize have proven impossible for numerous reasons, and the challenges seem insurmountable. Perhaps for these reasons, replacing the dollar with a BRICS currency was not even on the agenda of this most recent BRICS summit.

The first obstacle in abandoning the dollar is that countries would have to find or create an alternative. Currently, the dollar is the world's most useful currency; it is liquid and freely convertible, and accounts for about 90 percent of all currency trading.[505] Additionally, just under 60 percent of all foreign currency reserves held by central banks are in U.S. dollars or dollar equivalents (Reuters, September 30, 2023). Most commodities, including oil, as well as most international trade, is priced in dollars, and over 74 percent of foreign trade is settled in dollars.[506] And because investors want to avoid currency risk, governments around the world issue most of their foreign bonds and sovereign debt obligations in U.S. dollars.

---

[504] https://www.globaltimes.cn/page/202303/1288311.shtml
[505] https://www.globaltrademag.com/how-the-united-states-dollar-dominated-the-global-trade-space/
[506] Ibid.

One common argument given for de-dollarizing is that the U.S. dollar is not backed by gold. While this is true, it is also true of essentially all other currencies on Earth today. Paper currencies issued by governments are fiat currencies, meaning that they exist by government fiat, rather than being convertible into gold or silver. What gives the dollar its value is that the U.S. government can tax the American people. The United States is a nation of 335 million people with a median household income of around $69,000 per year.[507] Because the U.S. authorities are very good at collecting revenue for the government, any debt run up by the government can be repaid by taxing the American people.

Since there is no gold-backed currency in existence which could replace the dollar, the wealth of the American people and the full faith and credit of the United States government provide the best support for the currency. The other option would be to trust the full faith and credit of China, Russia, Brazil, India, or South Africa, all of which have smaller GDPs and currencies which are not particularly useful outside of their home market. If the world did demand a switch to a gold-backed currency, the U.S., with 8,133 metric tons of gold,[508] has more than twice as much as the next largest reserve, that of Germany. The combined gold reserves of the BRICS countries — 5,287 tons — is considerably less than U.S. gold reserves. So, even with a return to gold-backed currency, the U.S. dollar would be the soundest currency.

Ironically, most of the countries calling for the collapse of the U.S. dollar use the dollar to back their own currency, either directly or indirectly. Oil-producing nations like Saudi Arabia peg their currency to the dollar. The only BRICS currency which is a global reserve currency is the Chinese yuan, which is now at a

---

[507] https://worldpopulationreview.com/state-rankings/median-household-income-by-state
[508] https://www.madisontrust.com/information-center/which-world-countries-have-the-most-gold/

record low. Countries outside China hold only about 2.5 percent of their reserves in yuan. Significantly, most BRI, SCO, and BRICS members avoid holding large quantities of Chinese currency in their reserves.

The yuan is actually pegged to the U.S. dollar, but is allowed to fluctuate within a narrow band. Russia, India, Brazil, and South Africa do not peg to the dollar, but their currencies are considered only partially convertible or nonconvertible,[509] weakening their viability as international currencies. Furthermore, the foreign exchange reserves used to back the currencies of all of these nations are largely comprised of U.S. dollars and U.S. treasuries. This means that the value of the currency and the wealth of these countries is largely predicated on the quantity of U.S. dollars they hold. If the dollar collapsed, so would the foreign reserves of these countries, driving their own currencies down as well.

A final hurdle in creating an international currency to replace the dollar is that all the world's countries would have to agree. If BRICS made their own currency tomorrow, OPEC would have to agree to accept that currency for oil trades. The EU and ASEAN and other trading blocs and nations would have to agree to accept that currency for trade. If they did not, the currency would not be very useful and it would not be held in reserves. It is very unlikely that the world would agree to use a new BRICS currency led by Russia and China. Therefore, the other option, the one Xi Jinping really wants, is for everyone to agree to use yuan. And this raises the issue of sovereignty.

The very reason why many countries want to drop the dollar is to increase their economic independence. Adopting the yuan would not achieve this goal. These countries would be

---

[509] https://www.investopedia.com/terms/c/convertible-currency.asp

subjugating themselves to Beijing. Putin has begrudgingly accepted the use of yuan in some trade with China, because international sanctions related to the Ukraine War prevent Moscow from using dollars. It is unlikely, however, that he would give up the ruble. India, although a BRICS member, has an adversarial relationship with China and would reject any shift toward using the yuan. Despite its own debt issue, and a reputation for international interference, the world appears to favor Washington over Beijing. As a result, the dollar will remain the global currency until all of these problems have been addressed. And so far, no one — not even Xi or Putin — has a solution.

A Silk Road to Debt

The Belt and Road Initiative (BRI), also known as One Belt, One Road, is a vast economic and infrastructure development project initiated by China in 2013. That year, Xi Jinping stated that he was creating the BRI to enhance mutual prosperity and to help developing countries improve their economies. The initiative aims to bolster cooperation and connectivity among countries in Asia, Europe, Latin America, and Africa. The BRI has two main components: The Silk Road Economic Belt (focusing on connecting China to Europe through a network of railways, highways, and pipelines, following the historic Silk Road trade routes) and the 21st Century Maritime Silk Road (the sea-based element, linking China's southern coast to regions like Africa and Europe through a network of ports and shipping routes).

The initiative involves the construction of roads, harbors, and other infrastructure, along with trade agreements and economic cooperation efforts to boost trade, investment, and economic development among participating countries. The BRI has gained widespread attention due to its massive scale and potential impact on global economics and geopolitics. Its supporters say it will boost GDP growth in participating countries. However, in many countries, debt to China has increased, pollution has worsened, and the trade deficit with China has increased, while GDP growth has been elusive. Most of the money participating countries have received from China has been in the form of debt, rather than donations. According to a CNBC report (September 30, 2021), for every grant given by the PRC, it has made 31 loans.

Between 2000 and 2017, China financed at least 13,427 projects, totaling $843 billion, through more than 300 state-owned entities across 165 countries.[510] Between the launch of the BRI in 2013 and 2020, China provided funds totalling between $50 billion and $100 billion per year.[511] The loans are largely in dollars and more costly than funds from Western donor nations and institutions.

Debt to China is particularly problematic for developing countries because, unlike domestic debt, foreign debt must be serviced via exports. Consequently, there are definite limits as to how much debt poor countries can sustain.[512] Even more, a general global economic slowdown has reduced the amount of debt that is considered sustainable. The largest borrowers are African nations that are now in debt distress or at high risk of distress.

For datasets released September 29, 2021, AidData Research Lab at William & Mary's Global Research Institute determined that 42 low-and middle-income countries now have China debt in excess of 10 percent of their GDPs. For some

---

[510] https://www.aiddata.org/data/aiddatas-global-chinese-development-finance-dataset-version-2-0
[511] https://www.brookings.edu/articles/seven-years-into-chinas-belt-and-road/
[512] Ibid.

countries, the level of debt is even more onerous. For example, Laos owes over 30 percent of its GDP to China. Extreme examples include the Republic of the Congo, where debt to China went from 13.62 percent of gross national income (GNI) in 2014 to 38.92 percent in 2019; Djibouti, from 7.71 percent to 34.64 percent; and Angola, from 5.87 percent to 18.95 percent.[513] Other BRI countries with exceptionally large debts to the PRC include Pakistan, where around a third of the nearly US$125 billion owed to external creditors is China debt.[514] Kenya, which has been struggling with ballooning public debt, owes $6 billion to Chinese creditors.[515]

As loan repayments have kicked in, many nations face such overwhelming debt service payments that they are unable to continue with further investment. Among the hardest hit are Tonga, Djibouti, Cambodia, Angola, Comoros, and Maldives. As a result of a lack of transparency in BRI lending, official debt totals are often much lower than the real amounts. Lending on BRI projects comes not only from the CCP regime, but also from government-run agencies, state-owned enterprises, and private companies. The spaghetti-like structures of BRI lending arrangements include special purpose vehicles (a type of shell company, often created for the sole purpose of borrowing money, to keep it off of the balance sheet of the parent entity). The system is so confusing that even Chinese regulators do not know how much has been lent (*The Economist*, September 30, 2021).

In previous decades, PRC lending went to foreign governments. Under the BRI, however, AidData Research Lab found that "70 percent of China's overseas lending is now directed

---

[513] https://greenfdc.org/public-debt-in-the-belt-and-road-initiative-bri-covid-19/

[514] https://www.eurasiantimes.com/pakistans-economic-crisis-how-chinas-vicious-debt-trap/

[515] https://apnews.com/article/kenya-china-loans-economy-belt-road-debt-97e352532bf5db3bc40a7370116f4410

to state-owned companies, state-owned banks, special purpose vehicles, joint ventures, and private sector institutions." Due to the opaque nature of these loans, the BRI is now plagued by an estimated \$385 billion of hidden debt, *Wall Street Journal* reported on September 28, 2021.

China has been taking large chunks of equity in countries that cannot repay their debts, notably in Sri Lanka — where Hambantota port was leased to a PRC company for 99 years in 2017 after Sri Lanka was unable to pay back the money they borrowed to build it[516] — and in Laos. The latter is an excellent example of a confusing debt and equity structure; three Chinese state-owned firms took a majority stake in a joint venture which owes China \$3.6 billion. On the balance sheet, this will now appear to be a debt owed by a Chinese company (*The Economist*, September 30, 2021).

Polluting Projects

According to a study reported on by Reuters (September 29, 2021), 35 percent of BRI projects are impacted by corruption, unfair labor practices, environmental pollution, and protests. Stalled and abandoned projects are failing to generate promised GDP gains for host countries. Domestic industries do not benefit from the construction of projects, as only 7.6 percent of project contracts are awarded to local companies, while 89 percent are completed by Chinese firms (CSIS, January 25, 2018). Very often, local employment gets no boost, because even the laborers are flown in from China.

Environmental researchers have determined that China is also benefiting by exporting its carbon emissions to BRI

---

[516] https://www.voanews.com/a/chinese-funded-projects-deepen-sri-lanka-s-economic-woes-/6888652.html

countries.[517] Host countries are using up their carbon budget on BRI projects, while making China richer and themselves going into debt. China is reducing pollution at home by installing renewables, yet has sold coal-fired utility plants to Cambodia and other places. By 2016, China was involved in at least 240 coal projects in 25 BRI countries[518] — and many of the PRC-financed power plants are reportedly based on low-efficiency, highly-polluting, sub-critical coal technology.

Countries often join the BRI because they are unable to borrow elsewhere and because they believe that the economic growth generated by the completed projects will outweigh the cost of the debt. In reality, this GDP growth often does not come. For example, according to growth models used on the BRI, Pakistan should have expected to have a 5.18 percent increase in GDP.[519] The China-Pakistan Economic Corridor was launched in 2015, but in recent years the South Asian country has experienced a dismal economy.

According to World Bank Working Paper 8801 (April 2019), which attempted to quantify winners and losers from the BRI while focusing on transportation infrastructure, BRI countries should, on average, see a GDP increase of up to 3.4 percent. However, because trade gains are not necessarily equal to project investments, some countries will see a negative welfare effect. Yet all countries must repay the loans they took from China. Many countries are losing out, yet the PRC continues to profit. China's trade surplus with BRI states reached $199.2. billion in 2020,

---

[517] http://20.244.136.131/expert-speak/the-belt-and-road-initiative

[518] https://e360.yale.edu/features/how-chinas-big-overseas-initiative-threatens-climate-progress

[519] https://thediplomat.com/2019/12/the-belt-and-road-calculating-winners-and-losers/

accounting for 40.4 percent of its total trade surplus (Belt and Road Quarterly, Q4 2020).

Far from it being a benevolent endeavor, AidData Research Lab determined that, through the BRI, Beijing seeks to achieve three objectives: converting dollars earned through exports into foreign loans; providing work for the domestic construction and industrial sectors; and securing commodities. Another worrying trend is that 400 projects valued at $8.3 billion are linked to the Chinese military (*Wall Street Journal*, September 28, 2021).

The BRI appears to be stagnating, in part because the PRC economy is flagging. Chinese outbound investment reached a peak in 2016 and has been in decline since.[520] In 2020, China was the world's number-two outbound investor. In 2021, China slipped to fourth place behind the United States, Germany, and Japan. In 2023, facing inflation, unemployment, a debt crisis, and the economic fallout of Covid-19 restrictions, the CCP regime and foreign investment banks repeatedly cut China's GDP growth projections. Beijing is now focusing on attracting foreign investment, but it will be a hard sell. Because interest rates in the United States and in China have traveled in opposite directions, the U.S. is a more attractive destination for FDI than China.

Due to the PRC's economic woes, China's BRI investing in emerging markets has lagged far behind global FDI in emerging markets (excluding China). From 2020 to 2021, global FDI inflows into developing countries were up 40 percent while Chinese BRI investment in those countries had decreased by 25 percent.[521] This decline in investment is actually set out in China's 14th Five-Year Plan for 2021 to 2025.

---

[520] https://english.ckgsb.edu.cn/knowledge/article/the-end-of-china-odi/
[521] https://greenfdc.org/china-belt-and-road-initiative-bri-investment-report-h1-2022/

PRC investment in several countries, namely Russia, Egypt, and Sri Lanka, has fallen to zero. About 55 percent of China's total BRI investment has been in the Middle East.[522] The largest overall recipient of Chinese investment has been Saudi Arabia, which has received $5.5. billion. This investment is perhaps linked to the CCP regime's efforts to convince the kingdom to aid the yuan's internationalization by settling oil trades in Chinese currency. These negotiations have been in process for nearly a decade, but no agreement has been reached.

Chinese officials have repeatedly mentioned the possibility of expanding the BRI flagship project, the China Pakistan Economic Corridor, to include Afghanistan. However, the problems that prevent the PRC from expanding its investments in Afghanistan still exist.[523] These include operational and regulatory barriers, as well as security concerns. There is also a severe lack of infrastructure.

As part of its global domination strategy, the CPP regime has become one of the world's largest lenders to the least developed nations,[524] charging higher interest rates and demanding collateral in the form of ports, airports, minerals, and revenue streams.

Debt owed by the world's poorest countries to China increased threefold between 2011 and 2020.[525] *South China Morning Post* reported (April 22, 2022) that both the IMF and the World Bank had warned about record levels of global debt, particularly among developing countries. The U.S. and other

---

[522] Ibid.

[523] https://www.brookings.edu/articles/chinese-investment-in-afghanistans-lithium-sector-a-long-shot-in-the-short-term/

[524] https://www.devex.com/news/devex-invested-the-problem-with-hidden-chinese-debt-101750

[525] Ibid.

Western nations (BBC, November 30, 2021) have accused the CCP regime of debt-trap diplomacy and the seizure of key assets.

Debt-trap diplomacy is a powerful weapon in the CCP's arsenal. Like cheetahs singling out and stalking the sick gazelle in the herd, Beijing looks for countries close to breaking point. These are small undeveloped economies one loan away from collapse. China then offers them loans with oppressive terms, which ultimately allows Beijing to gain control of the country's assets or revenue streams.[526] The collateral can be ports, such as Piraeus in Greece or Gwadar in Pakistan. Beijing's investment and aid policy targets countries which can provide resources such as minerals, or countries like Djibouti which have strategic locations.

Beijing argues that, for many of the countries that have defaulted, China was not the first or largest lender (*Global Times*, January 12, 2022). The Western counterargument is that Chinese loans pushed these countries over the brink. The reason these countries seek loans from China is because the IMF, World Bank, Paris Club, and others have deemed them in danger of default. In many instances, these countries seek to borrow money to pay interest on previous loans.[527] Traditional lenders refuse to lend money to these countries for fear of worsening the situation.

Foreign aid accounts for roughly 1 percent of the U.S. federal budget[528] with half of this money being spent on poverty reduction. While American aid can come in various forms of international assistance, it does look like aid. With China, the line is blurred between aid and investment. China claims to be one of the largest donors, but it would be more accurate to call it a giant creditor. Much of what the PRC sees as aid, such as export credits and military assistance, does not qualify as aid under OECD

---

[526] https://www.tandfonline.com/doi/full/10.1080/03932729.2020.1855904

[527] https://www.cadtm.org/The-submerging-market-debt-crisis

[528] https://www.oxfamamerica.org/explore/issues/making-foreign-aid-work/

definitions. Beijing has a focused aid strategy which is wrapped up in its program of foreign investment and trade promotion.[529] Washington, on the other hand, does not seem to have a unified or codified aid strategy. Moreover, U.S. trade and investment are done by the private sector, with little or no government direction.

Under the Trump administration in 2019, the International Development Finance Corp. (DFC) was overhauled to help counter Beijing's influence. The DFC provides loans to help developing nations promote infrastructure improvements. *Financial Times* suggested (April 26, 2022) that U.S. aid and military aid should be coupled with a comprehensive trade policy. Without a trade component, foreign nations may question Washington's commitment to a long-term relationship. This is particularly true in Africa, Latin America, and Asia where investment and trade are desperately needed, and where China links its strategic and military goals to its trade and investment decisions.

The Atlantic Council recommended (April 25, 2022) that the U.S. adopt more of a private-sector mindset. Washington should aim to find out what the clients, foreign countries, need and want, and then provide it in such a way that helps solve these countries' problems, before Beijing arrives with its checkbook. Furthermore, the U.S. must be more unified across government agencies with all parts working together and in cooperation with the private sector.

China's Interactions with Countries Around the World

China's foreign policy is predicated on Beijing trying to improve its global position. This can mean, in an attempt to build coalitions

---

[529] https://www.atlanticcouncil.org/blogs/new-atlanticist/i-helped-defend-against-chinas-economic-hybrid-war-heres-how-the-us-can-respond/

and voting blocs in the UN, internationalizing the yuan, creating investment and employment opportunities for Chinese companies and citizens, or obtaining raw materials. Contrary to popular belief, China invests more in developed economies than in developing economies, because the risk is lower. Xi Jinping tries to position himself as the leader of the global south and the friend to the developing world, but in reality, Chinese investment in Africa and the developing world is a very small percentage of total investment and it tends to flow into resource-rich countries. Some examples of China's engagements with Africa, Latin America, the Pacific Islands, and Latina America and the Caribbean follow.

China's Destabilizing Role in Africa's Coup Belt

In the summer of 2023, military officers in Gabon placed the country's president under house arrest. Since 2020, there have been eight military coups in six African nations: in Mali in 2020 and again in 2021; in Guinea in 2021; twice in Burkina Faso in 2022; in 2023 in Sudan, when leaders of the 2020 coup turned on each other; in Niger in 2020 and 2023; and most recently in Gabon (Agence France-Presse, August 31, 2023). These nations share a number of similarities. They are all rich in minerals, but economically poor. Another commonality is that Chinese state-owned and state-backed firms are active within their borders. They have all participated in some form in the Forum on China-Africa Cooperation.[530] In terms of diplomatic ties, they all recognize the PRC, not Taiwan.

Most of them have also received Chinese loans and purchased weapons from China. Russia used to be the primary supplier of arms to Africa, but the Ukraine War has impaired Moscow's ability to export weapons. This has created a window of opportunity that Beijing has been quick to capitalize on. In

---

[530] http://www.focac.org/eng/

addition to creating markets for its weapons exports, this also intensifies relations with coup leaders already ostracized from the Western-led rules-based order. China needs minerals and the generals need cash and guns, so the relationship works for everyone involved. Only the common people will suffer, but Beijing is more concerned about expanding its influence than it is about human rights.

The frustration of coup leaders, common people, and international observers across Africa is that these countries, which rank among the world's poorest, are very rich in natural resources. Coup leaders claim to be anticolonial forces, liberating their countries from European domination, taking control of natural resources,[531] and sharing the wealth with the people. In practice, coup leaders rarely make good on such promises. After kicking out Western business partners and investors, they generally turn to China for concessionary loans. And the PRC winds up controlling those nations' mineral exports. Unlike Western lenders and investors, however, China does not demand a return to democracy.

For example, Mali is estimated to have 800 tons of gold deposits, 2 million tons of iron ore, 5,000 tons of uranium, 20 million tons of manganese, 4 million tons of lithium, and 10 million tons of limestone.[532] Beijing is interested in all of these minerals, and Chinese firms have already invested in the country's lithium mines.[533] The military government has purchased armored vehicles and all-terrain vehicles from China.

Guinea holds some of the world's richest bauxite and iron ore deposits, as well as gold and diamonds, graphite, manganese,

---

[531] https://www.reuters.com/world/africa/gabonese-military-officers-announce-they-have-seized-power-2023-08-30/

[532] https://www.trade.gov/country-commercial-guides/mali-mining

[533] https://asia.nikkei.com/Politics/Niger-tensions-threaten-Chinese-projects-as-dam-building-stops

nickel, and uranium.[534] In 2017, China loaned the nation $20 billion in return for bauxite and aluminum concessions (Reuters, September 6, 2017). Chinese extraction companies operating in the country include China Power Investment Corporation, Aluminium Corp of China, and China Henan International Cooperation Group. In early 2023, China's Baowu became one of several companies awarded the right to set up operations at Guinea's Simandou Iron Ore mine, believed to be the world's largest untapped high-quality reserve.[535] The two countries have a relatively balanced trade relationship worth about $4.5 billion annually. Chinese security companies are active in Guinea, and the nation is a purchaser of Chinese weapons, according to a 2022 Rand report.

Burkina Faso is rich in a number of different natural resources, including such as gold, zinc, copper, and manganese.[536] In 2018, when Burkina Faso broke off diplomatic ties with Taiwan, China pledged $44 million in aid.[537] Beijing has granted scholarships to the nation's soldiers to attend military academies in China.[538] The PRC has also provided the nation with some small arms, multiple rocket launchers, and recoilless rifles. Chinese investments include an optical fiber communications network as well as a security surveillance system. In July 2023, Burkina Faso's president met with China's special representative for Africa, to discuss strengthening security and economic ties between the two nations.[539]

---

[534] https://www.trade.gov/country-commercial-guides/guinea-mining-and-minerals
[535] https://www.afr.com/companies/mining/rio-tinto-in-157m-first-shout-for-simandou-20231006-p5ea82
[536] https://eiti.org/countries/burkina-faso
[537] https://www.vifindia.org/article/2022/china-s-great-game-in-the-sahel
[538] Ibid.
[539]
https://www.fmprc.gov.cn/eng/wjdt_665385/wshd_665389/202307/t20230710_11110999.html

In addition to petroleum, Sudan has small quantities of gold, iron ore, silver, copper, tungsten, mica, chromium ore, and zinc (AZO Mining, October 12, 2012). Since 2005, China has invested $6 billion in the country in mining, energy, construction, and agricultural projects, VOA reported on May 30, 2023. China National Petroleum Corp. (CNPC) is an investor in the country's oil industry and a joint owner of the Khartoum Oil Refinery. In 2021, China's exports to Sudan totaled $1.82 billion, while its imports were only $780 million. China has long provided weapons to the Sudanese military, in spite of allegations of gross human rights abuses. PRC state-owned enterprise Norinco has been selling arms to South Sudan, which broke away from Sudan in 2011, while CNPC has also funded militias that protect its oil field investment in South Sudan, Quartz reported on August 26, 2015.

Niger has large uranium deposits.[540] China Gezhouba Group is building an $808-million hydroelectric dam in the country, while a unit of CNPC is backing the construction of a $4-billion oil export pipeline.[541] China's Sinopec has signed agreements with Niger's government to work on oil and gas projects. Niger's arms imports from the PRC were negligible in 2022, but with Russian weapons exports dwindling, Chinese weapons sales are expected to grow.

Gabon produces about 200,000 barrels of oil a day, in fields operated by France's TotalEnergies and Anglo-French producer Perenco.[542] French miner Eramet extracts manganese. China purchases about half of Gabon's exports, accounting for $4 billion worth of commodities in 2022; Beijing also loaned money to

---

[540] https://apnews.com/article/niger-coup-west-africa-wagner-bazoum-c233b0d2becf61ebb00c5705941fc168

[541] https://asia.nikkei.com/Politics/Niger-tensions-threaten-Chinese-projects-as-dam-building-stops

[542] https://www.reuters.com/world/africa/gabonese-military-officers-announce-they-have-seized-power-2023-08-30/

Gabon for the completion of two hydroelectric dams and a 22-kilometer road project.[543] Since then, China has upgraded its relationship with Gabon to a "comprehensive strategic cooperative partnership" (CGTN, April 19, 2023).

Solomon Islands and Micronesia

The CCP regime has co-opted the Solomon Islands, and has its sights set on removing the Federated States of Micronesia from their Compact of Association with the United States. On March 25, 2022, the Solomon Islands confirmed that they were drafting a security deal with China, the BBC reported on that day. With this single contract, the U.S. loses a valuable ally in a critical part of the world, the PLA will gain a new overseas base, and Australia has been placed on alert knowing that the enemy is now in the backyard.

The strategic partnership with Beijing allows Honiara, capital of the Solomon Islands, to call for police or military assistance from China. It also provides the islands with economic development, trade expansion, and civil aviation services. In 2006, rioters burned down Honiara's Chinatown, accusing Chinese-linked businesses of having rigged a general election. In 2019, Honiara switched recognition from Taiwan to the PRC, the BBC report pointed out.

Unrest broke out again in 2021, as citizens expressed outrage at how close their government was becoming with Beijing. Protesters attacked Chinese-owned businesses. In the end, Australian peacekeepers and military police were called in to restore order, the BBC reported on November 25, 2021. Next time, it could be the PLA, as the country's agreement with Beijing

---

[543] https://thediplomat.com/2023/04/china-gabon-relations-get-an-upgrade/

specifically allows the PLA to "protect the safety of Chinese personnel and major projects… [and] preserve social order."[544]

The fall of the Solomon Islands to the CCP represents a breakdown in U.S. engagement with the Pacific Island nations. Washington's Indo-Pacific strategy has been heavily focused on the Quad, a security partnership dedicated to opposing the CCP. The Pacific Island Forum, however, has 18 members, all of whom are drifting further from Australia and New Zealand.

China is courting these developing nations by offering aid, investment, and loans. The U.S. has recognized that in order to counter the CCP regime's influence in the region, the U.S. must increase its direct involvement. This is particularly true of those nations where Washington believes Beijing wishes to establish PLA military bases.[545] China is building transportation infrastructure in those countries, and U.S. officials have warned that airstrips and aviation facilities built or expanded across the region by the CCP could be used by the PLA.

Secretary of State Anthony Blinken's visit to Fiji on February 12, 2022, where he conferred with 18 leaders from Pacific Island nations, was the first by a U.S. secretary of state for more than 40 years. He announced that Washington plans to reopen its embassy in the Solomon Islands, which has been closed for 23 years.[546] However, this gesture was too little, too late to prevent the Solomon Islands from slipping into China's orbit.

Meanwhile, another U.S. ally, the Federated States of Micronesia (FSM) is in danger of falling into the mouth of the dragon. On March 31, 2022, ABC Australia reported that the FSM

---

[544] https://www.abc.net.au/news/2022-03-31/federated-states-micronesia-solomon-islands-china-security/100955650

[545] https://www.reuters.com/world/asia-pacific/blinken-with-pacific-trip-aims-reaffirm-us-focus-asia-2022-02-07/

[546] https://www.bbc.com/news/world-asia-pacific-60359869

had asked the Solomon Islands to reconsider their security pact with China. FSM President David Panuelo said that while the people of the FSM consider themselves to be friends of China, they are allies of the United States. And with the two huge countries increasingly at odds, the unilateral decision taken by the Solomon Islands was "unprecedented," said Panuelo, expressing his fear that such agreements could fragment the Pacific Island nations into opposing camps acting at the behest of each respective great power (Agence France-Presse, March 31, 2022).

Despite a population of just over 100,000, FSM is one of the most important linchpins for the U.S. to maintain its hegemony in the Indo-Pacific. The FSM comprises more than 600 islands spread out over an area greater than 2,600,000 square kilometers (1,000,000 square miles) of the Pacific Ocean. The islands are situated within striking distance of Indonesia, Papua New Guinea, Guam, the Marianas, Nauru, the Marshall Islands, Palau, and the Philippines.

The relationship between the U.S. and FSM is governed by the Compact of Free Association (COFA). Under the COFA, the U.S. is responsible for the defense of FSM, which in return grants the U.S. exclusive rights to station military personnel and assets within the territory.[547] The FSM receives economic assistance from the U.S.; citizens of the FSM can easily join the U.S. military, immigrate to, or work in the United States.

For years, the CCP regime has been trying to increase its influence in the region through investment and soft power initiatives.[548] In addition to the strategic location, Pacific nations each get one vote in the UN General Assembly. Given their small size and lack of development, Beijing believes they can buy their allegiance and their votes cheaply. Pacific nations which have

---

[547] https://hir.harvard.edu/micronesia-the-next-us-china-battleground-2/
[548] Ibid.

already switched recognition from Taiwan to the PRC include Kiribati, Papua New Guinea, the Solomon Islands, Tonga, and Vanuatu. The FSM — which already recognizes Beijing rather than Taipei — are the CCP's next target for removal from the U.S. sphere.

China has given the FSM $100 million in aid since 1990, with Beijing funding government complexes, convention centers, and transportation infrastructure. In 2017, FSM joined the Belt and Road Initiative. The COFA, the FSM's contract with Washington, was eventually renewed in 2023, following delays because of the Covid-19 pandemic. The Marshall Islands extended its COFA with the U.S. at the same time; the COFA with Palau is set to expire in 2024, but Palau — which recognized Taiwan rather than the PRC — is planning to renew it.

Nevertheless, the extension of the FSM-U.S. compact may not completely shut the CCP regime out of the region. Chuuk, a part of the FSM which lies very close to the U.S. territory of Guam, has been the recipient of much of Beijing's economic aid.[549] On three occasions since 2015, Chuuk has scheduled, but failed to carry out, independence referendums. If Chuuk quits the federation, they would, theoretically, be free to enter into an agreement with China, perhaps meaning the PLA would be able to establish a base there.

The loss of the Solomon Islands to Beijing should serve as a wakeup call for the Biden administration. Losing the FSM would be disastrous and steps need to be taken to prevent this. Washington needs to increase its engagement with all of the Pacific Island nations and provide significant economic aid; otherwise, Beijing will. Indeed, it can be argued that President Trump's 2017 decision to withdraw the U.S. from the Trans-

---

[549] Ibid.

Pacific Partnership (TPP, now called the Comprehensive and Progressive Agreement for Trans-Pacific Partnership), while perhaps correct from an economic standpoint, sent a signal of abandonment to Washington's allies in the Pacific.

Since the Solomon Islands deal, however, Beijing has struggled to make progress. On May 30, 2022, CNN reported that PRC Foreign Minister Wang Yi had failed to persuade ten island nations to agree to a sweeping trade and security communique. Shut out of President Biden's Indo-Pacific Economic Framework, the CCP regime is pushing forward with the China-led Regional Comprehensive Economic Partnership (RCEP), which the U.S. has refused to join. Signed by China, Japan, South Korea, New Zealand, Australia, and the ten ASEAN member states, RCEP appeared to have an immediate impact on trade flows. It came into effect at the start of 2022, and data from that year's first quarter showed China trade with member countries grew 6.9 percent year-on-year. RCEP has been touted as the world's largest free trade bloc (Al-Jazeera, November 15, 2020).

At the fourth Quad Summit in Tokyo on May 24, 2023 the Biden administration launched the Indo-Pacific Economic Framework (IPEF). It has since been joined by seven of ASEAN's ten members, the four Quad members, South Korea, and New Zealand. This development demonstrates Washington's determination to expand its regional presence beyond the Quad, AUKUS, and the Five Eyes, all of which have a defense-related purpose. Even though the IPEF is not a trade agreement, it does cover issues of economics, supply chains, and security.[550]

The grouping is significant because the IPEF is the first economic multilateral arrangement in the Indo-Pacific that India has joined.[551] Additionally, IPEF is one of the first U.S. groupings

---

[550] Ibid.
[551] Ibid.

to include South Korea. The presence of economic powerhouse Japan and the solid support of Australia is now being complemented with the economic and military strength of South Korea. However, it is also true that several members of the IPEF are also part of RCEP.

The Taliban, China, and Russia Forge Closer Ties

The Taliban government of Afghanistan is expanding its trade and cooperation with both Russia and China, but a true alliance is unlikely. At the start of 2023, Kabul and Beijing signed a $540 million deal to develop Afghanistan's oil and gas fields, *Wall Street Journal* reported (January 5, 2023). This is the biggest deal the Taliban has signed since taking control of the country in August 2021. After the U.S. pulled out, the economy collapsed. Because the regime has not been recognized by any Western government, and the Taliban is designated as a global terrorist organization, sanctions restrict flows of cash into the country. Washington has frozen Afghanistan's foreign currency reserves, totalling around $7 billion, held in the U.S.[552]

Around 95 percent of Afghanistan's population say they have recently experienced hunger,[553] and the country has become completely dependent on foreign aid. The U.S. is the largest provider of humanitarian aid to Afghanistan but the Treasury Department has set strict rules on the provision of aid, to ensure that it gets to the people rather than to the regime. At the same time, many international aid organizations are reviewing their support for Afghanistan because the Taliban has tightened the restrictions on women's participation in public life. The WHO released a statement (December 28, 2022) saying that if women are

[552] https://edition.cnn.com/2022/02/11/politics/executive-order-afghanistan-9-11-humanitarian-aid/index.html
[553] https://news.gallup.com/poll/390008/afghanistan-failing-economy-taking-afghans.aspx

not permitted to participate in NGO work, then certain aid programs would have to be halted.

Afghanistan's mineral reserves, including rare earths, are estimated at $1 trillion.[554] Sanctions prevent Western countries from investing in extraction projects, opening the door for Chinese investment. One PRC company has signed an oil deal, and a state-owned mining company is negotiating with the Taliban about extracting copper.[555] However, there are still major security issues. The Taliban controls most of the country, but Islamic State (IS) is still actively opposing Taliban rule and Chinese presence. Near the end of 2022, IS attacked a hotel in Kabul that housed several PRC citizens (VOA, December 12, 2022)

In addition to the threat of IS attacks, another wrinkle in the Taliban-Beijing dynamic is Afghanistan's harboring of the Turkistan Islamic Party, formerly known as the East Turkestan Islamic Movement,[556] a separatist terrorist organization opposing repression in China's Xinjiang Uyghur Autonomous Region. Beijing's engagement with the Taliban is also compromising its relationship with Islamabad. Pakistan has been plagued by terrorist attacks carried out by the Tehreek-e-Taliban Pakistan (TTP), the Pakistan Taliban,[557] which is closely aligned with the Taliban in Afghanistan. The TTP's stated objective is to defeat the Pakistan army and establish itself as the ruler of the Afghanistan-Pakistan region. Islamabad worries that money flowing from Beijing to Kabul will ultimately support terrorist attacks in Pakistan. The Pakistan military has been clamoring to engage in preemptive strikes against TTP cadres inside Afghanistan. The Taliban, while

---

[554] https://www.wsj.com/articles/chinese-firm-signs-540-million-oil-and-gas-deal-in-afghanistan-11672934543

[555] https://www.bbc.com/news/business-64183083

[556] https://www.eastasiaforum.org/2022/11/03/russia-and-afghanistans-partnership-of-convenience/

[557] https://sundayguardianlive.com/news/kabul-beijing-oil-deal-limits-paks-options-tackle-ttp

claiming neutrality in the dispute, has made it very clear that they would not tolerate a breach of its national borders by Pakistan's army.

The Taliban has managed to sign trade deals with a number of countries, including Kazakhstan, Turkmenistan, and Iran.[558] Meanwhile China and Russia have all expressed interest in investing in Afghanistan. Russia, like China and Iran, does not officially recognize the Taliban government, although its leaders have been guests at the Kremlin (Reuters, September 28, 2022).

There appears to be growing cooperation between states outside of the U.S.-led Western order, namely Iran, Russia, China, Afghanistan, and Pakistan. While they share a common distrust or even hatred of the United States, their fundamental interests are not clearly aligned. Tensions and disputes among them are also preventing them from forming a real alliance. For the time being, it looks like Beijing may throw a lifeline to Afghanistan, and Kabul will help Russia keep afloat by buying its oil, but the formation of a politically and economically meaningful bloc seems unlikely.

Riyadh Reluctant to Accept Yuan for Oil

China sees Saudi Arabia as a key to both OPEC and the Middle East in general. Beijing would like to convince Riyadh to accept yuan for oil when trading with China and, more broadly, to price all oil in yuan, as well as to keep the yuan as its reserve currency, and to have China replace the United States as the kingdom's security partner. However, Saudi Arabia is unlikely to accept yuan for oil despite strengthening ties with China.

The 2022 deal between Saudi Arabia and China for Huawei to provide the kingdom with 5G equipment was signed despite

---

[558] Ibid.

protests from the U.S.[559] — and Saudi Crown Prince Mohammed bin Salman's warm welcome of Xi Jinping was in sharp contrast to the lukewarm meeting with President Biden that BBC reported on July 15, 2022. Biden's relationship with Saudi Arabia has been rocky since he took office. Biden began the meeting by fist bumping the prince rather than shaking hands. This insult came in the wake of Biden's pre-election comment that he would make Saudi Arabia "a pariah state" due to its human rights record.

Biden's requests for Saudi Arabia to increase oil production and thus boost efforts to isolate Russia were ignored. However, Riyadh working with the United Arab Emirates eventually secured the release of WNBA player Brittney Griner from a Russian prison (CNN, December 8, 2022), so at least the president did not walk away empty handed.

The day after the Huawei deal was signed, Xi delivered the opening remarks at the first China-Gulf Cooperation Council Summit in Riyadh. He recommended that Saudi Arabia and other oil producers begin transacting China's oil purchases in yuan: "China will continue to import large quantities of crude oil on a long-term basis from GCC countries and purchase more LNG... the Shanghai Petroleum and Natural Gas Exchange platform will be fully utilized for [yuan] settlement in oil and gas trade."[560]

That platform is a Chinese exchange with a spot pricing index for LNG imports quoted in U.S. dollars. The exchange's ten shareholders are all PRC state-owned enterprises. Established in 2021, the purpose of the exchange is to encourage the internationalization of the yuan and the use of the yuan in the energy sector. So far, there has been very little movement on either front. For years, Xi has been urging the Saudis to accept yuan for

---

[559] https://www.reuters.com/world/saudi-lays-lavish-welcome-chinas-xi-heralds-new-era-relations-2022-12-08/
[560] https://www.fmprc.gov.cn/eng/zxxx_662805/202212/t20221210_10988408.html

oil to break the dollar's hold on global commodities. There has been a lot of fervor in the press suggesting that this is likely to happen, yet there is no indication so far that Riyadh will go along with Beijing's proposal.

For more than 40 years, Washington has agreed with Riyadh that, if the kingdom prices its oil in dollars, the United States will provide them with military protection and sell them weapons.[561] So far, no country has agreed to allow PLA troops to replace American troops on their soil. Consequently, Saudi Arabia needs to maintain its relationship with the U.S. The agreement also allows Saudi Arabia to purchase U.S. government bonds (treasuries) before they go to market (Bloomberg, May 31, 2016). Just like no country wants Chinese troops on their soil, no country is leaping to replace U.S. government bonds with Chinese bonds in their currency reserves. The IMF and most countries keep less than 3 percent of their reserves in yuan.[562]

Saudi Arabia's foreign currency reserves are mainly U.S. dollars and U.S. treasuries. The kingdom held $117 billion of treasuries in September 2023,[563] and the Saudi riyal, is pegged to the dollar, like the currencies of most GCC countries. With oil, foreign currency reserves, and a national currency all dependent on dollars, neither Saudi Arabia nor any Gulf nation would benefit from a weak dollar or from an influx of yuan.

Like a troubled marriage, the Washington-Riyadh relationship has hit a rough patch. But this has happened before, and in the end, the U.S. can offer Saudi Arabia security and wealth

[561] https://carnegieendowment.org/2018/02/27/what-has-49-billion-in-foreign-military-aid-bought-us-not-much-pub-75657

[562] https://data.imf.org/?sk=e6a5f467-c14b-4aa8-9f6d-5a09ec4e62a4

[563]

accumulation — something the CCP regime cannot. Xi will find out that the red carpet can be used for both entrances and exits.

The Iran-Saudi Deal

The March 2023 China-brokered peace deal between Saudi Arabia and Iran has implications for U.S. influence in the Middle East. The announcement that Saudi Arabia and Iran would resume diplomatic relations severed back in 2016[564] is meant to reduce tensions and improve security in the Gulf region. However, the situation remains complicated, because the U.S.-Israel relationship still defines much of Washington's engagement with other Middle Eastern nations.

The Abraham Accords, signed by Israel, the United Arab Emirates (UAE), and Bahrain, and witnessed by President Trump,[565] went into effect in late 2020. Since then, Israel has signed a free trade agreement with the UAE, the largest such agreement with an Arab nation, Al-Jazeera reported on May 31, 2022. But the deal with Iran meant that any hope Saudi Arabia would also join the Abraham Accords — which would be a major step toward ensuring peace in the Middle East — seemed slim, even before the October 7, 2023 Hamas attack on Israel.

From Washington's perspective, the Riyadh-Tehran agreement is troubling as it is the latest step in Beijing's campaign to bring the Middle East into its political orbit. The wording of the joint statement by China, Saudi Arabia, and Iran sounds exactly like CCP rhetoric about "respect for the sovereignty of states and the non-interference in internal affairs of states."[566]

---

[564] https://www.cnbc.com/2023/03/10/arch-rivals-iran-and-saudi-arabia-agree-to-revive-ties-reopen-embassies.html

[565] https://www.state.gov/the-abraham-accords/

[566] http://tr.china-embassy.gov.cn/tur/zgyw/202303/t20230311_11039241.htm

This verbiage has repeatedly been used in official Chinese foreign policy statements to deflect challenges to the annexation of Taiwan, the repression of democracy and freedoms in Hong Kong, condemnation of the repression and genocide against Uyghurs in Xinjiang, and criticism of cultural genocide in Tibet and Inner Mongolia. The CCP stance is that these are internal affairs and outsiders should not meddle.[567] The regime includes similar language in many of its international agreements such as BRICS, the BRI, and the SCO. By co-opting a growing number of countries into signing documents forbidding intervention in another country's sovereignty, the CCP regime is hoping to prevent these nations from voting against China in the UN Security Council or United Nations Commission on Human Rights.

Since the U.S. became largely oil independent, China has displaced the U.S. as the greatest importer of oil. This makes China a larger economic partner for many Middle Eastern countries and strengthens Beijing's influence. While the U.S. may have less influence as a buyer, the U.S. still holds two advantages.

The first is that oil is priced in dollars, and that, because all countries need oil, most countries have the U.S. dollar as their reserve currency. For Saudi Arabia and other oil producers, pricing and collecting oil sales in dollars eliminates currency exchange risk and prevents their central banks from having to go on foreign currency markets to buy dollars. Many Middle Eastern countries also peg their currency to the dollar.[568]

Being a weapons supplier is part of the United States's second advantage over China. The U.S. maintains bases in Saudi Arabia, the UAE, Oman, Turkey, Syria, Lebanon, and Israel,

---

[567] http://gb.china-embassy.gov.cn/eng/PressandMedia/Spokepersons/202303/t20230314_11040256.htm
[568] https://www.investopedia.com/articles/forex/061015/top-exchange-rates-pegged-us-dollar.asp

providing physical security to its regional partners. If the Iran-Saudi Arabia agreement holds, these countries may feel they no longer need American protection, and may choose to be in Beijing's orbit. But this remains to be seen and is part of a far off and hypothetical future. Even then, there would still be the issue of dollar dominance, which Beijing is powerless to resolve.

The Hamas Attacks and China's Diplomatic Wins in the Middle East

The October 7 Hamas attack on Israel has improved China's position in the Middle East. A few weeks earlier, Saudi Arabia was formally invited to join BRICS.[569] Riyadh has not so far agreed to price oil in yuan, hold yuan as its reserve currency, or accept China as its security partner, but U.S.-backed normalization talks with Israel have been put on hold (Al-Jazeera, October 14, 2023). Saudi Arabia moving forward with an Israeli peace deal would have been seen as a betrayal of the larger Muslim world. The kingdom's refusal to engage with Israel is a diplomatic failure for the U.S. and a win for China.

In the absence of a peace deal with Iran, Saudi Arabia needed U.S. military protection at home, as well as U.S. support for a Saudi-led coalition in Yemen, fighting the Iran-aligned Houthis (Al-Jazeera, October 14, 2023). Beijing hoped that the Iran-Saudi peace deal would render U.S. military assistance to the kingdom unnecessary.

Since the October 7 incursion by Hamas, China's wumao army has been busy on social media, amplifying messages about civilians killed in Gaza. Beijing is also taking the moral high ground, blaming the U.S. for supporting Israel's actions. Chinese social media is brimming with expressions of support for

---

[569] https://edition.cnn.com/2023/08/24/business/saudi-arabia-brics-invitation-intl/index.html

Palestine.[570] At the same time, American and Western cities have seen clashes between Palestine supporters and Israel supporters. While the U.S. must brace itself for terrorist attacks, China is unworried. The only attack so far has been on an employee of the Israeli embassy, not a Chinese target.[571]

China has refused to condemn the October 7 attack for a number of reasons. First, China is a major economic partner of Iran.[572] China helps Iran bypass Western sanctions, buying cheap oil and selling Iran technology that is used in drones and missiles. The CCP regime has also provided Tehran with cyber technology, allowing the country to become a major cyber security threat. Iran's Islamic Revolutionary Guard Corps supports Hamas with equipment, intelligence, weapons and training. Meanwhile, Tehran provides Hamas with 70 percent of its funding.[573]

Beijing's propaganda apparatus is promoting China's humanitarian aid efforts in Gaza, while emphasizing China's solidarity with Muslim communities worldwide. The United Front Work Department has been diligent in shaping favorable portrayals of Xinjiang, showcasing content featuring smiling Uyghurs in traditional attire engaged in joyful dancing. These videos are typically accompanied by narratives discrediting Western reports of alleged genocide in Xinjiang as misinformation orchestrated by the CIA.

As further proof of Beijing's sincerity regarding the Muslim cause, Taliban representatives attended the October 17-18, 2023 Belt and Road Forum in Beijing. The previous month, China

---

[570] https://www.businessinsider.com/china-weibo-social-media-israel-palestine-support-blame-war-gaza-2023-10

[571] https://apnews.com/article/israel-palestinians-hamas-war-china-attack-d572e4169dd7f451cb2b2197506bc74c

[572] https://nationalinterest.org/feature/beijing%E2%80%99s-middle-east-policy-running-aground-206857

[573] https://foreignpolicy.com/2023/11/21/hamas-israel-gaza-war-tehran-palestinian-authority-arab-league-oic/

became the first country to officially name a new ambassador to Kabul, Reuters reported on September 13, 2023.

The Israel-Gaza situation is upending the Biden administration's Middle East policy agendas, aimed at countering China (Bloomberg, October 13, 2023). Any hope for a Saudi-Israel economic corridor linking India to Europe now seems distant. But, on the other hand, what has China really won? Those skeptical that Beijing is making real progress point out that the PRC lacks global military power and does not have friends throughout the world. So far, neither Saudi Arabia nor any other country in the Middle East has been willing to allow the PLA to replace American troops as security providers. Most countries prefer U.S. weapons to Chinese weapons, and want to hold U.S. dollars in reserve, rather than yuan.

For now, it seems that the CCP regime may be gaining ground in the realm of propaganda and garnering support from certain Middle Eastern nations. Nevertheless, the extent of this victory remains uncertain. Notably, Saudi Arabia has not indicated a rejection of its relationship with the United States. On the other hand, Europe and the G7 countries are aligning with the U.S. and Israel. In broader global power dynamics, the United States was unlikely to win favor with the Taliban or with South Africa, a BRICS member which has strongly criticized Israel.[574] Ultimately, Washington retains its preeminent position on the global stage, while Beijing continues its pursuit of the top spot.

To curry favor with Middle Eastern nations, the PRC has repeatedly demanded that Israel grant independence to Palestine. In early 2023, Xi Jinping also tried to build his cachet as a peacemaker by attempting to broker an Israel-Palestine peace

---

[574] https://www.politico.com/news/2023/10/11/israel-hamas-china-middle-east-policy-00120995

deal.[575] Part of Xi's plan for peace included Israel allowing Palestine to establish its capital in Jerusalem. However, Israel has officially relocated its capital to Jerusalem, rendering this proposal untenable. During President Trump's term, the U.S. officially recognized Jerusalem as the capital of Israel and moved its embassy there, in contrast to most other countries that maintain their embassies in Tel Aviv.

Although China is Israel's third-largest trading partner, the Israeli government initiated an investigation into Chinese investments within Israel, citing national security concerns. Because Israel is unlikely to align with China's sphere of influence, it would be in the best interests of Beijing to support Palestine, cultivate relations with other Middle Eastern nations, and view Israel as a write-off. When Xi met with Palestinian President Mahmoud Abbas in Beijing, the two signed a strategic partnership. In return, Palestine joined 53 nations, signing a joint statement in support of the CCP's genocide in Xinjiang (VOA, June 23, 2023). Abbas also supported Chinese efforts to suppress pro-democracy protests in Hong Kong.

Law Enforcement Diplomacy

Latin America is a new frontline in the war for influence between the United States and China, warned the head of Southern Command (VOA, March 16, 2021). One aspect of the threat is Beijing's law-enforcement partnership program in the developing world.

The CCP initiative, called International Law-Enforcement Cooperation (LEC), consists of providing materials, equipment, inexpensive digital tools, and training to foreign police officers,[576]

---

[575] https://www.aljazeera.com/opinions/2023/6/22/why-china-cant-broker-peace-between-israel-and-palestine

[576] https://www.brookings.edu/articles/extending-the-long-arm-of-the-law-chinas-international-law-enforcement-drive/

as well as advice on legislation. These programs include installing Xinjiang-style surveillance systems, enabling autocratic regimes which partner with the CCP to increase its surveillance and social control over its own people, according to a chapter in *China's Global Influence: Perspectives and Recommendations*.

While the program may not pose an immediate or direct threat to the U.S., it does pose a threat to the development of democracy and the maintenance of freedoms throughout the developing world — and this trend is particularly worrying in Latin America, as it brings China's surveillance capabilities right to the southern border and the Caribbean coast.

In its 2008 and 2016 Latin America policy white papers, the CCP stressed the importance of "judicial and police cooperation." And at the 2019 and 2021 forums for China and the Community of Latin American and Caribbean States, the Chinese regime prioritized fighting organized crime and corruption. The increasing presence of Chinese companies in the region, as well as international crime, have become pretexts for Beijing to get more involved with local law-enforcement and security forces.

The expansion of Chinese organized crime into Latin America has motivated local governments to organize joint-operations with PRC counterparts. In June 2010, Brazil's National Secretary of Justice Romeu Tuma Jr. was fired for connections with the Chinese mafia.[577] In 2016, Chinese security forces cooperated with local authorities in Argentina to counter a Chinese gangster. Similar cooperation has taken place in Panama and other nations.[578]

Increased Chinese investment outside the PRC has positioned a growing number of Chinese people and business

---

[577] https://g1.globo.com/English/noticia/2010/06/justice-minister-dismisses-national-secretary-justice.html
[578] https://www.csis.org/analysis/chinese-security-engagement-latin-america

interests in dangerous places. The CCP public-private partnership structure provides government support for private firms which make the country richer. Apart from financial subsidies and soft loans from state-banks, this support extends to physical security. Consequently, the PLA and security forces conduct training, preparing to engage on foreign soil to rescue citizens or to protect Chinese businesses. Chinese petroleum and mining firms operate in remote regions of war-torn or unstable countries, sometimes encroaching on indigenous land, making them vulnerable to violent attacks or kidnapping for ransom. The PLA had to intervene when Chinese workers were attacked in South Sudan.[579] In Yemen and Libya, the PLA Navy evacuated Chinese citizens.[580] Similar risks also exist in Venezuela and other parts of Latin America, such as when Chinese oil projects came under attack in northern Ecuador.[581]

As part of the LEC program, Chinese companies have donated police vehicles and equipment to countries in Latin America and the Caribbean (CSIS, November 19, 2020). The U.S. House Foreign Affairs Committee has been told that, in Panama's Colon Free Trade Zone, Huawei "Safe City Technology" has been installed, including facial recognition cameras, similar to those used to oppress the Uyghurs in Xinjiang. ZTE helps Venezuela control their populace through smart ID cards (Reuters, November 14, 2018). A ZTE team is now stationed in the Venezuelan state telecommunications company. Argentina was considering buying a similar system from ZTE, Reuters reported on July 5, 2019.

---

[579] https://www.crisisgroup.org/africa/horn-africa/south-sudan/intervene-or-not-chinas-foreign-policy-experiment-south-sudan-raises-questions

[580] https://www.bbc.com/news/world-middle-east-32173811

[581] https://news.mongabay.com/2017/01/conflict-erupts-between-chinese-mining-company-govt-and-indigenous-communities-in-ecuador/

In 2017, the PRC sold 51 Chery Tiggo armored vehicles to Uruguay's national police,[582] and donated 2 Marcopolo omnibuses as well as 10 armored trucks. The PRC also provided the police with 4,000 surveillance system components, 1,000 of which were deployed on the Brazilian border. The rest went to the capital, Montevideo, as part of the national response system. In addition to surveillance technology, Uruguay is also deploying Chinese biometric systems.[583] Chinese security products now have 53 percent of the Uruguayan market (U.S. Department of Commerce, September 22, 2022).

Through international police exchanges and training, the CCP regime strives to "normalize" technology-based social control systems. Addressing the 86th Interpol General Assembly, Xi Jinping said that the Chinese model is a more efficient system which should be used for global security and social management, Brookings reported on January 15, 2021.

Non-democratic actors, such as Vietnam, are following China's lead, adopting cybersecurity laws modeled on those of the PRC. Since 2008, around 80 countries have adopted Chinese surveillance tools. The spread of CCP's security model throughout the world is having a negative impact on human rights and rule of law, as well as the security of U.S. citizens at home and abroad. Countering the negative influence of the LEC, the U.S. offers the International Law Enforcement Academies, to enhance the skills of Washington's foreign criminal-justice partners, as well as improve coordination in combating international crime. These academies aim to enhance democracy by supporting the rule of law, and to use improved legislation and law enforcement to better the functioning of free markets, to maintain social, political, and

---

[582] https://theglobalamericans.org/2021/06/uruguay-exemplifies-how-to-deal-with-china/
[583] https://www.biometricupdate.com/201904/serbia-and-uruguay-deploy-chinese-biometric-and-surveillance-technology-amid-growing-controversy

economic stability. Over the past 20 years, 60,000 officers from 85 different countries have graduated from ILEAs (State Department, undated). However, the battle for influence is difficult, as partnership with China is often accompanied by loans, grants, and investments.

Beijing Losing Diplomatic Steam

While China remains a major threat to the United States and other countries, its economy is slowing, and — as a consequence of Xi Jinping's leadership — its once-robust soft power and diplomacy are waning. Initiatives like the BRI, SCO, and BRICS show signs of diminishing influence. China surpassing the U.S. on the global stage seems unlikely.

Launched by Xi in 2013, the Belt and Road Initiative (BRI) aimed to create a global infrastructure network encompassing roads, railways, ports, and special economic zones.[584] Originally called the New Silk Road or One Belt, One Road, the project was initially greeted with enthusiasm, and some 147 countries across six continents joined.[585] Over time, concerns grew as countries realized that China would be the main beneficiary and that many participant nations would wind up losing out.

The core of the BRI model involves China lending money for infrastructure projects in BRI nations. Typically, the loans stipulate that PRC firms will handle construction, often using Chinese labor. This has resulted in limited local job creation, with China quickly receiving loan repayments through state-affiliated construction firms. Nonetheless, the loan remained, requiring countries to make payments. Given their existing economic difficulties, BRI nations accepted these loans. Furthermore,

---

[584] https://www.cfr.org/backgrounder/chinas-massive-belt-and-road-initiative
[585] Ibid.

projects often faced delays when countries could not meet payment deadlines. As a result, many nations now grapple with crippling debt and unfinished, non-functioning infrastructure. In 2021, China had to provide 128 rescue loans to 22 debtor nations.[586] Roughly 60 percent of BRI nations are experiencing economic distress, and China is increasingly seen as the cause. Fewer countries are now showing interest in the initiative, some projects have been canceled, and a few countries — like Italy — have formally exited.

Xi's Global Security Initiative

"The Global Security Initiative is another global public good offered by China, as it contributes Chinese solutions and wisdom for solving security challenges facing humanity," regime mouthpiece Xinhua claimed (April 23, 2022). At the Boao Forum for Asia (BFA) Annual Conference 2022, Xi Jinping, without actually naming the United States, blamed the U.S. for war and the state of the global economy while pledging the Global Security Initiative. This is another vague plan for the CCP's global expansion.

The BFA is an annual PRC-led forum of 28 countries modeled on the World Economic Forum held annually in Davos, Switzerland. The gathering is named after Boao on China's Hainan Island; its headquarters operates in Beijing.

The 2022 BFA was titled "The World in Covid-19 and Beyond: Working Together for Global Development and Shared Future." According to the full text of his opening speech, published by Xinhua on April 21, 2022, Xi talked about cooperation and integration as well as trade and economics. His language was a

---

[586] https://www.ifw-kiel.de/publications/news/belt-and-road-bailout-lending-reaches-record-levels/

veiled attack on the U.S., which the CCP regime portrays as isolationist and protectionist, despite PRC tariffs on U.S. imports being higher than U.S. tariffs on Chinese imports.[587] Furthermore, China has virtually unrestricted investment and market access in the U.S., whereas Chinese markets are heavily restricted.

Along with blaming Washington for impeding world trade, Beijing criticizes the Federal Reserve and the European Central Bank (ECB) for raising interest rates. In fact, one forum session focused on "Global Inflation, Interest Rate Hikes and Economic Stability." The Fed, like the ECB, raised interest rates to combat inflation.[588] By contrast, China has been cutting interest rates to compensate for the negative impact of Covid-19 lockdowns in major cities (BBC, August 21, 2023).

In a move toward Chinese-led globalism, Xi said that the world should "embrace a global governance philosophy" (Xinhua, April 21, 2022). The CCP leader went on to say that nations must "firmly safeguard the international system with the UN at its core and the international order underpinned by international law." Although the regime talks of supporting the UN and international law, the CCP refuses to condemn the Russian invasion of Ukraine or the coup in Myanmar that ousted an elected leader.

Xinhua reported (April 21, 2022) that Xi used the phrase "territorial integrity." This was a subtle reference to Taiwan, implying that the U.S. should not interfere if China invades the island. He also urged nations to "reject the Cold War" as well as "group politics" and "bloc confrontation," hinting at NATO, the Quad, the Five Eyes, and AUKUS. He also repeated the

---

[587] https://www.piie.com/research/piie-charts/us-china-trade-war-tariffs-date-chart
[588] https://www.nbcnews.com/business/economy/how-raising-interest-rates-helps-fight-inflation-high-prices-recession-rcna33754

"legitimate security concerns" verbiage that the CCP had previously deployed to justify Russia's invasion of Ukraine.[589]

While there was nothing new about the CCP blaming the U.S. for most of the world's ills — including those that China is guilty of — what was most noteworthy was the unveiling of the Global Security Initiative. Not much concrete detail was given, but Xi used the term "indivisible security" (Reuters, April 22, 2022). Perhaps significantly, Putin used the same term to justify his confrontation with Ukraine in a February 2, 2022 phone call with the UK's prime minister.

At the BFA and in later statements published by Xinhua (April 23, 2022), PRC Foreign Minister Wang Yi provided greater detail about the initiative, saying: "The initiative contributes Chinese wisdom to make up for the present peace deficit." *The Global Times* (April 24, 2022), interpreted this statement as "China will never claim hegemony, seek expansion or spheres of influence, nor engage in an arms race," even though the CCP regime has done and is doing all of those things. The CCP mouthpiece subtly accused Washington of undermining the global security order by seeking hegemony in the name of democracy.

One of the six component areas of the Global Security Initiative is "stay committed to taking the legitimate security concerns of all countries seriously, and uphold the principle of indivisible security" (Xinhua, April 23, 2022). Once again, the key words "legitimate security concerns" and "indivisible security" were present. Although it is unclear exactly what form this initiative will take, clearly it seeks to legitimize Moscow's invasion of Ukraine and support Beijing's position on Taiwan. Geopolitical scholars around the world, including Europe,[590] agree that these two stances are the greatest threats to global security.

---

[589] https://www.aljazeera.com/news/2022/1/27/china-warns-us-over-ukraine-interference-in-winter-olympics
[590] https://euobserver.com/world/25981

10

Issuing a Red Alert

In the aftermath of World War II, the global community saw the emergence of two superpowers, the United States and the Soviet Union, each possessing immense military power and ideological influence. This unique bipolar dynamic of the Cold War, with Washington and Moscow as the primary antagonists, shaped global geopolitics for decades, fueling competition in areas such as the nuclear arms race, space exploration, and proxy conflicts, while also fostering alliances and diplomatic maneuvering on a global scale. The tension between these two formidable nations not only defined the era, but also influenced the strategic thinking and foreign policy of the United States, as it navigated a world dominated by two behemoth adversaries.

With the collapse of the Soviet Union in 1991, the United States emerged as the world's sole superpower. This newfound status positioned the U.S. as the dominant global force across political, economic, and military spheres. While the United States did face challenges to its national security, including threats from Islamic extremists and terrorism, it did not encounter a near-peer adversary that could rival its comprehensive power on the scale of the Cold War. This unipolar moment allowed the U.S. to exert significant influence on international affairs, shape global institutions, and establish itself as a primary driver of the post-Cold War world order.

This period of unchallenged American supremacy persisted until around 2012, marked by Xi Jinping's ascension to power and

China's pronounced rise on the world stage. Over the three decades of America's singular dominance, China had quietly expanded its economy and bolstered its military strength. However, Xi's leadership brought a significant shift in ambition. He set a clear goal for China to become a superpower, contesting the rules-based international order that largely revolved around U.S. leadership. While U.S. lawmakers envisioned friendly competition between the two nations, Xi left no room for ambiguity. He aimed for China to surpass the United States economically, militarily, and diplomatically by 2049. In the interim, he sought to reshape the international rules-based order to align with the vision and interests of the People's Republic of China. This transformation marked the onset of a new era in great-power competition, where China emerged as a central player challenging the established global order.

Xi's ambitions cast a comprehensive shadow of threat that touches virtually every corner of the world. This includes Africa, Asia, and South America, as well as within the American homeland. He deploys a wide array of tools, including cyber espionage, hacking, information warfare, industrial and economic espionage, and the illicit acquisition of technology. All the while, the PRC's economy has grown, with the proceeds fueling the relentless expansion and modernization of the People's Liberation Army. Xi sees this build up as preparation for an inevitable showdown with the United States.

The realization of Xi's grand ambitions hinges on a prerequisite of consistent and uninterrupted economic growth. The modernization of the PLA and the establishment of global coalitions through loans and investments are exceptionally costly endeavors. Additionally, Xi is well aware that to sustain a possible confrontation with the United States, he must have adequate reserves to provide for the well-being of China's massive population of 1.4 billion. Paradoxically, the PRC's economic growth relies heavily on U.S. consumers who purchase Chinese-made products, U.S. investors and pension funds that invest in Chinese stocks and bonds, and American entrepreneurs who engage in business in China.

China stands as a near-peer competitor equipped with both the aspiration and the capability to reshape the international order while posing a substantial threat to the United States. The consensus within the U.S. Intelligence Community is that China is the most significant national security concern. To safeguard U.S. interests and limit the ascent of the PRC, the regime's income must be curtailed.

The Trump administration's imposition of historic volumes of tariffs on Chinese imports, and the expansion of the powers of the Committee on Foreign Investment in the United States (CFIUS) to restrict Chinese investment in the U.S., represented effective steps in this direction. And the Biden administration wisely continued and intensified these tariffs and measures.[591] In recent years, the White House has amplified the authority of CFIUS and imposed sanctions on an increasing number of Chinese companies. The SEC's enforcement of audit regulations will further push many Chinese firms to delist from U.S. securities markets, while President Biden's chip ban is expected to hinder China's capacity to advance next-generation technologies.

At the 2023 G7 conference, the world's most advanced nations collectively resolved to embark on a systematic process of de-risking from the PRC, effectively initiating a gradual decoupling. This strategic shift entails diminishing investments in China, reshoring or friend-shoring manufacturing, and rerouting trade toward friendly nations. This approach serves several key objectives, including reducing supply-chain overreliance on China,

[591] https://www.reuters.com/markets/us/biden-administration-maintain-china-tariffs-while-review-continues-2022-09-02/

decreasing interdependence on the regime in Beijing, and simultaneously bolstering the economic development of nations such as India and Vietnam.

In addition to implementing measures aimed at curbing Chinese economic growth, the United States must bolster its cybersecurity capabilities to protect against cyber threats emanating from China. This should be accompanied by a reduction in immigration from China, including a decrease in visas issued to students and researchers. A comprehensive moratorium on direct investments by Chinese entities within the United States is imperative for safeguarding national security. Furthermore, the definition of a foreign agent should be expanded to encompass all members of the CCP, the PLA, and their families, as well as employees and officers of state-owned and state-backed enterprises.

PRC companies headquartered outside of the United States — even in locations like the Cayman Islands — should no longer be permitted to register on U.S. exchanges. The IRS should prioritize thorough examination of bank accounts and money transfers linked to Chinese entities operating in the U.S. Lastly, it is vital that the Federal Government collaborates with state governments to enforce China-related investment rules. State governors and members of Congress should refrain from undermining U.S. foreign policy by engaging in official meetings with Xi Jinping, as California Governor Gavin Newsom did in October 2023,[592] or visiting China unless specifically designated to do so by the Federal Government.

The American public must be educated on the extent and relentlessness of the China threat, to counteract CCP propaganda disseminated on social media platforms. U.S. universities,

---

[592] https://www.gov.ca.gov/2023/10/25/governor-newsom-meets-with-chinese-president-xi-jinping/

especially those offering majors in national security, military science, and related fields, should introduce courses focusing on China's economy, politics, and military. Securing the southern border is of paramount importance, and not only to disrupt the fentanyl trade, in which China is complicit. U.S. intelligence agencies have cautioned that Chinese agents, spies, and criminals exploit the border to enter the country, bypassing visas and background checks. The CCP's exploitation of American rights and freedoms poses a direct threat to U.S. national security, underscoring the urgency of comprehensive measures to safeguard the nation's interests and values. In conclusion, it is time to issue a red alert on China.

Glossary

AUKUS – A trilateral security partnership between Australia, the United Kingdom, and the United States announced in 2021.

BRI – The Belt and Road Initiative, China's massive infrastructure project spanning the globe

BRICS – A political grouping initially composed of Brazil, Russia, India, China, and South Africa, expanded in 2023 to include six new member states.

CCP – The Chinese Communist Party; the term is also used to refer to China's government.

CFIUS (The Committee on Foreign Investment in the United States) – An inter-agency committee of the U.S. government which reviews the national security implications of foreign investments in the United States.

Comprehensive National Power (CNP) – A framework used to assess and measure the overall strength and capabilities of a nation, across multiple domains, including military and economic power, resources, and influence.

CSIS (Center for Strategic & International Studies) – A Washington D.C.-based think tank focused on political, economic, and security issues throughout the world.

CSTO (Collective Security Treaty Organization) – An intergovernmental military alliance consisting of six post-Soviet states: Armenia, Belarus, Kazakhstan, Kyrgyzstan, Russia, and Tajikistan, formed in 2002.

DHS – The United States Department of Homeland Security.

DOD – The United States Department of Defense

DOJ – The United States Department of Justice.

FDI (foreign direct investment) – Investment which flows into a country from abroad.

Five Eyes (FVEY) – An intelligence alliance comprising Australia, Canada, New Zealand, the United Kingdom, and the United States.

Military-Civil Fusion (MCF) – China's development strategy to coordinate military and civilian sectors and bolster military procurement and R&D.

PLA – The People's Liberation Army, China's armed forces including its air force and navy

PMESII-PT (Political, Military, Economic, Social, Infrastructure, Information, Physical Environment, and Time) – A tool developed by the U.S. military to organize information and build a strategy.

PRC (The People's Republic of China) – The government established in Beijing in 1949.

Quadrilateral Security Dialogue (QSD or the Quad) – A strategic security dialogue between Australia, India, Japan and the United States.

RCEP (The Regional Comprehensive Economic Partnership) – A free trade agreement among Indo-Pacific nations.

ROC (The Republic of China) – The government established in China in 1911 and based in Taiwan since 1949.

SCO (Shanghai Cooperation Organization) – A China-led Eurasian political, economic, international security and defence organization.

TRA (Taiwan Relations Act) – Act of the United States Congress officially defining the substantial but non-diplomatic relations between the U.S. and Taiwan.

UFWD (United Front Work Department) – A CCP unit which gathers intelligence on, manages relations with, and attempts to win influence over individuals and organizations inside and outside of the PRC.

Index

www.ingramcontent.com/pod-product-compliance
Lightning Source LLC
Chambersburg PA
CBHW072114270326
41931CB00010B/1555